Comparative Criminal Justice

Third edition

Francis Pakes

Routledge
Taylor & Francis Group

LONDON AND NEW YORK

First published by Willan 2004
Third edition published 2015
by Routledge
2 Park Square, Milton Park, Abingdon, Oxon OX14 4RN

and by Routledge
711 Third Avenue, New York, NY 10017

Routledge is an imprint of the Taylor & Francis Group, an informa business

British Library Cataloguing-in-Publication Data
A catalogue record for this book is available from the British Library

Library of Congress Cataloging-in-Publication Data
Pakes, Francis J.
Comparative criminal justice / Francis Pakes. -- Third Edition.
pages cm
1. Criminal justice, Administration of--Cross-cultural studies. I. Title.
HV7419.P35 2014
364--dc23
2014023256

ISBN: 978-0-415-82627-3 (hbk)
ISBN: 978-0-415-82629-7 (pbk)
ISBN: 978-0-203-43136-8 (ebk)

Typeset in Bembo
by Saxon Graphics Ltd, Derby

Printed and bound in Great Britain by
TJ International Ltd, Padstow, Cornwall

To Suzanne

Contents

Tables

Chapter 1

Making sense of local and global criminal justice

There is much to be discovered through examining how justice is done and social control given shape in places far from home. We can marvel at diversity. It can be difficult to comprehend how profoundly different arrangements are when we look elsewhere. Where do these differences come from? What social, cultural, historical or political factors have been at play in shaping them? Equally we are frequently struck by the discovery that justice systems in remote areas in fact share many similarities with domestic systems. What factors bring about these similarities? For instance, why do we have police forces in virtually every place on earth? Surprisingly perhaps, they often sound very similar, something like police in English-speaking countries, polícia in Portugal, polis in Indonesia or полиция in Bulgaria. But are the police in the UK, Portugal and Indonesia as similar as they sound? Probably not. David Nelken, without doubt one of the foremost scholars in comparative criminal justice, argues that comparative work is both 'about discovering surprising differences and unexpected similarities' (Nelken, 2010: 34). They certainly can intrigue in equal measure.

Differences and similarities may be superficial or profound: different organisations may perform similar functions, and terms such as 'police' that sound the same may actually represent rather different entities. As such, appearances may easily deceive. It is therefore important that comparative research is thorough, sensitive to nuance, with reference to local customs, histories and a range of influences. Only then can we really appreciate the blend of similarity and difference that we tend to observe around the world. This is true for any comparative endeavour but perhaps particularly so in the contested and complex area of criminal justice. We can certainly provide a compact definition of criminal justice. Criminal justice forms part of the set of processes, bodies and institutions that aim to secure or restore social control. Social control is defined as 'the organised ways in which society responds to behaviour and people it regards as deviant, problematic, worrying, threatening, troublesome and undesirable' (Cohen, 1985: 1–2). However, that does not make it easy to decide what counts as part of such 'organised ways'. In this book I take a broad perspective on criminal justice. Criminal justice goes well beyond the traditional institutions such as police, courts and prisons. This book therefore includes a discussion on private policing and other forms of private security and also on extra-legal means of institutionalised social control such as for instance those in place in remote areas of Alaska. We also must not forget that much goes on in the shadows of criminal justice such as torture, various forms of state crime and administrative detention. These certainly should not be ignored.

This broad perspective is not just a matter of taste. The comparative project should not limit itself to criminal justice in a narrow sense. To do so is to miss out on identifying key aspects of crime, justice and control. These include hidden measures carried out in secrecy. Comparative research should therefore focus on harm inflicted and not just on crimes committed. In addition, justice is increasingly international, with international arrangements influential in shaping national criminal justice as well as dispensing justice directly via international criminal tribunals such as for the Former Yugoslavia or in East Timor or dispensed through the International Criminal Court. This book therefore looks at international crime, international policing as well as international courts to emphasise that comparative research must include the analysis of transnational and international arrangements. At the same time, we must appreciate that justice and social control frequently remain local matters. Certainly at the level of the city a lot of exciting comparative research has taken place (e.g. Wacquant, 2008; Body-Gendrot, 2000). It shows that the essential loci of comparative analysis are changing. It is not just about comparing countries with other countries. We also compare cities, parts of cities and geographic or conceptual regions. This has made comparative criminal justice more varied and also more challenging (Aas, 2007).

The utility of the comparative project

There are theoretical as well as practical incentives to the comparative study of criminal justice but there is also a moral imperative. That said, a useful starting point is simply curiosity. For example, if you're most familiar with Anglo-Saxon systems of justice you might wonder how the Dutch manage to operate a criminal justice system without the involvement of a jury anywhere in their criminal justice process. Such a state of affairs raises various questions. First of all, how exactly does this work? Comparative research would discover that it is professional judges (individual judges in the case of minor offences and a panel of three judges for serious offences) who reach verdicts and impose sentences. That might raise suspicion: would seasoned judges perhaps be highly prone to convict? This is an argument often heard in favour of the jury. Subsequently, we might wonder about how the jury-less state of Dutch criminal justice is perceived by defendants, the legal profession and by society at large (see Tak, 1999; Kelk, 2007). Conversely from a Dutch perspective the jury is only known from TV: an exotic oddity for which there is no place at home.

In Britain any attempt to tamper with the right to trial by jury is likely to be met with protests from the legal profession and civil liberty organisations alike (see Lloyd-Bostock and Thomas, 2001, on the state of the jury in England and Wales). There seems to be widespread agreement within these groups that the jury represents a pillar of the criminal justice system: the jury symbolises fairness and impartiality. It begs the question of whether similar opinions are held in the Netherlands and to what extent these opinions inform law and policy-making. That might lead to a better perspective on criminal justice in the Netherlands as well as on the value of the jury in a more general sense. At a higher level of abstraction such debates can be enlightening as to what the key features of justice actually are.

A similar argument can be applied to sentencing practices in Saudi Arabia (Souryal et al., 1994). The lay impression is that these are harsh, with frequent reports of executions and body mutilations. However, we need to know more about these practices before we can reach a balanced judgement. In Saudi Arabia these punishments are justified by reference to the country's low crime rates, which are claimed as a sign of its success. When potential offenders realise that they might lose a hand as a result they might think twice before committing theft. The second argument to justify severe sentences carries even more weight. It relates to the fact that law in Saudi Arabia is to a large extent based on the Qur'an and therefore strongly dogmatic. The sentencing practices derived from the Muslim holy book are considered appropriate, regardless of their effectiveness. Any discussion about their utility is not very meaningful in the light of that, in the strongly religious state of Saudi Arabia (Souryal, 1987). That said, this does not mean that places such as Saudi Arabia are immune to change. We see this in relation to women's rights: the Arab Spring has taught us that we cannot look at the Middle East without adopting a dynamic approach. At present Saudi Arabia is the only country in the world where women are not allowed to drive a car. However, it is thought that this may change. In September 2011, King Abdullah announced that women would be allowed to vote and run for office in the 2015 municipal elections. There is a degree of hope that the Arab Spring will open up areas for change that previously did not exist, even in Saudi Arabia. That said, framing any issue as one of religion remains an effective way of stifling developments and nullifying opposition, and public protest in Saudi Arabia remains a dangerous pursuit. In 2014, women who drive (many do and provocatively post videos on YouTube) can still expect punishment.

Comparing is not easy. The academic endeavour of comparative criminal justice requires detailed understanding of not just criminal justice processes but also the actors involved in it and the society that forms the backdrop to these processes. Often history is important in order to understand how particular arrangements have come about in the first place. Criminal justice arrangements need to be contextualised so that we can understand how they work in relation to each other and how the nuts and bolts of arrangements fit together. We also need to find ways of deciding how criminal justice arrangements fit a country, a culture or a legal tradition. As Fairchild and Dammer put it, 'The fact is that a nation's way of administering justice often reflects deep-seated cultural, religious, economic, political, and historical realities. Learning about the reasons for these different practices can give us insight into the values, traditions, and cultures of other systems' (Fairchild and Dammer, 2001: 9). Acquiring such knowledge has the added benefit of preventing *ethnocentrism* from occurring. Ethnocentrism refers to sentiments that regard domestic arrangements as necessarily 'normal' and 'right', and other cultures or customs as 'weird' or 'wrong'. It occurs frequently in the spheres of culture and religion and is no stranger to criminal justice either (Birkbeck, 1993; Nelken, 2009).

Another impetus for comparative study is of a more practical nature. Knowledge of systems in neighbouring countries has been vital in securing basic levels of cooperation. Longstanding agreements exist, for instance between Belgium and its neighbouring countries with regard to limited cross-border powers. These have been in place with France since 1919, with Luxembourg since 1920 and with the Netherlands since 1949. Such arrangements are handy, for instance when dealing with bank robbers who manage to flee into a neighbouring country while being chased by the police. They ensure that police activity does not come to a complete stop when the border is reached (Geysel, 1990). Such arrangements are of a local nature. More overarching transnational arrangements exist, which include, for instance Europol which is a cooperative body within the European Union (see Anderson et al., 1995) and Interpol, a policing organisation that is operative on a global scale.

There is no doubt that crime has increasingly acquired a global dimension. This is particularly true for crimes such as terrorism and cyber-crime. We must however note that much international crime only exists due to the restrictions of movement brought about by the existence and enforcement of borders. Also, state crime and forms of environmental crime can be of truly global proportions. It is a truism to say that increasingly offenders commit their crimes in more than one country, cross national borders themselves or reap the benefits of their crimes in another country. International cooperation is increasingly necessary in order for offenders to be apprehended, tried and convicted. Because officials of different systems cooperate with increasing frequency, a certain level of harmonisation of laws and procedures is beneficial. In order to achieve this, a certain level of understanding and appreciation of their similarities and differences is important. Harmonisation without understanding will always be very difficult indeed.

However we also must note that what travels is not just crime or criminals. Melossi, Sozzo and Sparks (2011) argue that it also is 'the criminal question' that has travelled. Pitch is quoted as arguing:

> To study the criminal question is different from studying crime. It means that crime is not considered independently from the procedures by which it is defined, the instruments deployed in its administration and control and the politics and debates around criminal justice and public order.
>
> (Pitch, 1995: 52)

The criminal question is therefore wider and urges us to consider: 'how do the many ways of circulating images of and responses to crime and punishment internationally flow and owe their contemporary shape to the cultural and economic transformations now widely known as "globalisation?"' (Melossi et al., 2011: 3). Comparative research therefore goes well beyond crime into something that is neatly encapsulated in 'the criminal question': the constellation of images, ideas, processes and attitudes towards crime, safety, punishment, control and fear that are fundamental in shaping social control more generally and criminal justice in particular. That is the focus of comparative criminal justice research – and seeking to uncover its essence, drivers and consequences a key objective.

A further benefit of comparative research is simply to learn from the experience of others. This is the realm of policy transfer. A highly current example is the policing of public protests (Pritchard and Pakes, in press). These are particularly politicised in the case of protests surrounding G8 summit meetings, as they have taken place in Genoa, Seattle and Gleneagles in Scotland in recent years. Also anti-austerity protests have become widespread. Although superficially, there are similarities in how these events have been policed, at the same time it is important to take note of the fact that the policing of such events is informed by local history (Gorringe and Rosie, 2008). When Gleneagles in Scotland hosted the G8 in 2005 an attempt was made to learn lessons from earlier G8 Summits such as in Genoa in 2001 where a protestor was shot dead by police (Della Porta and Fillieule, 2004). This highlights that debates in criminal justice are informed or even instigated by developments abroad, and experiences gained elsewhere might serve to inform decision-making at home.

Criminal justice systems around the world are likely to face similar challenges and globalisation is likely to have intensified this. It might therefore be instructive to investigate how other systems tackle some of their problems, not just in major events, such as political events or sports tournaments but also with regard to more persistent issues. It is safe to assume that England and Wales are not the only jurisdiction whose race relations, in the context of criminal justice, have proved to be a challenge. It might be instructive to see what, for instance, the opinions in Australia are on the over-representation of Aboriginals in their criminal justice system. Is there recognition of 'institutionalised racism' in Australia? Perhaps lessons could be learned from there.

A further incentive for comparison relates to the question 'Where do we stand?' In order to gain insight into states of affairs at home it might be helpful to examine matters abroad. Prison populations are a good example. In England and Wales the prison population is rising and has been for some time (see www.hmprisonservice.gov.uk for data and information). One way of making sense of prison populations is by taking a comparative perspective. The first and obvious place to look might be the so-called league tables that present detention ratios for various countries (e.g. Walmsley, 2013). These statistics invariably show that both the USA and the Russian Federation have a lot more people incarcerated (as calculated over their total population) than the UK. It is equally obvious that there are many countries with smaller numbers of prisoners on, as well as outside, the European continent. Additionally, such statistics are helpful in dispelling the myth that prison rates in every Western country are on the rise. In Finland, in particular, prison rates have gone down for decades, a development that is attributed to the political determination to use incarceration sparingly (Törnudd, 1993; Von Hofer, 2003). Such, possibly atypical, examples help to put the case across that not every country appears to be heading for a crime complex in which mass incarceration is the knee-jerk reaction to growing public feelings of insecurity and fear of crime (Garland, 2001). John Pratt's penal exceptionalism thesis (Pratt, 2008a, 2008b) also shows this clearly. He studied the Nordic countries of Finland, Norway and Sweden and considered the causes for their very different approach to punishment as compared to the USA or the UK. As Garland himself emphasises, the American way does not necessarily have to be *the* way.

Statistical comparisons may seem relatively straightforward. However they frequently are not. A simple comparison of, say, prison figures in isolation is not particularly informative as they can only say so much. For a proper comparison on, for instance, nations' tendencies to use imprisonment as a means of social control, more information is required than just prison rates. This information should at least include crime figures, but we might also wish to include information on the relative wealth of countries and the distribution of wealth in society. Unemployment rates and information about political stability might also be relevant in understanding comparative prison rates. The same is true for policing and sentencing practices. Do similar crimes attract similar sentences in different countries? What about the differences between sentences imposed and actually served? What alternatives to prison are there for sentencers to consider?

A further consideration is the extent to which these figures themselves are comparable. Do they include only convicts, or remand prisoners as well? Are those involuntarily detained in mental hospitals incorporated in the figures? The comparison of criminal justice statistics across countries is fraught with difficulty, as any available data require a great deal of interpretation (see Nelken, 2009). That requires intimate knowledge about the acquisition of the data itself and a thorough understanding of both the system and the society that produced them. We will explore these methodological issues further in Chapter 2.

Criminal justice systems are undoubtedly less self-contained than they have been in the past. Laws in England and Wales nowadays are strongly influenced by international treaties and by European Union legislation and rulings. Comparative criminal justice is an enterprise that increasingly involves the study of such transnational and international arrangements. A good knowledge of the bodies and processes that make international law is therefore vital in order to understand how criminal justice is developing across the globe. It is already clear to see that it is impossible to gain that understanding without a good appreciation of what is commonly referred to as *globalisation*. We see globalisation in action in many ways in criminal justice: it is not just that criminals travel and cross borders, but so do notions and understandings of what criminal justice is and how it is done, and probably increasingly so. Globalisation exerts further effects, such as the movement of people and legal and illegal goods. But there also is the mobility of economic opportunity: large factories that were in, say, Sheffield 50 years ago may have moved to Slovakia 25 years later only to be uprooted and moved to Shanghai next. Production moves around leaving communities, even whole economies in their wake. Such drastic changes have consequences and justice systems are frequently called upon to deal with exactly those. Globalisation is a multi-faceted concept, with some obvious expressions such as transnational offending but also many subtle consequences that do not relate to the international scene but rather to how globalisation affects local communities. We will discuss this more fully in Chapter 2.

Globalisation not only has a profound impact on criminal justice arrangements but it also has consequences for the field of comparative criminal justice research. In the past comparing justice may have mainly involved the comparison of entirely distinct and unconnected states of affairs (Nelken, 2011). Straightforward country by country comparison was the standard way in which this occurred. This is far less likely today, because of policy transfer (Jones and Newburn, 2007) and the spread of ideas about how criminal justice should be organised: the travels of 'the criminal question' have changed all that. Criminal justice systems everywhere are affected by these travels. Because of it Sheptycki (2005) speaks of 'diffusely intermingled difference' (p. 83) as opposed to pure difference. That makes the task of comparing and contrasting such arrangements more difficult (Aas, 2007). But no doubt it also makes it more current, and more interesting.

What this book is about

A text on comparative justice can be written from various perspectives. In these perspectives certain themes might receive emphasis, possibly at the expense of others. First, this book focuses more on procedural aspects of justice than on substantive issues. For instance, prosecution systems and the way trials are conducted are analysed in depth, but, for example, the difference in legal definitions of murder and manslaughter in various jurisdictions is not discussed. Nevertheless, it would be nonsensical to adhere over-rigidly to that distinction, and I have no intention of ignoring comparative matters of substantive law. Legal definitions of criminal behaviours are of particular interest in certain contexts. This includes, for example, the definition of genocide as adopted by the Yugoslav War Crimes Tribunal in The Hague in the Netherlands.

Similarly a comparative book could primarily examine either criminal justice structures or criminal justice processes. Criminal courts can serve as an example here. A structural description would involve a description of higher and lower courts and their relative competencies. A related distinction is often made between law in the books and law in practice. Law in the books is obviously written up in codes, acts and constitutions. It would however be naive to assume that what it says in the law books is the sole (or even the main) determinant of how justice is actually administered. There are extra-legal arrangements that do not occur in statutes but which have, nevertheless, gained widespread acceptance within criminal justice systems. Similarly, any law book contains many a dead letter. In the UK there are many local laws stemming from centuries back that are no more than inconsequential remnants of days past. Nevertheless, not every so-called dead letter should be considered meaningless. In many countries where the execution of convicts is no longer the practice the death penalty might still linger in the law books. While on the one hand it could be said that it is merely a harmless trace of a more punitive past, it could, on the other, be argued that such dead letters could be resurrected relatively easily, so that a reinstatement of the death penalty in such countries would be easier – and therefore possibly more likely – than in countries with no such relics left in the law books.

Additionally, the treatment of offenders receives more attention than that of victims in this book. This is arguably against the worldwide trend of securing a more prominent place for victims throughout the criminal justice process (see Tapley, 2005). However, an exhaustive review of comparative criminal justice is simply impossible. It is equally impossible to include each and every development in all corners of the globe, which is why the choice is made for this more traditional emphasis on criminal justice with the perspective on the offender. In its defence I would argue that criminal justice, although no doubt more victim aware than before, has shifted its emphasis towards security, surveillance and the control of dangerous populations. That emphasis limits the extent to which criminal justice systems have truly become victim-centred. How such shifts play out in different locales is an important area to consider.

I have opted for a thematic approach. This is as opposed to a country-by-country approach, in which descriptions from a limited set of countries are utilised throughout the book. The rationale behind this choice is that I assume the reader to be more interested in general issues in criminal justice rather than in criminal justice in specific countries. Therefore, this book will use examples to fit the issue to be discussed, rather than exclusively focusing on a pre-determined set of countries. For that reason, Japan will feature in detail when we discuss policing styles. However, when it comes to prosecution, we will look more in depth at the state of affairs in the Netherlands. Suitable examples are often typical examples, although on occasion it makes sense to discuss the exception to the rule and use deviant cases instead, and the process of decarceration in Finland serves as such a case. In other areas I have chosen to discuss the archetypical example, the example that bred a category. The jury in England and Wales constitutes one of those, as does the practice of zero-tolerance policing in New York City. When we discuss genocide, emphasis will be lent to the recent genocides in the Former Yugoslavia and the central African state of Rwanda.

This thematic approach is carried out in what can be called a kaleidoscopic fashion. While some of the major criminal justice systems in the world receive extensive coverage, I have attempted not to stick to these. Australia, England and Wales, Japan, France, the Netherlands and the USA do feature in various chapters. However, arrangements in many other countries have also been examined. In making such choices I have aimed to highlight the diversity found in criminal justice arrangements around the world. This is why the rise of the gender balance of the judiciary in the Czech Republic, prisons in the Philippines and police misconduct in Brazil are all discussed.

Diversity is a key word in comparative criminal justice. Despite or perhaps even thanks to globalisation, the way in which justice is administered around the world is surprisingly diverse and there is no need to travel far to encounter this diversity. Not many people, even in England and Wales, might appreciate the substantial differences in arrangements between England and Wales, Northern Ireland, Scotland, the Isle of Man, and the Channel Islands of Jersey and Guernsey. This is true in particular when we look at the jury system. The composition of the jury in these places is spectacularly different, even though they are geographically and culturally very close. The same argument applies to the federal states of Australia and the USA, where many arrangements are made at a local level, allowing for substantial differences across the country, or even within the same state or territory.

Federal and local law enforcement in the USA

A circumstance that complicates foreign understanding of the US criminal justice system is the distinction between federal law enforcement, and state and local criminal justice. At one point in time, probably at least a century ago, this distinction was quite straightforward. The bread and butter of everyday law enforcement were local matters. Only when the position of US states was at issue in some shape or form or when a crime was clearly transcending state borders was there a reason for federal (roughly speaking, national) law enforcement to get involved. Counterfeiting, for instance was seen as an offence of federal importance. The same was true for offences involving mail. These offences and their effects were likely to affect not simply individual states, but the USA as a whole. The protection of the president also was a federal matter. However, the distinction between what is federal and what is local in terms of law enforcement is no longer sharply defined:

> Explaining the boundary that separates Federal enforcement concerns from state and local is a daunting task indeed. The more one knows,

the harder it gets. Federal agents still seek out counterfeiters. But they also target violent gangs and gun-toting felons of all sorts, work drug cases against street sellers as well as international smugglers, investigative corruption and abuse of authority at every level of government, prosecute insider trading, and pursue terrorists. Until recently, about the only area of criminal enforcement that seemed immune from Federal activity was domestic violence.

(Richmond, 2000: 82)

The areas of federal involvement have tremendously increased and the Federal Bureau of Investigation (FBI) has grown accordingly. Federal legislation is now seen to supplement local legislation in many areas, so that crime can be dealt with more effectively. This state of affairs regularly raises issues relating to competencies on the one hand and to the harmonisation of local and federal rules of procedure on the other hand. There is certainly room for tactical decision-making about whether to deal with a crime as a local or a federal matter. Laws of evidence and resource allocations are not necessarily identical so that practical considerations might be decisive in the determination of whether an offence should be dealt with by the local or the federal law enforcement machinery. This is called 'forum shopping'.

Richmond (2000) argues that the increased federal involvement in criminal justice is the result of a shifting of the balance of power between the states and the federal government. Over the last century, this balance has shifted toward the federal government along with the construction of crime, law and order as national if not global issues.

Shifts of power from local to national and vice versa occur regularly in most criminal justice systems. A movement towards localisation is often motivated by the intention to better serve local communities' needs. A shift towards centralisation might occur because of central government's desire to control criminal justice matters more tightly. That desire for control might originate from the wish to enhance the extent to which the criminal justice system serves the interests of the state, or might stem from tendencies to secure a more uniform treatment of offenders and offences throughout the country. Finally, such dynamics are not unique to the USA although they are perhaps most visible there. In other federal states such as Australia and Germany similar tensions may occur.

A notable tension between local, state and national governance in the USA involves the regulation of cannabis. Two US states, Washington and Colorado, voted to legalise recreational use of cannabis in 2012. That is despite a federal prohibition, opening the door for legal wrangling in order to exactly establish the state of law. In the state of Washington a new law allows for one ounce to be possessed by people of age 21 and older. Colorado's new Amendment 64 also allows for someone over 21 to own six cannabis plants in a locked space. Cannabis regulations do differ from state to state in relation to medicinal use of cannabis products. Clearly cannabis is an area where the tug of war between local, state and national is currently being played out, not just in the USA but also elsewhere such as the Netherlands and the UK (Pakes and Silverstone, 2012).

Throughout this book, case studies such as the one above serve as examples. In many instances they pertain particularly to the issues described in the main text. Sometimes, however, case studies are included for illustration or general interest purposes. Depending on the issues concerned the comparative approach is sometimes quantitative and sometimes qualitative in nature. A discussion about policing styles and principles is almost inevitably qualitative, as they require a deeper understanding of the contexts in which they are applied. I have therefore chosen to conduct a limited number of in-depth case studies and focused comparisons, to illustrate styles of policing in the context of different societies. In other areas a more quantitative approach was the appropriate choice. A discussion regarding rates of imprisonment is likely to feature prison ratios at least as a starting point. It is important to reiterate that the collection of such numerical information does not usually suffice to answer any question. Nevertheless, such figures do provide for a foundation on which meaningful comparisons can be made.

Criminal justice systems in Scotland, and England and Wales

People outside the United Kingdom could perhaps be forgiven for assuming that criminal justice in Scotland is identical to that in England and Wales; but it is not. Whereas England and Wales constitute one criminal justice system, Scotland has a separate system with its own characteristics. Whereas Wales does not have a separate police service, court or prison system, Scotland has, and it has evolved quite separately from those of its southern neighbours. Scottish scholars tend to argue that there is an additional difference in criminal justice culture. Scottish criminal justice is often said to be less adversarial, less punitive and more welfare-oriented (see Duff and Hutton, 1999). A number of specific differences between the two systems can easily be identified.

In Scotland, a jury can return three verdicts: *guilty*, *not guilty* or *not proven*. Guilty and not guilty are essentially the same as elsewhere, but the third category, not proven, is probably unique to Scotland. The not proven verdict is returned quite frequently and it results in the acquittal of the accused, so that it is to virtually all intents and purposes identical to a verdict of not guilty. The answer to why this verdict exists lies in history. There was a time that the only verdicts a jury could return were proven or not proven. While the verdict of proven has long since been replaced, that of not proven has survived the test of time.

The suggestion is that when a jury returns a not proven verdict instead of a not guilty one, they might nevertheless feel that the accused actually committed the offence but that there is insufficient evidence to justify a conviction. A not guilty verdict could then be taken to mean 'really' or factually not guilty. But it has been argued that the 'not proven' verdict is only confusing. Proponents, however, stress the purity of the not proven verdict. After all, the role of the jury is not to decide on guilt but on whether the prosecution has proved the charge beyond reasonable doubt. A verdict of not proven might more accurately reflect the actual decision that jurors are asked to make (Duff, 2001).

Whereas in England and Wales there are 12 jurors, in Scotland a jury consists of 15 members. They are randomly pulled from the voters' register in the jurisdiction of the court where the accused stands trial. Until recently, both prosecution and defence had the right to peremptory challenge. Nowadays, however, prospective jurors cannot be removed easily before trial and this action requires both parties' agreement. In Scotland there is no need for a unanimous verdict. For a guilty verdict a simple majority of eight versus seven will suffice. Because there is a choice of three verdicts, it could, for instance, happen that seven jurors favour a guilty verdict, five a verdict of not guilty, and three a verdict of not proven. If this is the case a not guilty verdict should be returned. An accused is not convicted unless at least eight jurors find him or her guilty (Maher, 1988). In England and Wales a unanimous verdict is preferred but a 10 versus 2 majority is possible. The Scottish simple-majority verdict is not uncontroversial. Observers have argued that when 7 of the 15 jurors are not prepared to render a guilty verdict that by itself might constitute some form of reasonable doubt (see Duff, 2001).

Unlike in England and Wales, a prosecution service that receives cases from the police has been the state of affairs in Scotland for a long time. The head of the service is the Lord Advocate, who is a government minister. His deputy, the Solicitor General, is also a government appointee. Most prosecutions take place in sheriff's courts or district courts through local prosecuting officials called Procurators Fiscal. The term 'Fiscal' relates to their past function, to do with the collection of tax revenue (Moody and Tombs, 1982; Duff, 1993, 1999). The Procurator Fiscal is wholly independent. That protects the service against pressure from outside, but it also means that it is almost impossible for victims to challenge a decision made by the Procurator Fiscal.

There are other differences between England/Wales and Scotland that deserve brief mention. The accused in Scotland does not have a say in the mode of trial decisions, unlike suspects in England and Wales for the middle range of offences. In Scotland, mode of trial is always a decision for the prosecution. Finally, lawyers in Scottish courts (those who are called barristers in England and Wales) are called advocates in Scotland and do not make opening statements.

The source of many of the differences between Scottish criminal justice and criminal justice in England and Wales is historical. Scotland became part of the United Kingdom in 1707. A separate criminal justice system existed before that, and while it has been kept separate ever since, the subsequent laws for Scotland were made by the UK parliament in Westminster, London. The 1707 union was the start of a long period in which the similarities between both systems increased. Arguably, at this moment there might be more scope for divergence than there has been for centuries. Scottish devolution and the instigation of a Scottish Parliament in Edinburgh in 1999, which can pass laws on criminal justice matters, gives Scotland opportunities for taking matters in their own hands in a way not possible in the 300 years that went before (Duff and Hutton, 1999; McAra, 2008). Whilst a referendum on Scottish independence failed to yield a majority vote for independence, further powers will be handed to the Scottish Parliament as part of a process of devolution. Whether that will lead to further divergence of arrangements north and south of the English/Scottish border remains to be seen.

Finally, it must be said that a single-author text on comparative criminal justice does require the author to attempt to be a bit of an expert on everything. It has already been recognised by others that this obviously can never be fully achieved (e.g, Mawby, 1999b). It is therefore inevitable that I rely mostly on areas with which I am familiar; my experience and knowledge inevitably have coloured this book. In Chapter 2, I declare my hand with regards to methodological and positional issues in order to position myself more explicitly within the field.

Traditionally, comparative research was perhaps a luxury. It served to broaden one's horizons and to establish if elsewhere there might be success stories in criminal justice worth adopting at home. Today, comparative research is a necessity. The only way to effectively prevent and combat crime on the world stage is via the harmonisation and the coordination of national and international efforts. That requires up-to-date and intimate knowledge of criminal justice arrangements abroad. And with that comes, one hopes, an appreciation of meaningful and valuable differences, stemming from culture, history and social discourse which help shape criminal justice arrangements in places quite different from our own. At the same time, the exotic might be strangely familiar and where it is, this tells us something about influences and interconnections. Uncovering that blend of the familiar with the exotic is both the essence, and the joy, of the comparative project.

Further reading

Aas, K.F. (2007) *Globalisation and crime*. London: Sage.
Melossi, D., Sozzo, M. and Sparks, R. (Eds) (2011) *Travels of the criminal question: Cultural embeddedness and diffusion*. Oxford: Hart.
Nelken, D. (2010) *Comparative criminal justice: Making sense of difference*. London: Sage.

Study questions

1   What accounts for similarities between remote criminal justice systems? Consider at least three reasons.
2   What sort of factors account for important differences? Consider at least three reasons for this.
3   What are three key reasons for comparative research?

Chapter 2

Conducting comparative research in a globalised world

Comparative criminological research is centuries old but as an academic enterprise it seems to be in a perennial state of having a point to prove. We must emphasise that comparative research should not be nor should it be perceived to be 'an excuse for international travel' or 'an exotic frill', or even 'a luxury that serious social scientists leave to dilettantes' (Bayley, 1999: 241). Such sentiments (not in fact held by Bayley) are notwithstanding the early efforts of comparatists such as penal reformer John Howard (1777), who visited many prisons in Britain and in mainland Europe. Howard was inspired, passionate even, about prisons and those held in them. Having been imprisoned in Northern France while on his way to Portugal may well have ignited a humanitarian spark that led to such seminal work. Howard's comparative work had a strong normative component. He was appalled by his own experience of prison but also of the conditions that he witnessed in the UK. Where he saw more favourable conditions, such as in gaols in Belgium and the Netherlands, he made political efforts to have such conditions replicated in the UK (Howard, 1777). Howard's life work comprises comparative criminology and criminal justice in a nutshell. His aims of comparison were clear in his life and work, in a way that made him both an insider and an outsider when it comes to judging what goes on behind the closed doors of prison establishments. It goes without saying that Howard serves to debunk the 'dilettante' accusation very effectively as he combined years of prison visits at home and abroad with acute analysis and political activism. Plenty of contemporaries agree with the fundamental value of comparative research, not least Nelken (2010, 2011), Muncie (2011) and Savelsberg (2011). Other strong comparative work has been carried out by for instance Body-Gendrot (2000) and more recently again, Wacquant (2008). Crawford's recent edited collection on comparative research and urban governance is also compelling and informative (Crawford, 2011). However, the fact that comparative research is open to such suspicions at all makes it all the more important to explain both the 'why' and the 'how' of comparative research in detail.

The aims of comparison

All sociology is comparative, argued Durkheim (1895). From that perspective it would follow that the aims and methods of comparative study would be the same as for other forms of social study. Indeed many of the methodological foundations of general criminology do apply *mutatis mutandis* to comparative study. However, where research is explicitly comparative it is important to be clear in terms of its aims.

A relatively modest aim is that of classification, to provide order to what can be perceived as a bewildering variety in criminal justice arrangements. Classification systems have highlighted fundamental objects and relations between objects in particular areas of knowledge with great success. In biology Linnaeus' classification of species is a good example but the most celebrated example is probably the periodic table that systematically orders chemical elements (see Scerri, 2006). The realm of chemistry classification seems an excellent vehicle for the ordering of our world which at the same time brings predictive value as the ordering is based on very clear principles such as the elements' atomic number. The periodic table can rightly be called a masterpiece of structured information of our physical world.

In social science its utility is likely to be more limited. However, classifications of criminal justice systems or styles of policing are popular and enduring. For instance, Cole and colleagues (Cole et al., 1987) classify criminal justice systems as follows. First, there are so-called common-law or adversarial systems. The three examples they mention are England and Wales, the USA and Nigeria. Originating from the British Isles, they are found in all English-speaking countries, with the possible exceptions of Scotland and South Africa. Second, there are civil law or inquisitorial systems. These originated in continental Europe and have been exported to other parts of the world as well. The third group consists of socialist law systems. Cole et al. describe the systems of the former USSR and Poland. Their book was published in 1987, two years before the fall of the Berlin Wall, and is obviously dated in some respects. In this book we do not discuss socialist law systems, although it would be wrong to assume that this legal tradition has died out completely. In Cuba, the legal system still has a strong socialist orientation. However, in place of these we discuss Islamic legal systems. These occur widely in the Middle East but also elsewhere such as in Nigeria. So-called Sharī'ah law is subject to controversy, because of the perceived harshness of some punishments, the criminalisation of certain behaviours, the subordinate role of women and the archaic nature of its procedures and its laws of evidence.

In a sense the debate whether certain legal systems, such as Japan, can be called inquisitorial or not is moot. There are hardly any 'pure' legal systems. Instead most systems are hybrid mixes of various orientations that often have developed over time and more often than not in a haphazard fashion. That is particularly true of Japan. Thus, the classification of legal systems into a few discernible categories does have a degree of heuristic value but on the other hand, is it clear that most systems are mixed. In addition there is a great deal of legal pluralism going on where different systems operate alongside each other. Thus, legal systems cannot be organised in the same way that chemical elements can. Categorisation runs the risk of obscuring the diversity within categories as well as underplaying the fact that many cases could arguably be placed in either. Because of that, classification can only be an early milestone in our understanding of social arrangements. Classification is risky: it may obscure as much as it can reveal due to the fact that many criminal justice arrangements often simply defy simple categorisation. Detailed scrutiny remains required further to that.

Research orientations

The detailed scrutiny needed for gaining a rich and full understanding of initially unfamiliar arrangements will often require sustained liaisons with those arrangements. Perhaps the oldest academic endeavours involving such immersion come from anthropology. Anthropology is the science of humanity, or more specifically the scientific study of the origin, the behaviour and the physical, social and cultural development of human beings. In the first half of the twentieth century many anthropologists studied exotic communities, often on sunny islands far away from Europe or the USA, where many anthropologists undertaking that research were based. These distant communities at the time were often referred to as 'primitive', a characterisation that carries a sizeable value judgement. The most famous exponent of this tradition is probably American anthropologist Margaret Mead. She spent a great deal of time in South Pacific communities. During her career she conducted field studies on islands such as New Guinea, Bali and Samoa (Mead, 1928, 1935).

An anthropologist tends to be particularly concerned with understanding human behaviour in the context of history, culture and social structure. Anthropology endeavours to illuminate dissimilarities and to sharpen contrasts, which is a focus that can be applied to the study of criminal justice as well. Immersion in one's own criminal justice system tends, inevitably, to solidify assumptions and blunt critical faculties. Laws appear 'natural', modes of implementation 'inevitable' and relationships between criminal justice agencies 'necessary'. The anthropological-research approach guards against such tendencies and emphasises the view that everything in social reality is relative.

Such research is often furthered by a method called *ethnography*. This involves sustained immersion in the culture or context to be studied. Margaret Mead once famously wrote that 'The way to do fieldwork is never to come up for air until it is all over' (1977: 136). Ethnographic studies aim to come to a holistic yet localised understanding of processes, meanings and arrangements. Ethnography involves the sustained immersion in other cultures, frequently in the role of participant observer. It tends to include extensive observations, in-depth as well as casual conversations and interviews in order to find meaning behind everyday interactions (e.g. Hodgson, 2000). The aim of this type of research has been summarised by Dixon, not without a hint of pathos, as the attempt to 'maximise understanding of alien cultures by honest-to-God field work, moral charity, intellectual humility and a determination of the taken-for-granted assumptions of both his own and others' cultural milieu' (Dixon, 1977: 76).

A classic ethnographic work is Whyte's study of Italian immigrants in Boston in the USA: *Street corner society* (1943). It examines individuals' roles and values surrounding gang membership. Whyte actually lived in the area for a few years, part of which he spent living with an Italian family. That is indeed the 'sustained immersion' required so that the 'lived experience' of the communities studied can be laid bare. Wacquant's resolute deconstruction of 'the pugilistic point of view', from boxers in Chicago, is another strong example (Wacquant, 1995).

Although by no means by necessity (Nelken, 1997, 2009), ethnography is often the preferred methodology of those with a relativistic view of society. Often the argument is made that the way societies are organised does not correspond to certain templates or principles but is rather a function of the environment. The arrangements in place therefore depend on habits, culture and history. Thus, because society in the UK works in a certain way that does not mean that other societies would even remotely work in the same fashion. After having learned how societies are organised abroad, one can look on one's own society with a new perspective and realise that the way society is organised is not the only way, not necessarily the best way, and certainly not cast in stone.

In contrast to relativism stands the positivist approach. The philosophy underlying this approach is that criminal justice can be best understood by focusing on commonalities, on those characteristics that criminal justice systems share. The assumption is that, at a certain level, we can find 'universals' in how justice is administered or how social control is given shape. Social control is a phenomenon that occurs in any society, so that, consequently, justice or social control can perhaps be understood in general terms. A main aim of positivist comparative research is identifying the core set of principles underlying criminal justice and distinguishing them from those traits that are merely external features. When Mannheim wrote his classic *Comparative criminology* in 1965 he argued that the aim of the project should be the identification of generally applicable knowledge.

Positivism dates back to the nineteenth century through the work of Auguste Comte. In his view, sciences could be more or less 'positive' depending on how well they explain the phenomena in their realm. In this perspective, the aforementioned periodic table would represent a high level of positivity, whereas social sciences tend to have less predictive and explanatory power and are therefore less positive. Positivism therefore is the approach to social science that strives to formulate precise definitions, exact predictions to be tested through controlled studies. It leans to quantitative research methods. The term positivism therefore is associated with progress, away from teleology (explanations by reference to a higher end or religious being) and towards an exact and precise understanding of social structure and process. It corresponds to an optimistic and, according to many, naive conception of science: that it is progressing towards ever more precise descriptions of reality through a process of advancement that is steady and inherently rational. In some sort of contrast, social scientists frequently subscribe to *social constructivism* that suggests that we construct our social reality as much as social science discovers it. That is at odds with a resolute positivistic stance that the laws of social science are there to be discovered to an ever more precise degree (Bryman, 2012).

To be fair the aims of many comparative projects are more modest and down to earth. Such comparative projects tend to be more practical and often inspired by current issues. Often there is a domestic problem identified in need of scrutiny. That might prompt a desire to look elsewhere for ideas as to how the identified problem is tackled elsewhere. In such research projects, arrangements elsewhere are given meaning in relation to domestic arrangements. The relativist position, in contrast, would be that arrangements should be given meaning in their own context and that we should not assume that what is effective in one context can be lifted into another. Thus, for the ethnographer, the idea of policy transfer will often be anathema. These struggles are reflected in comparative criminological research.

In this chapter, however we will look at comparative methods to the extent that they are specific to comparative research. At this point, the key distinction between positivist/quantitative approaches and interpretivist/qualitative approaches is important. The former are more likely to focus on areas such as murder rates or prison rates, that is, the more 'countable' phenomena, whereas the latter are more likely to be followed by those intrigued by the less countable and more fluid and elusive phenomena such as cultures, taboos and contradictions involving issues such as crime, order, security, justice, retribution and reconciliation. Comparative students should be finely attuned to these orientations as they are often tacit but nevertheless inform both the content, tone and the method of comparative research.

Doing comparative research

Comparative research can take place using a range of methods. We have already discussed ethnography which arguably is both a methodology and a research philosophy. In this section we will be discussing a few more methods. It has been argued that methodology in comparative criminal justice is underdeveloped, and the following outline borrows therefore from methodologies in comparative politics (e.g. Hague et al., 1998). The research methods in this area are to a large extent valid for studies in comparative criminal justice as well. In turn, I will address case studies, focused comparisons and statistical analysis.

Case studies

It is perfectly feasible to carry out a comparative study that treats only one country or jurisdiction in depth. In order for such a case study to be meaningful the case should be picked carefully and with justification. For instance, when a researcher is interested in examining suspects' rights in inquisitorial criminal justice systems, picking 'any old inquisitorial system' is not sufficient. Such a choice has to be justified. Either the study aims to elicit localised knowledge or alternatively the case can be taken to represent a wider category. Following Hague et al. (1998) I distinguish four types of case to be selected for a case study. They are representative cases, prototypical cases, deviant cases and archetypical cases.

A *representative case* is a typical example of a wider category. It is the bread and butter of comparative research. A comparative study involving a country with a low crime rate may choose to focus on Japan, well known (at least until fairly recently) to have a low rate (see, e.g., Komiya, 1999; Ellis and Hamai, 2006). Similarly, a study involving high rates of imprisonment may consider the USA for much the same reason.

Prototypical cases are cases that might be expected to become representative cases in the future. Prototypical cases are often frontrunners with regard to particular developments. In certain countries decriminalisation of euthanasia (often referred to as 'mercy killing' or assisted suicide, i.e., helping another to die) might be at an advanced stage of development. These countries may serve as examples and lead the way for others as to how to go about decriminalising medical life-ending conduct. Study of such prototypical cases might yield valuable insight for policy-makers in countries tending in the same direction but which have not quite proceeded as far.

Deviant cases are selected to yield insight into the atypical or unconventional. They can shed light on causal relations, or the lack of them. For instance, it is often thought that crime rates cause rates of imprisonment, so that when crime rates go up one would assume that imprisonment rates would follow. The study of what seemingly is an atypical case, such as the Netherlands between 1950 and 1975, might show that this relationship is not one of causality, as imprisonment rates in this period went down while the crime rate consistently went up (Downes, 1988).

Archetypical cases are cases that generate a category. The French inquisitorial system of criminal procedure is a good example: all other European inquisitorial systems are more or less derived from it. Thus, when studying inquisitorial modes of justice, the French one would be an appropriate choice, as it can be said to be the quintessential inquisitorial system. Similarly, England and Wales could be said to be the archetypical adversarial system of justice.

Focused comparisons

Focused comparisons are like case studies, but include more than one case. Most often the number of countries compared is two or three. As with case studies, the key question is how to select jurisdictions for study. We will discuss two techniques: the 'most-similar' and the 'most-different' designs. Hague et al. (1998) define them as follows:

A most similar design takes similar countries for comparison on the assumption that the more similar the units being compared, the more possible it should be to isolate the factors responsible for differences between them. By contrast, the most different design seeks to show the robustness of a relationship by demonstrating its validity in a range of contrasting settings.

(Hague et al., 1998: 281)

Most-similar designs tend to be easier to achieve. They often involve neighbouring countries or countries in which the same language is spoken. Most-similar designs can involve former colonies as well. Most-different designs are often more difficult to carry out, as they tend to involve a selection of at least one jurisdiction that is alien to the researcher, with all the associated problems of familiarising oneself with such a system and all its intricacies. Leishman (1999) calls such problems the 'gang of four' because they often co-occur: problems with gaining meaningful access, cultural literacy, ethnocentric bias and problems of language.

Smith (2011) calls focused comparisons 'parallel studies' and distinguishes parallel studies undertaken by a single researcher from projects where two researchers conspire to undertake the same study, each in their own locality. She argues that both researchers need to agree on concept equivalence: what exactly is being studied? She continues that 'anything short of a detailed and complete description will leave ambiguity at multiple steps through the remainder of the project' (Smith, 2011: 220). Others however would argue that such ambiguities are unavoidable and 'complete' descriptions run the risk of positivist over-simplification. Smith also makes a point about cultural differences. Here again she argues that each cultural difference must be identified and documented prior to the commencement of the research. Relativists would again argue against the very feasibility of this. Finally, Smith mentions language differences but here she is quite emphatic about the multitude of problems involving translation. Clearly, when conceived of as an individual or as a shared project, focused comparison can throw up many a challenge. A philosophical point refers to whether these can be mitigated (more reminiscent of a relativist point of view) or completely solved (more in correspondence with a positivist perspective).

Statistical analysis

Statistics may occur in any comparative study. The description of crime rates in any country will probably involve at least descriptive statistics to describe the prevalence of various forms of crime. In this context, however, statistical analysis is meant to mean statistical testing as a main research methodology. The aim of such analysis is to explore the relation between two or more variables, which can be measured quantitatively. An example might feature the size of a country's police service (in terms of personnel) and its prison rates. That might help us decide whether more police would lead to more arrests being made, and ultimately more people in prison.

Via statistical means insight can be gained into the relationship between such variables in a range of jurisdictions. It must, however, be borne in mind that the existence of a statistical relation does not necessarily mean that there is a causal one. Other factors may be at work behind the scenes that actually cause the effect to occur. A relation that seems to imply a causal relationship but actually does not is called 'spurious'.

Examples of spurious correlations are plentiful. For instance, the more surgeons in an operating theatre, the more likely it is that the patient dies. This is a real statistical relationship. However, this obviously does not mean that these surgeons would actually cause the patient to die. The mediating factor is of course the seriousness of the patient's condition. In criminal justice the positive relation between public approval ratings of the police and reported crime rates is argued to be spurious. When the public have high confidence in the police they might be more willing to report crimes because they feel that the police will be able to do something about them. The inference that the relation between the two might be causal – that a more positively rated police service causes crime rates to increase – is obviously not valid.

One particular kind of statistical analysis is called 'meta-analysis' (Rosenthal, 1991). It aims at integrating research findings from a large number of empirical studies in a statistical fashion. The procedure is for researchers to collect a large amount of experimental data on a particular subject, such as the effectiveness of prison sentences as compared to community sentences when measured by rates of recidivism. When the data is reported in sufficient detail, these results can be statistically combined and different outcomes might be explained by differences in certain characteristics of the various studies. In comparative criminal justice, meta-analysis studies have been influential in the theoretical underpinning of effective programmes for working with offenders (Lipsey, 1995). Two recent examples are Deković et al. (2011) on early intervention programmes and Fazel and Yu (2011) on the relation between psychosis and repeat offending.

Using criminal justice statistics comparatively

The use of official statistics in criminal justice is fraught with difficulty. While these difficulties are commonly acknowledged, it is worth emphasising that many of them get amplified in comparative research. We know that official statistics cannot and will not tell the whole story of the extent of crime in society. A main reason for this is underreporting. There are many reasons why crimes are not always reported to the police. In order for a victim to go to the police a number of criteria have to be met. The victim must realise he/she is a victim of a crime; victims might not notice items lost that have been stolen, or might not realise that what has happened to them constitutes a crime. Victims (or witnesses) usually take the step of reporting only when they feel that there is a certain benefit to be gained from it. Such benefits are obvious in the case of an insurance claim, but often a victim may feel that the authorities may not be able or willing to do anything about the crime, let alone solve it. The extent to which the police are judged to be capable of doing something about crime differs considerably among countries. As an illustration, see Table 2.1 on the percentage that think the police do a good job, based on International Crime Victimization Survey data (Van Dijk et al., 2008).

When a crime is reported that does not mean that is it recorded properly, which means that it might not be investigated, and that a suspect might not be identified. An identified suspect might not be found or apprehended; their case might be discontinued because of lack of evidence or for other reasons. And when cases come to trial, they might not result in a conviction. Thus, crimes are filtered out of the criminal justice system at various stages, while a significant number of crimes never enter the system, and hence the statistics, in the first place.

Table 2.1 Percentage of people that think the police do a good job in controlling crime in their area

Hong Kong (SAR China)	94
Finland	89
USA	88
Canada	86
New Zealand	84
Australia	82
Denmark	82
Austria	81
Scotland	79
Ireland	78
England & Wales	75
Germany	74
Norway	73
Belgium	71
Hungary	70
Netherlands	70
Northern Ireland	70
Switzerland	69
Portugal	67
Italy	65
Sweden	65
Luxembourg	62
France	60
Spain	58
Greece	57
Bulgaria	53
Estonia	47
Mexico	44
Poland	41

Source: Van Dijk et al., 2008.

The functioning of any criminal justice agency depends partly on its workload. This is affected significantly by crime rates and by the extent to which the public report crimes to the police. The performance of these agencies has to be viewed in the context of such indicators. For many countries, those indicators are available. For many others they are not. The selective reporting and recording of crimes probably happens everywhere. The crux is, however, that it is often very difficult to tell whether this happens at the same points in the system, for the same reasons and to the same extent in the different jurisdictions. Thus, while dealing with official figures is hazardous in the first place, it is doubly so in a comparative context.

Even when official figures are available and reliable that does not mean that comparison necessarily becomes straightforward. Take the following example. In higher courts in France the conviction rate is extremely high: in total, 90 per cent or more of all defendants appearing before these courts are found guilty (Hodgson, 2001). In comparison to England and Wales this proportion seems staggeringly high. Based on the Judicial Statistics in 2001, only 39 per cent of Crown Court cases ended in a conviction; 36 per cent were discharged or acquitted by the judge, while 25 per cent led to a jury verdict of not guilty (Home Office, 2001). This difference, when taken at face value, should raise questions about the treatment of defendants in French courts, who seemingly stand a poor chance of acquittal.

The key question here relates to what these figures represent. An examination of trial procedures in France and England reveals important differences that put these figures into context. In France there are no separate procedures for defendants who do not protest their innocence. There is no such thing as a guilty or not guilty plea so that all defendants face a trial regardless of whether they admit their guilt or not. That certainly helps explain the high conviction rate. A further explanation might be found in the role and functioning of police and prosecution in France as compared to England and Wales, discussed in later chapters. But there are additional areas worth investigating in order to make sense of the French conviction rate. We may have to consider the role and functioning of jury trials, which are more common in England and Wales than in France. Perhaps we would also need to look at the different rules of evidence in the two systems. Thus, in order to compare statistics, we need to know how these figures came about and what they represent. Simply comparing figures on an assumption of like-for-like may give an impression of accuracy and precision that might well prove to be deceptive.

There is a further epistemological issue relating to the use of statistics. It relies on the availability of statistics in the first place. That availability is not random or 'natural' but depends on what is considered worthy of collecting statistics about. On some crimes or behaviours data are vigorously collected in some jurisdictions but not others, for example on truancy. The consequence of this is that those who utilise official data for their research will inevitably follow official agendas. This is evident when we look at areas that fall outside national data collection efforts. We could consider statistics on migration deaths (Weber and Pickering, 2011). Similar issues appear in the investigation of deportations (Weber and Pickering, 2013). The researchers' work cannot rely on official statistics, typically because there aren't any. Because of the lack of official data, the size of the problem is difficult to gauge, a situation that may in fact suit those in power. The general point to make is that working with official statistics does not only expose the researcher to the limitations of those data (see Bennett, 2011 for a review). They must also accept that they risk working to official priorities. Those priorities may obscure questions that perhaps urgently need to be asked but aren't, as the work of Weber and Pickering demonstrates. In summary, the very availability of statistics carries judgements and values about what is deemed important to know and comparative research should reflectively consider such value judgements.

Comparative criminal justice and globalisation

Globalisation refers to the growing interconnectedness of states and societies (Held, 2000) and it comes in many guises. It is brought about by mobility of people, goods, information and ideas. It has led to a state of affairs where global issues are local ones and vice versa. When global news stories break, wherever they are in the world, almost instantly the whole world is watching, via radio, television and the internet. Because of that, globalisation is said to have compressed space and time and to make both, as it were, less important to our existence: we can therefore say that life is to an extent despatialised.

Geographic distance is less of an issue as we can build and maintain personal relationships via telephone and social networking websites (Aas, 2007). This has allowed us to utilise our caring capacity for happenings and people elsewhere, where much of our belonging is now anchored: with family in another country, friends who moved away and online pals we have never met in person: what we care about most can be far removed from us. At the same time, much of what displeases us remains very local: antisocial behaviour, noise pollution and neighbourhood decay are eminently local features. Despite the force of globalisation, most people cannot take themselves away from their local surroundings. After all, the ability to travel or to move to your desired location is the preserve of the 'happy few'. For many others borders are firmly closed and areas economically out of reach. Thus, globalisation enhances issues of equality: a minority of world citizens move themselves to where they want to be, but a majority is locked into poverty and deprivation.

Globalisation is something you must be aware of when conducting comparative research (Nelken, 2011; Savelsberg, 2011; Sheptycki, 2011). The classic anthropological game plan of visiting isolated communities and gaining insight into the lived experience of locals via sustained immersion is less appropriate than it once was. Communities are connected via mass media, and happenings such as the Olympic Games and natural disasters are experiences that are vicariously shared all over the world.

In one respect globalisation has served comparative research well. Much research relies extensively on the internet, through which official data, statistics, academic publications and also newspapers and television coverage are available. The internet allows the comparative researcher extensive exposure to the issues that they study by simply clicking their mouse. In that regard, comparative research is now more the province of the web-savvy than of the intrepid explorer. But how do we study interconnected rather than isolated contexts? Hardie-Bick et al. (2005) argue that globalisation should be a focal point for criminology. Comparative research should examine 'how criminology's global context encourages the transgression of boundaries: national, cultural and theoretical' (Hardie-Bick et al., 2005: 7). From this perspective, key objects are phenomena created or enhanced by globalisation, such as transnational offending, the crossing of borders and the relations between crime, fear and mass migration (Aas, 2007). Sheptycki (2011) argues that comparative criminology finds 'old habits' hard to shift. That includes taking the state as the standard comparative unit of analysis and focusing on the relative preponderance of various common offences through statistical indicators. He argues that in a world of diffuse and complex interrelations the old fashioned 'compare and contrast' method runs a risk of ignoring interrelations. He concludes by saying that comparative criminology needs to adapt to take account of these changed circumstances.

At the same time, we can continue to look at national or local arrangements (Sheptycki (2011: 147). Sheptycki calls them 'somewhat useful' but we must be aware of the fact that globalisation impacts on those arrangements. New police uniforms in West Africa rather resemble police uniforms worn by US officers. That is not a coincidence: US cop shows that are shown around the world will have shaped perceptions of what a police uniform ought to look like. Thus, when investigating policing in West Africa we must not only take into account the socio-cultural context in which it is set and the impact of the colonial past but at the same time we must appreciate that new directions are shaped by the fallout of globalisation: global mass media shapes our cultural imagination. The meta-narrative therefore is not one of diversity in isolation, it is about local arrangements given shape in relation to local traditions, historical factors and the diffuse cultural, economic and normative influence that is exerted via mass media, visiting experts, travel experiences, and that is heavily affected by globalisation.

The doom scenario of globalisation turning comparative research into an anachronism because it will obliterate diversity is not coming to fruition. Instead, globalisation can bring about local defiance (Pakes, 2007d) so that local differences get increasingly valued and sometimes enhanced. Savelsberg (2011) also highlights the remaining importance of national contexts and argues that broader comparative analysis is still required. He argues that cross-national comparative studies remain crucial as it is there where the differential impacts of globalisation can be discerned: 'Global scripts encounter local cultural conditions, rooted in religion and collective memories, and distinct institutional arrangements' (Savelsberg, 2011: 82).

In addition, the fact is that the benefits of globalisation are unevenly distributed and this should drive comparative research. Some regions are reaping its benefits whereas others are excluded. Such bifurcations do not only occur between whole continents, but also occur within societies and local communities. Globalisation favours the active, the educated, the mobile, the entrepreneur and in particular the wealthy (commonly referred to as the 1 per cent). But those without the required skills and assets justifiably feel in danger of being left behind. For some globalisation is a promise, of cosmopolitan life experiences and business opportunities. To others, it is a force set to destroy their way of life. The differential impact of globalisation on local communities is a key area of comparative research.

Methodological hazards

Zedner (1995) notes the following risks involved in comparative research. The first is what she calls 'criminological tourism'. This is a trap into which it is relatively easy to fall. Going abroad often occurs in a positive frame of mind. We feel free of the worries and commitments of everyday life and are set to enjoy ourselves. It is then easy to find the locals friendly, helpful and hospitable without realising that our own positive attitude (not to mention our tourist money) might bring about such feelings. Zedner warns of the possibility of misreading or simplifying local customs and regarding exotic arrangements uncritically. In particular, when reading reports on countries that traditionally receive praise, a critical attitude is necessary. That includes policing in Japan as well as soft drugs policy in the Netherlands, where at times particularly rosy accounts have been provided by foreign observers, sometimes vehemently protested against by native scholars (e.g. Franke, 1990).

The second caveat relates to linguistic difficulties, one of the afore-mentioned pitfalls cited by Leishman (1999). Zedner (1995) takes the position that anything less than complete fluency leaves one vulnerable to misinterpretation. This, however, has not stopped many a prominent scholar from writing books about foreign systems without having mastered the native language. In countries where most people speak English as a second language the English-speaking researcher is probably in a less vulnerable position than in countries where the researcher's language is not widely spoken. Thus, although the advantages of speaking the indigenous language are obvious, an inability to do so should not automatically disqualify anyone from engaging in comparative research.

The third difficulty relates to what might be called 'touching base'. It relates to questions such as: who do you talk to? What do you read? What do you observe? Many aspects of criminal justice worth looking into are controversial. It is therefore important to try to assess both sides of any argument and not limit oneself to talking to a restricted range of people with a shared set of opinions and knowledge. This need is closely related to what Leishman calls 'meaningful' access (Leishman, 1999). The touching-base caveat becomes more poignant as a function of the intensity of contact with the people and culture that is being investigated. Participant observation carries its own set of risks, including that of going native, that is, the over-identification with the population studied at the expense of one's critical faculties (Bruyn, 1996; Jorgensen, 1993).

There are sceptics who argue that the entire enterprise of the comparative analysis of foreign criminal justice systems is flawed. Stephen argues in relation to comparing the systems of France and England and Wales that:

> The whole temper and spirit of the French and the English differ so widely, that it would be rash for an Englishman to speak of trials in France as they actually are. We can think of the system only as it would work if transplanted into England. It may well be that it not only looks, but is a very different thing in France.
>
> (Stephen, in Vogler, 1996: 17–18)

Similarly, Vogler emphasises that comparative research involves 'many attempts to translate the untranslatable' (Vogler, 1996: 18). It might well be impossible to reach a complete understanding of foreign systems, just as it might be impossible to completely understand another person. But that should not stop us from attempting to get to know others, and learning from their experiences. The same is true for the study of foreign criminal justice systems.

In order to undertake such study responsibly and ethically it is important to reflect upon one's own position. Heidensohn (2006) distinguishes nine different types of comparative researcher. I will pick out five that are discussed in Heidensohn (2007) and add a further one. Perhaps the most important group in British criminology are *refugees*. Refugees did not leave their home country by choice but once displaced learn the local language and can make profound academic contribution to the state of knowledge of their area. Heidensohn mentions Mannheim and Radzinowicz who both escaped the rise of Fascism in mainland Europe. Another category is referred to as *rendez-vous-ers*, those who make brief visits to their subject area as a substitute for sustained immersion. *Reformers* are those who travel abroad in order to find answers to questions raised at home. These comparatists will often look for possibilities of policy transfer, that is, to capture arrangements elsewhere and, as it were, take them home for implementation. Shopping around for ideas without much regard for context is hazardous yet not uncommon. Another group of comparative researchers are called *armchair travellers* by Heidensohn. These researchers study arrangements elsewhere without ever leaving their base. Finally, there are *global theorists* who seek to present theories that transcend national or local contexts and are universally applicable.

Declaring my hand as a Dutch national who has been based in the UK for over 15 years I would add the category of the *expatriate*. The 'expat' combines many virtues: intimate knowledge of their home country but having moved abroad, combined with the ability to look at developments in '*la patrie*' from a distance (my reading of Van Swaaningen, 2011: 131 is that he agrees). That brings a perspective that is both sensitive to nuance and detail but that at the same time can be broad brush and holistic. It is a perspective that is no longer characterised by sustained immersion but can rather be described as the ability to 'hover above' a society or community to identify patterns that are not easily discernable by either the stranger or the local. The expat is well suited to undertake comparative research, as long as unwarranted tendencies to either romanticise or vilify the home nation can be avoided.

A very specific comparative method: in defence of prison tourism

Some of the oldest comparative research on conditions in prison relied on prison visits. We have already noted the work of penal reformer John Howard who was a prolific prison visitor. In his book (Howard, 1777) he gives brief descriptions of what he found. He was particularly interested in the economics of prisons, which often depended on prisoners paying fees. However, he also demonstrated a good eye for prison conditions even if many of his visits were brief. He commented on a lack of water, sewage and fresh air in some of the prisons he visited, and on occasion despaired at the gambling and debauchery. In the Netherlands, in contrast, he noted: 'prisons … are so quiet, and most of them so clean, that a visitor can hardly believe he is in a gaol' (p. 119). Prison visits can certainly garner strong impressions and feed the comparative imagination.

David Downes (1988) similarly visited numerous prisons in the Netherlands in the early 1980s, and he was also impressed with what he saw; more recently differences between UK and Netherlands prisons were revalidated by Kruttschnitt and Dirkzwager (2011). The prison visit as a means of research was also successfully utilised by John Pratt to investigate *penal exceptionalism* in Finland, Norway and Sweden, which led to high profile publications and a degree of debate on the prison visit method (Pratt, 2008a, 2008b).

The prison visit method can of course easily be criticised as it may lead to biased impressions. First, there is the choice of prison. Authorities will be most eager to show visitors their flagship establishment and that may skew observers' views on the prison system as a whole. In addition, one is typically shown round by the governor or a substitute. These individuals will be both wanting and able to cast the prison in a favourable light. They may showcase what is good and hide what isn't. When speaking with inmates (a staple of such visits) their selection will almost inevitably be biased. Thus, there is plenty of opportunity for such visits to lead to an unwarranted rose-tinted view of these establishments.

Pratt and Eriksen (2012) however, defend the method and argue that as long as one visits a number of establishments and one does not solely rely on these visits as data they are most informative and certainly allow for an insight into key aspects of prison life. Prison architecture cannot be faked, and the language in which the establishment is discussed, the obvious safety measures that are present or absent all provide valuable information. Declaring my hand as a keen prison visitor myself, I would agree that the prison visit is a valuable tool, albeit one that cannot trump prison ethnography proper (e.g., Shammas, 2014). Through a visit one discovers the smells and noises of prisons (they do differ considerably between establishments and countries), the degree of safety measures and the degrees of freedom the visitor is afforded. Chats with inmates may just provide an insight into staff–inmate relationships. Conversations with prison staff may do the same. In short, although not the best comparative method, prison tourism should not be dismissed as inherently flawed. It does allow for a peek into the kitchen of penal policy and the knowledgeable observer may derive some rich and meaningful information from it.

Conclusion: a cosmopolitan turn?

People look at other countries and contexts for differing reasons and to avoid the pitfalls of 'tourism', the purpose of the comparison should always be made clear. The risk for anthropological research is that one gets too engrossed in the new, the exciting and the exotic. The risk of positivistic research is that there will be too little actual immersion. As with so much, it is about striking a balance. Zedner (1995) describes the reality of comparative criminal justice research as follows:

Doing comparative research rarely entails selling one's own home and tearing up one's passport, forever to live among the drug dealers of Delhi or the detectives of Düsseldorf. Neither can one, with credibility at any rate, write about continental criminal procedure without stepping outside the ivy-clad walls of an Oxford college. Rather the research process entails developing a general theoretical (but distant) understanding at home-base, punctuated by a series of forays (often of increasing duration) into the terrain of study. This itinerary is matched by an intellectual journey which takes one from the perspective of global structures to the minutiae of local detail and back and forth over the course of the research in 'a sort of intellectual perpetual motion' (Geertz, 1983: 235). While periods of fieldwork provide for immersion in local culture (the court, the prison, the police station), the journeys between make possible an intellectual distancing. Once more library-bound, the researcher can engage in the detached reflections and distanced evaluation which are the very stuff of comparison.

(Zedner, 1995: 19)

Finally, it is important to remember that globalisation is changing comparative research profoundly. Beck and Sznaider (2006) argue that social research therefore requires what they call a 'cosmopolitan turn'. They critique methodological nationalism which carries the assumption that societies are bound by states, arguing that in our globalised world that simply is no longer the case. As globalisation happens, they argue, cosmopolitanism should follow: a perspective or a mind-set that allows us to illuminate the transnationality that we see around us. Methodological cosmopolitanism requires new, non-national units of research. Another issue is how to 'understand' phenomena from a cosmopolitan perspective. Can we still, as Mannheim argued, look for universal truths? Or is knowledge essentially local? Beck and Sznaider (2006) argue that there is, or should be, a universalistic minimum: there are substantive norms (that some might call human rights) that should be held up as universal. But beyond that, the picture is unclear: can there be multiple cosmopolitanisms? Can cosmopolitanism be essentially local or does that negate what cosmopolitanism is all about? Clearly the methodological and epistemological challenge proffered by globalisation is far from put to bed. It is however clear that globalisation is changing comparative criminal justice research (Nelken, 2011; Pakes, 2013). It is likely to revitalise it.

Further reading

Nelken, D. (Ed) (2011) *Comparative criminal justice and globalization*. Farnham: Ashgate.

Pakes, F. (2010) The comparative method in globalised criminology. *Australian and New Zealand journal of criminology, 43,* 17–30.

Sheptycki, J. (2005). Relativism, transnationalism and comparative criminology. In J. Sheptycki and A. Wardak (Eds), *Transnational and comparative criminology*. London: GlassHouse, 69–88.

Study questions

1   What are the two main theoretical perspectives on comparative research? Describe both with examples.
2   How does globalisation complicate comparative study?
3   Describe in outline the three main methods of comparative research.

Chapter 3

Comparing crime

Finding patterns, uncovering meaning

There is a widespread desire to establish the rate of crime across countries or jurisdictions. The benefit of such data is obvious. They help us chart the 'state of crime'. They can provide us with information on the relative effectiveness of certain measures against crime. We can also study the relation between rates of crime and geographic, cultural or governmental variables. These latter variables can include population data, measures of wealth or economic conjuncture or type of government. Differences in crime rates between countries can also help give us insight into configurations of social control and work towards assessing their impact. In summary, comparative crime data can further our understanding of deviance and social control in a variety of ways and it is therefore no surprise that many studies, varying from the strictly local to the truly global have been conducted in order to capture differences and similarities between rates of crime.

We saw in the previous chapter that comparative research frequently struggles in ensuring that comparisons are like for like. There are many reasons why comparing crime is often difficult. Crime definitions change from country to country; what is legally performed euthanasia in one country can be murder or complicity in murder in another. Homosexuality and adultery are prohibited in many countries in the Middle East and Africa but not in most others. Thus, when comparing crime rates, an obvious disparity relates to differing criminalisations. It reminds us of the fact that crime is not a natural category but a social construction that is to an extent, perhaps to an increasing extent, arbitrary, contested and negotiable.

In addition we must appreciate that understandings of crime may differ as much as crime definitions. In the UK it was discovered that one in three victims of a sex offence did not regard that offence as a crime but rather as 'something that happens' (Walby and Allen, 2004). That is a disturbing finding. Similarly, offences such as stalking may not be recognised as such by victims. That makes it unlikely that such offences would feature reliably in self-report data let alone official reporting. In a comparative perspective, these problems are always compounded as offences but are less likely to carry the same cultural meaning in various parts of the world. A sex offence in Oslo is unlikely to be viewed identically to the same physical behaviour in Oman or Osaka. Comparative research needs to be sensitive to that but we shall see that that is not always the case.

Many criminologists would make the argument that reducing criminal acts to something we should count actually strips it of meaning. Our preoccupation with counting crime not only produces data that is irrelevant, they would argue, but it also provides knowledge on crime that simply misunderstands the very phenomenon it is meant to capture.

With that in mind, let us examine crime trends, the way they have been investigated and the meaning that can be attached to them.

Comparing official statistics

The principal drawback of official statistics in a comparative context is that they are compiled in differing ways and for varying reasons. That makes comparison inevitably hazardous. That said there are studies that do compare such statistics with a certain degree of accuracy and consistency. The sceptical case (Young, 2004) against the value of such statistics is easily made. First, the 'dark figure', that is, crime never reported to the police, does not feature and in addition, it is thought that official statistics frequently reflect police action and priority rather than rates of victimisation. For some crimes, for example drink driving, that is more the case than others, such as burglary. The sceptical case is well rehearsed in criminology but we must not forget about the value of official statistics. Official statistics are often the most comprehensive source of data and often quite easily accessible. Because these statistics are periodically reported they also lend themselves to the analysis of patterns over time. Young (2004) therefore argues that such data provide for important raw material for theory construction: statistics do not provide all the answers but ignore them at your peril!

The very existence of international crime statistics signals the internationalisation of criminal justice. It is clear that the last 20 to 30 years have seen an enormous institutionalisation of international crime data agencies. Supranational bodies such as the United Nations, the Council of Europe and Interpol and Europol all hold crime data. HEUNI is the European Institute for Crime Prevention and Control, affiliated with the United Nations. HEUNI in Finland is the European link in the network of institutes operating within the framework of the United Nations Crime Prevention and Criminal Justice Programme. It was founded in 1981. The primary objective of HEUNI is to promote the international exchange of information on crime prevention and control among European countries. There are a number of such institutes in various parts of the world. For example, based in Japan, UNAFEI focuses on technical cooperation including training and research to promote the sound development of criminal justice systems in Asia and the Pacific Region. ILANUD is based in Costa Rica and is the UN affiliated Latin American Institute for the Prevention of Crime and the Treatment of Offenders. In Uganda in Africa there is UNAFRI, the United Nations African Institute for the Prevention of Crime and the Treatment of Offenders.

HEUNI's data on official crime in Europe and North America are widely used. Although there are prevalence data of many recorded crimes it is possibly the most serious crimes such as murder that are most reliably recorded by the police. Table 3.1 compares murder rates in 27 countries in 1995 and 2004 (Aromaa and Heiskanen, 2008). When looking at Table 3.1 do bear in mind that murder is not defined equally across jurisdictions. Homicide in the UK comprises murder, manslaughter and infanticide. It may well be different elsewhere. In addition, as the report acknowledges, some countries include attempted homicide, whereas others do not. That of course affects the figures but it is important to note that it does so in more than one way. First, if you count all homicide as well as all attempted homicides, the prevalence will inevitably be higher. In addition, whereas homicides can be subject to issues of definition this is even more the case for attempted homicide. It may require

Table 3.1 Homicide rates in 1995 and 2004 (per 100,000 population)

Country	Homicide rate 1995	Homicide rate 2004
Norway	1.0	0.8
Denmark	1.1	0.8
Ireland	1.2	0.9
Belgium	1.4	2.1
England and Wales	1.4	1.6
Cyprus	1.4	1.9
Germany	1.7	1.0
Czech Republic	1.7	2.2
Netherlands	1.8	1.3
Canada	1.8	2.0
Italy	1.8	1.2
Poland	2.2	1.7
Slovenia	2.2	1.5
Hungary	2.9	2.1
Finland	2.9	2.8
France	3.0	1.7
Romania	3.3	2.4
Croatia	3.6	1.9
Portugal	4.1	1.8
Azerbaijan	5.8	2.4
Bulgaria	5.9	3.1
United States	8.2	5.5
Ukraine	8.5	7.3
Belarus	9.3	8.3
Latvia	11.6	8.6
Lithuania	13.8	9.4
Estonia	16.6	6.7

Source: Aromaa and Heiskanen, 2008.

intent in some jurisdictions but not others, for instance. Also, attempted homicide might, in a plea bargaining situation, be bargained down to a violent crime rather than a 'life' crime. Thus, attempted homicide is more susceptible to definitional and re-definitional negotiations that render such figures much less reliable.

Looking at the data and bearing in mind the caveats listed above, the safest comparison is within jurisdictions over time (obviously after having checked that criminal definitions and criminal justice practice have not meaningfully changed over this period). It is clear that in most countries listed, the murder rate is going down. The HEUNI report seems to argue that a proper level of analysis is not country by country, but in fact by clusters of nations or per region. We can distinguish four regions, North America, Western Europe (those within the EU when it consisted of 15 Western European countries), Eastern European countries that became part of the enlarged EU, and finally non-EU European countries. The 'old' EU countries have by far the lowest homicide rate (Aromaa and Heiskanen, 2008). Country clustering can of course be performed in many different ways. Messner and Rosenfeld (2007) classified countries by their levels of social welfare protection whereas other classifications, by legal tradition, or distribution of wealth are also possible. We can also compare below the level of the nation state. City to city comparisons are increasingly carried out, not least in victimisation surveys. With all that said, the substantial and widespread drop in murder rates does seem highly noteworthy.

A more recent HEUNI publication (but based on data from the same period) provides somewhat more sensitive data. The overall reduction in intentional homicide may obscure increases in certain sub-regions. This is particularly the case for the Caribbean and Central America. The author points to drug trafficking, organised crime and gang activity as probable causes (Malby, 2010). When looking at the percentage of homicide using firearms, regional differences become quite stark. It is particularly striking that in the sub-regions where homicide has been on the increase, homicide by firearm is most prevalent; close to 80 per cent of all homicides involve firearms. Contrast that with the situation in Europe, Asia and Oceania where the figure is less than 20 per cent. However, Malby does add the caveat of differing counting methodologies and differing national capabilities for the production of statistics when we interpret these figures.

Alvazzi del Frate (2010) discusses the ways in which UN agencies compile criminal data and the challenges that that brings. She argues that solid systems of crime statistics rely on a) the availability of specific data collection methods and instruments, adapted to the local context; b) the availability of technical expertise and/or equipment to carry out data collection and analysis; and c) the commitment and motivation of relevant government agencies to introduce a strategic approach to the collection and analysis of crime and criminal justice statistics. It is clear that often this is still lacking.

The researchers do play down the difficulty of asking respondents such questions over the telephone: 'Contrary to popular belief, there is no indication that asking for victimisation by sexual offences over the phone causes problems, provided skilled interviewers are used for the fieldwork' (Van Dijk et al., 2008: 77).

However, it is noteworthy that ICVS findings on rates of sexual victimisation are at odds with United Nations data (United Nations, 2006). The latter found sexual victimisation most prevalent in developing countries, a finding that the ICVS fails to replicate. That does cast doubt on the validity of these data. You might even wonder whether it is feasible in the first place to ask such personal questions in a way that assures universal interpretation across cultures and continents. To be fair, more recently Van Dijk (2010) has conceded that other instruments (he mentions the International Violence Against Women Survey (Johnson et al., 2007)), are preferable.

There is now a wealth of victimisation data away from Western industrialised nations. Burglary rates in parts of Asia, Africa and Latin America are presented in Table 3.3 (from Alvazzi del Frate, 1998).

It is interesting to note the low burglary rate in Brazil, particularly in the light of the earlier finding of high robbery rates in major Brazilian cities. Taking a further perspective, in Chapter 4 we will discuss Huggins' work on the Brazilian police, with its rich history of torture and abuses of power. You might expect that in that context, self-report data are much more reliable than official police statistics as citizens might be highly reluctant to report crimes to the police.

Table 3.3 Burglary rates in countries in Asia, Africa and Latin America (per 100,000 population)

	Burglary	Attempted burglary
Asia		
Indonesia	3.9	2.5
China	2.3	0.2
Philippines	2.0	1.6
India	1.4	2.0
Africa		
Tanzania	19.0	12.9
Uganda	11.7	11.7
Zimbabwe	10.7	9.0
Botswana	10.4	4.6
South Africa	6.3	3.7
Tunisia	7.2	3.6
Egypt	2.6	4.4
Latin America		
Paraguay	8.2	6.5
Costa Rica	7.3	8.5
Bolivia	6.7	8.5
Colombia	6.0	9.7
Argentina	5.5	5.5
Brazil	1.9	2.8

Source: Alvazzi del Frate, 1998.

An interesting recent outcome of several sweeps of crime victimisation surveys is that it has spurred publications seeking to explain what seems to be a *global crime drop* (Van Dijk et al., 2012). This is perhaps a counterintuitive but in fact rather strongly evidenced finding. In all European countries for which they have sufficient data, crime has dropped and this is true for violent as well as non-violent crime. The drop in crime was particularly noticeable in some Eastern European countries such as Poland and Georgia. In fact only Belgium did not show a reduction in crime in the years preceding 2004/5.

Van Dijk and Tseloni (2012) also found drops in burglaries from the 1980s onwards. They list that burglary rates in Argentina, Brazil, the Philippines and Uganda have come down substantially to evidence that the crime drop is not restricted to the West. Furthermore they also note a lowering of the rate of assault in many non-Western major cities such as Buenos Aires and Johannesburg. Van Dijk and Tseloni therefore speak of a semi-universal drop in the volume of crime that occurred after 1995 or somewhat later. This is true for homicide and the volume of crime and tells us something quite important about the state of crime across the world. What the exact causes are, however is not easy to disentangle. An intriguing hypothesis might be one of displacement, either towards transnational offending, or towards emerging offence types such as fraud. But then again, perhaps the world simply experiences less crime.

Specialised international statistics

Specialist agencies tend to hold data on particular forms of crime. These are often crimes with a strong transnational or international component and crimes that are difficult to count through official statistics. EMCDDA, the European Monitoring Centre for Drugs and Drug Addiction (see www.emcdda.europa.eu) collects and disseminates data on various aspects of drug usage, trade and legislation. The Annual Report on the state of the drugs problem in Europe presents the EMCDDA's yearly overview. It is highly elaborate and available in no less than 22 languages. EMCDDA relies on a network of about 30 national monitoring centres to gather and analyse country data according to common data–collection standards and tools. The results of this national monitoring process are analysed and form the building blocks of the Annual Report. It is important to note that these drug reports do not focus on one particular type of crime. The drugs trade can violate many laws and we must remember that the legal status of drug possession and usage differs considerably between countries and policing practice may vary from place to place even within the same jurisdictions.

The Cannabis section of the report looks at self-report user data, but also at number of seizures, the price and potency of cannabis products and legislative changes in the various European States. The state of cannabis usage of 15–34 year olds in Europe is summarised in Table 3.4 (EMCDDA, 2012).

Table 3.4 Cannabis usage in Europe

15–34 years	Lifetime usage	Last year
Estimated total number of users in age group	45 million	16 million
European average	32.5%	12.4%
Range	3.0%–49.3%	0.6%–20.7%
Lowest prevalence countries	Romania (3.0%) Greece (10.8%) Bulgaria (14.3%) Poland (16.1%)	Romania (0.6%) Greece (3.2%) Poland (5.3%) Hungary (5.7%)
Highest prevalence countries	Czech Republic (49.3%) France (45.1%) Denmark (44.5%) Spain (42.4%)	Czech Republic (20.7%) Italy (20.3%) Spain (19.4%) France (17.5%)

Source: EMCDDA, 2012.

We can see that the prevalence of cannabis use among young people in Europe is high but that the rate differs quite dramatically from country to country. Nearly half of all people between 15 and 34 in the Czech Republic report having used cannabis products, with prevalence rates in France and Denmark not much lower. Rates in the Southern European nations of Malta, Greece and Cyprus are much lower evidencing an effect of region in cannabis usage patterns. In most countries rates of usage are either stable or slightly decreasing. The decrease might have something to do with decreasing rates of smoking of regular cigarettes, a facilitator for the smoking of cannabis products. Cannabis in schoolchildren within the European Union is particularly high in the Czech Republic, France, Slovakia and the Netherlands (as well as the United States). Norway ranks lowest.

Table 3.5 Cocaine usage in the European Union

15–34 years	Lifetime usage	Last year
Estimated total number of users in age group	8 million	3 million
European average	6.3%	2.1%
Range	0.7%–13.6%	0.2%–4.4%
Lowest prevalence countries	Lithuania, Romania (0.7%) Greece (1.0%) Poland (1.3%) Czech Republic (1.6%)	Greece, Romania (0.2%) Lithuania, Poland (0.3%) Hungary (0.4%) Czech Republic (0.5%)
Highest prevalence countries	Spain (13.6%) United Kingdom (12.8%) Ireland (9.4%) Denmark (8.9%)	Spain (4.4%) United Kingdom (4.2%) Italy (2.9%) Ireland (2.8%)

Source: EMCDDA, 2012.

The corresponding figures on cocaine are listed in Table 3.5. Overall prevalence figures are much lower. It is perhaps interesting to note that some high prevalence countries in terms of cannabis usage score low on cocaine usage, such as the Czech Republic. Conversely, Spain and Denmark score high on user rates for both.

The EMCDDA Annual Report documents further regional differences in other types of drug use across Europe. In Eastern Europe, amphetamines are more prevalent than cocaine but in Western and Southern Europe the situation is reversed. Usage patterns of amphetamines at country level are not dissimilar to that of cannabis. High prevalence countries include the United Kingdom, Denmark, Norway and Ireland. Lowest rates of prevalence were obtained from Greece, Malta, Cyprus and Romania. That situation is more or less the case for cocaine as well, with a few European countries accounting for the majority of cocaine use. Overall, just over one in twenty individuals between 15 and 34 years old say that they have used cocaine in their lifetime. The Annual Report argues that the vast majority of cocaine comes from Colombia, Peru and Bolivia which arrives in Europe via trade routes utilising the Caribbean region or, increasingly, West Africa (EMCDDA, 2008).

The United Nations Office on Drugs and Crime (UNODC) collects and disseminates data on drugs on a global scale. However, its remit has become wider than that. Due to the perceived nexus between the drugs trade, organised crime and terrorism, UNODC is also mandated to assist member states in their struggle against illicit drugs, crime and terrorism. It is funded by contributions (mostly voluntary) by UN member states. An important publication is the World Drug Report that is produced annually. Like the EMCDDA Annual Report it examines both trade and consumption but the World Drug Report has a stronger focus on the production of drugs.

As far as cannabis is concerned, in 2006 most cannabis was produced in the Americas (55 per cent) and Africa (22 per cent). However, the cannabis market is highly regionalised. Cannabis can be grown almost everywhere and countries mainly producing for export remain limited: a number of African countries including South Africa, Nigeria, Ghana and Morocco and a few Asian countries including Afghanistan, Pakistan and Kazakhstan (UNODC, 2008).

The situation is different for opium/heroin. It is particularly Afghanistan and Myanmar (often referred to as Burma) where the growth of opium poppy takes place. Afghanistan in particular accounts for 82 per cent of the global area under cultivation. Whereas cannabis production worldwide is in a phase of slight decline, opium poppy cultivation is on the rise. Further evidence of the importance of Afghanistan as a cultivation and production centre comes from analysing the geography of heroin seizures. About 80 per cent of global opiate seizures were made in Asia in 2006. The bulk of global opiate seizures took place in the countries surrounding Afghanistan which together accounted for 73 per cent of global opiate seizures in 2006.

From the area of drugs we have entered the world of international and transnational crime. Transnational crime such as drug trafficking cannot easily be studied using self-report statistics, so that official measures such as for seizures are an important indicator for trends in prevalence, but of course not without limitations. It means that policing imperatives and border control activity will seriously affect the estimates of prevalence of such behaviours.

Within the European Union there is the European Organised Crime Threat Assessment (OCTA), produced by the European police office Europol. The report seeks to assess the development of groups, where the groups' leaders and assets are placed, where and how effectively they use corruption and violence and other structural factors (OCTA, 2008)

For instance, when looking at Trafficking in Human Beings, the Report lists a few key variables that will shape developments in Trafficking in Human Beings. One of these factors is the pool of potential victims or illegal immigrants in Eastern European countries such as Ukraine, Belarus, Moldova and Russia. Romanian and Lithuanian organised crime groups are well placed to capitalise on that. Other factors include dynamics linked to the African continent. Every year, tens of thousands of people from Africa attempt to enter the EU. Sadly, many lose their lives in the process. Africa is also being used as an area of transit by larger organised crime groups involved in smuggling immigrants from other continents. The role of Africa in Trafficking in Human Beings for sexual exploitation in the EU seems to be mainly played by Nigerian organised crime groups. Finally, another crucial variable is illegal immigration from China. Chinese organised crime networks facilitate the illegal immigration of Chinese people into the EU, according to OCTA (2008).

Although the report speaks with great authority it is not always clear how the data that support it are obtained or exactly how the analysis has been carried out. It has led to fierce criticism by Van Duyne (2007), who wrote of the 2006 OCTA report:

> About this accountability I can be short: there is none. The reader is supposed to feel satisfied with the statement: 'The OCTA is based on a multi-source approach, including law enforcement and non-law enforcement sources. These sources include various European agencies as well as the private sector. A specific emphasis is put on elaborating the benefits of an intensified public–private partnership.' What the input of the various law enforcement agencies and private sector is remains hidden. … Hence, there is no way to determine the reliability of the data input, the processing of the data, and therefore the reliability of the findings and the validity of the conclusions about the stated threats.
>
> (Van Duyne, 2007: 121)

He also finds the report obscure on previous research and often rather stating the obvious: 'one general statement of irrefutable truism about threats and unspecified threatening OC groups is followed by another' (Van Duyne, 2007: 127).

This goes to show that the exact establishment of the state of affairs in the murky world of transnational organised crime is not at all easy. It is also contested, with investigations hampered by the vested interests of organisations involved with tackling it and the impact that such phenomena can have on public opinion and international relations.

For the EMCDDA Annual Report standardised reporting is used, in order to overcome the substantial legal disparities between the various European states. That increases the reliability of the data reported. However, in the area of terrorism, definitional issues are possibly more pertinent due to the strong ideological connotations that the term carries. Let us examine a key publication that seeks to establish the rate of terrorist acts. Europol produces an annual report that works to national definitions. It is the EU Terrorism Situation and Trend Report (TE-SAT) 2008. By adopting national definitions, an element of standardisation has been lost but the trouble does not end there. The member states are, for instance, asked to report the number of arrests for and individuals charged with terrorist offences. Two difficulties are immediately apparent. The first is that the term 'arrest' and its legal meaning vary considerably between countries and the same is true for 'charge'. This is not just a matter of legal translation: measures in different countries operate along different lines, making such terms to an extent untranslatable. In addition, terrorism laws may be evoked in cases that for all intents and purposes have nothing to do with terrorism as most people understand it. Anti-terrorism laws can, and are, used in public order situations in many countries. That could skew the data, and a complicating factor is that that is likely to happen more in some countries than in others. This highlights the fact that official data reflect official behaviour, not just criminal behaviour. A further practical drawback is that not all member states have submitted data.

These limitations aside, the report documents 583 terrorist acts in Europe in 2007 and that number includes foiled and failed attacks. Overwhelmingly, these acts took place in France (253) and Spain (264) and concern acts by separatist movements. No more than four Islamic terrorist acts were documented, less than 1 per cent of all reported terrorist acts. Two of those were in Britain. Across Europe over a thousand individuals were arrested for alleged terrorist offences; there were 331 convictions (TE-SAT, 2008).

There are many more crime databases, some local; some global. Some are only accessible for operational purposes. That includes a number of databases held by international police organisation Interpol. It has a database of child sexual abuse images, one of stolen travel documents, and it has also produced a CD-ROM on Stolen Works of Art. This CD-ROM contains information which Interpol's member countries have provided. The CD-ROM is designed for police and customs services, museums, auction rooms, antique dealers, collectors and lists about 31,500 works of art and cultural property. There are also databases that have a national basis but concern crimes or issues of transnational concern. NAPTIP in Nigeria, for example, is the National

substitute for understanding it. Heidensohn is critical of the zeal with which crime counting takes place and highlights the extra layer of complications brought about by cross-cultural comparisons. She argues:

> These studies seem sometimes to be pursuing a holy grail that we were all taught long ago to be sceptical of: the perfect, accurate measure of crime, and in the case of cross-cultural comparisons, the precise measure that can be applied across the board to crime around the world. But there are surely serious problems of positivistic oversimplification going on here? A further issue is that the standardisation may not catch the interesting, complex facets of the crime problem.
>
> (Heidensohn, 2007: 211)

In short counting crime is not the same as understanding crime. Crime is both a local and a global phenomenon, and we cannot strip either the local context or the global picture away if we want to truly understand it.

Criminology is obviously not only concerned with establishing the rate of crime. To use a meteorological metaphor, it is not just about counting rain drops, it is about understanding climates. We must remain alert to meaning. A senior law enforcement officer from the Netherlands once relayed the following story about antisocial behaviour in Singapore. Singapore is tightly governed, and has heavy penalties in place for relatively trivial offences.

> Singapore society does not easily compare to my background in the Netherlands. On the last evening of my stay there was an open air cultural event that I went to see. Lots of young people had gathered and in many countries, the police would be focused on crowd control. But I was struck how tidy and civilised it all was. No litter, no disorder, nothing. But then, I saw a few youths anxiously looking around, as if they were up to something. And they were. A few moments later, a couple of empty drink bottles were thrown into a river. It was the only bit of antisocial behaviour that I've seen. It made me smile: a bit of juvenile rebellion Singapore-style.

The point of the story is of course that throwing litter in Singapore constitutes a much edgier counter-cultural expression than it would ever be in the Netherlands. Simply comparing rates of litter is not getting to the heart of that difference. It is not that levels of litter differ but that meanings of litter differ alongside that. You can make similar observations about many crimes, from sex offences to honour killings: you can count them all over the world but their meaning is rooted in local circumstances. That is the challenge of researching crime in a comparative context: the global context bears down on it, but the local context cannot be forgotten either. A cosmopolitan outlook, as advocated by Beck and Sznaider (2006) is certainly required to consider both the local and the global with acuity.

Further reading

Crawford, A. (Ed) (2011) *International and comparative criminal justice and urban governance.* Cambridge: Cambridge University Press.

Van Dijk, J.J.M., Tseloni, A. and Farrell, G. (Eds) (2012) *The international crime drop.* London: Palgrave MacMillan.

Young, J. (2004) Voodoo criminology and the numbers game. In: J. Ferrell, K. Hayward, W. Morrison and M. Presdee (Eds) *Cultural criminology unleashed.* London: GlassHouse, 13–28.

Study questions

1   What could be the reasons underlying the global crime drop?
2   Why is comparing international official statistics so hazardous?
3   Can we really unambiguously establish the global rate of crime?

Chapter 4

Crime fighters, social workers, torturers

Comparative policing

Popular images of the police are commonplace in television and fiction. Police television series, from *The Streets of San Francisco* to *Miami Vice* and more recently *CSI* and *Life on Mars* have an enduring global popularity. The police intrigue both in fiction and in reality (see Reiner, 2000b, for an overview of police depictions in the media). The police are the most visible manifestation of the criminal justice system. They also symbolise the power that the state can exert over its citizens. This hands enormous social and cultural significance to the task of policing and the nature of police organisations.

What are the police for? This is a surprisingly nebulous question. Stock answers include to fight crime, or to maintain law and order. Reference is frequently made to serving communities, preventing crime, helping solve conflicts or assisting those in need. Within Western democracies the prevailing view seems to be that the police have a serving role to play and that that role is best implemented through community policing through which some or all of these competing tasks can be implemented.

> ### Missing persons in comparative perspective
>
> Dealing with missing persons is an interesting case in point when it comes to considering what the police's core business is. In many countries the police get notified of tens of thousands or more instances of individuals who have gone missing. People may go missing through their own volition whereas others may be lost, injured, abducted or murdered. They may be children or the elderly missing from care homes or hikers who got lost in the wilderness. They may also be teenagers overstaying Saturday night curfew. In short, many instances of missing may involve harm or crime, but many will not. What are the police to do? Comparative research in the USA, UK, Canada and Australia found that in these countries, missing persons are a policing matter, but that many activities are carried out in a multi-agency setting: 'police work with non-governmental agencies to identify people at risk of going missing, with an

aim of reducing missing person incidents'. 'Police rely on other agencies … to disseminate information about missing persons. Throughout investigations, police agencies involve other organizations to help police discover information about missing persons, locate missing persons, and support missing persons on their return' (Missing Women Commission of Inquiry (Canada), 2012). This highlights three aspects of such police work. The first is that whereas we can distinguish 'crime' policing and 'non crime' policing in principle, in practice that distinction is frequently blurred. The second is that policing is increasingly, and probably essentially, multi-agency work where boundaries of responsibility and modes of interaction and exchange are continuously negotiated. The third is that much police work is reactive, further to calls from the public, which means that often the police job is to do what it is asked to do. These facets make it virtually impossible to place clear boundaries around any tasks that are deemed to be 'natural' police work.

The conceptualisation of policing as crime fighting, law and order and community service tends to be applied to Western democracies where something resembling policing by popular consent takes place. Unfortunately, examples where police forces do not quite fit the community they police are plentiful. Colonial police forces around the world often primarily had the interests of the colonial power at heart (see Cole, 1999, for an overview). The same is true for police forces in dictatorial or authoritarian states, whose main job is to ensure a tyrannical regime stays in power. Their style and organisation are often of a military or para-military nature and set against citizens who are seen to constitute an insidious threat. In such contexts, community concerns come second place at best. New democracies often face the challenge of transforming a police force that traditionally operated against the people into one that actually serves them. Needless to say, such new identities are not achieved overnight. The police force in Argentina, for instance, is still regarded by many as heavy handed and the state continues to be seen as authoritarian: even though the country has been a democracy for some time there remains considerable distrust of those in power (Ebbe and De Olano, 2000). Ebbe has argued that in such countries as Argentina, Nigeria and Brazil the police continue to be viewed as instruments of repression, antagonistic to the general public and estranged from the communities in which they operate (Ebbe, 2000a).

Violence workers: police torturers in Brazil

Why and how do ordinary people become torturers? Huggins et al. (2002) interviewed two dozen police officers in Brazil whom they characterise as 'violence workers'. Some of them had been involved with torture whereas others claimed they did not actually engage in torture themselves but could be regarded as torture facilitators during the Military Rule in Brazil between 1964 and 1985. Huggins and her colleagues found that torture was looked upon from an instrumental perspective: torture as a means, applicable in a continuing struggle against subversive elements in society. Police officers argued that they were engaged in an ideological war and that torture in order to 'break' individuals to gain information was sometimes judged necessary. It was also found that five patterns facilitate widespread atrocities committed by police or other state forces. These are secrecy, occupational insulation, personal isolation, organisational fragmentation and a public rendered impotent due to fear. That is a setting in which it is relatively easy to avoid personal or political responsibility for such atrocities. Such closed worlds allow for individuals to operate as if in a separate moral universe (Huggins, 2003) where everyday rules of social interaction can be suspended. Huggins has warned about the dangers of situations with the above characteristics such as in Guantanamo Bay or Abu Ghraib Prison in Iraq, where isolation and secrecy can be conducive to violent excesses.

Police and policing

It is important to distinguish between police and policing (Reiner, 2000a). Policing implies a set of processes with specific social functions. Reiner (2000a) describes policing as the attempt to maintain security through surveillance and the threat of sanction. Jones and Newburn (2006: 4) utilise the following definition:

> Organised forms of order maintenance, peacekeeping, rule of law enforcement, crime investigation and prevention and other forms of investigation and associated information-brokering ... undertaken by individuals or organizations, where such activities are viewed by them and/or others as a central or key defining part of their purpose.

Policing clearly is a broad concept, which encompasses a wide range of activities and personnel. The nature of policing is frequently discussed with reference to the elusive 'police function'. What is it that police officers are meant to do? It is true that the police face contradictory demands (see Robinson and Scaglion, 1987). Robinson and Scaglion refer to this contradiction as 'coercive kinship', to serve the people but with means to exert power over them at the same time. This contradiction is at the heart of much writing about the nature of policing, which makes it difficult to pinpoint what the police are about: it varies over time and culture so that any undisputed police core function is nigh on impossible to identify. Possibly as a result, descriptions of the essence of policing vary widely. Storch (1976) refers to nineteenth-century English officers as domestic missionaries, moulding and improving the lives and habits of the working classes. At the same time these officers were referred to as a plague, 'blue locusts' (Ignatieff, 1979), warning of the threat felt by the 'to-be-policed' regarding the new institution. In contrast, the caring side of policing is referred to by Cumming et al. (1965) who call the police officer 'philosopher, guide and friend' and state that half the time police officers function as 'amateur social workers', which is also emphasised by Punch and Naylor (1973). The policing function, therefore, from a comparative perspective is an area of diversity and contest: sadly, police practice ranges from social work and street corner psychiatry to torture, brutality and murder.

The police in contrast refer to the institution – the force or the service. The police are the modern specialised body of people who carry out much of the policing function in today's society. The police assume a unique position within criminal justice. They face unique pressures as they form the primary interface between the public and the criminal justice system. Police officers on a daily basis face myriad difficult tasks and situations. Compare this to the role of judges: the number and types of defendants in front of them may vary widely but the format in which they deal with those defendants is highly scripted. Police officers on patrol enjoy no such structure. They have to take each situation as it comes. The present chapter will focus largely on the police; but we should bear in mind that the police are rarely the only official body engaged in policing in any society. I will examine private policing and emerging architectures of security and community safety as well.

Police numbers and policing tasks

The sentiment seems to be the same wherever citizens are asked about the size of their police force. They want more police officers on patrol, or, as the phrase goes in the UK, more 'Bobbies on the beat'. The rationale for the sentiment is obviously that more police officers on patrol will make for safer streets. The number of police officers per 100,000 population is shown in Table 4.1 for a number of European countries. It seems that in many states the number of police officers ranges somewhere between 200 and 500 officers per 100,000 population but in some places is considerably higher.

Police ratios in Europe tend to vary between just under 200 police officers per 100,000 population and just over 600 per 100,000 population. Latvia is situated near the top end as is Cyprus with 609.3. However Montenegro tops that with 890.9. Sweden and Denmark and most notably Finland represent the low end with 192.2, 197.8 and 157.9 officers per 100,000 respectively. In other parts of the world police ratios are much higher. Three countries in fact report having over 1,000 police per 100,000. They are Bahrain (1866.7), Brunei Darussalam (1086.5) and Kuwait (1065.2). Such high numbers of police officers probably reveals something about the uneasy relation of the rulers of these

Table 4.1 Police ratio in a number of European countries (per 100,000 population)

Country	Number
Germany	303.8
Denmark	197.8
France	210.2
England and Wales	263.4
Netherlands	215.5
Spain	313.0
Italy	549.9
Norway	248.3
Poland	233.8
Sweden	192.2
Romania	309.0
Montenegro	890.9
Greece	376.4
Finland	157.9
Latvia	604.8
Belarus	325.5
Cyprus	609.3

Source: Harrendorf et al., 2010.

countries with their population and the role that the police play in subduing protest. Taking a global perspective there are regional differences that are summarised in Table 4.2.

Police numbers are open to a variety of interpretations. Low police numbers such as in Africa may refer to paucity of public resources. In places like Bahrain, the high police numbers add to the story of the police forming part of a machinery (together with army and security forces that are more or less indistinguishable) that serves to protect the ruling elite from popular challenge. That became painfully clear during the Arab Spring when Bahraini forces were able to suppress a popular uprising with recourse to police and security forces. Farmanfarmaian

Table 4.2 Average police ratios in global regions (per 100,000 population)

Country	Number
Africa	186.8
Oceania	187.0
Asia: South	202.0
Americas: Canada/USA	207.5
Americas: Latin and Caribbean	283.9
Asia: East and South East	299.1
Europe: West and Central	311.5
Asia: Central	326.6
Europe: East and South East	389.7
Asia: Near and Middle East	435.5

Source: Harrendorf et al., 2010.

(in press) argues that unlike in Libya or Egypt, where governments were overthrown, security forces in Bahrain soon got the upper hand, with the help of outside forces from, for example Saudi Arabia. Particularly scandalous in Bahrain was the arrest, detention and conviction of doctors and nurses for providing medical treatment to injured anti-government protesters (Devi, 2012).

Another point to make is that national figures do have a tendency to obscure important local or regional differences. One such pattern of difference involves rural versus urban policing. In Australia, the thinly populated but vast Northern Territory has the highest number of officers (491 per 100,000) but at the same time the lowest density of officers per square kilometre. The picture for the Australian Capital Territory (ACT) is reversed: the lowest ratio of officers per population but no fewer than 329 officers per square kilometre. The data from Venezuela obscure inequality of a different sort: affluent areas are policed more intensely than poor areas. For example, the wealthy Caracas business district of Chacao has 1,228 police officers per 100,000, whereas the poor municipality of Libertador in the nation's capital only 63 per 100,000. That carries the implication that policing in Venezuela might be more about protecting business than protecting the poor.

The quintessential activity for a police officer is to be 'on the beat'. Police officers walk the streets and deal with problem situations as and when they encounter them. Bayley (1991) found that in many countries the majority of a police officer's time is indeed spent patrolling. Police presence is regarded as a deterrent for the commission of crimes and other disturbances and police officers on the beat can deal with any crisis situations swiftly. Such police presence should therefore be a potent reducer of crime rates. However this is 'a neat idea but unfortunately not one that corresponds to reality' (Waddington, 1999: 6).

Research from the USA helps to illustrate this point. In the 1970s, in Kansas City, an experiment was carried out in which the patrolling time was systematically varied. Odd as it may seem, it had no discernible effect on crime levels. Although there were some methodological issues raised, the experiment did provide evidence for the fact that levels of patrolling might actually not make much of a difference to levels of crime (Kelling et al., 1998). Greater numbers of police on the streets fail to reduce crime. This lack of effectiveness raises further questions as to how the police ought to go about their business and further highlights the elusive nature of that core business.

Various classifications of police tasks or policing functions exist, but the distinction between the maintenance of public order and investigating crimes, or more broadly crime control, is probably most important (Waddington, 1999, 2000). Waddington has stressed the fact that first and foremost the police are the agents that enforce the power of the state over its citizens. When investigating crimes the police, in the first instance, represent the state: a theft is therefore not just an issue between victim and offender; it is also and perhaps primarily framed as an issue between the state (embodied in institutions such as the police, prosecution office and courts) and the wrongdoer. The argument for this arrangement is that an offence is not only an offence against the victim but also a violation of society's legal and social order. In that light, crime control is a particular type of public order maintenance (Waddington, 1999). When the state has certain aspirations with regard to issues of crime or social control it looks primarily to the police. McKenzie and Gallagher (1989) argue that a key difference between the police services of England and Wales and the USA reflects a difference in the traditional emphasis on crime control on the one hand and public order on the other. English 'Bobbies' are there traditionally to keep the peace. In the USA the police came into existence with an emphasis on crime control. Public-order maintenance could too easily clash with the American ideal of the freedom of the individual and would therefore constitute insufficient *raison d'être* for the US police.

The conceptual distinction between crime control and public order maintenance has been emphasised due to their varying political potency. The authority of the state is much more easily threatened by riots and mass protests than it is by criminal activity. Crimes generally do not overthrow governments, but riots and protests can and do. States, therefore, have a vested interest in suppressing mass dissent. In doing so, the police are one of their most powerful tools. On the other hand the fact that crime may not bring a government to its knees is not quite a given in so-called *weak states*. A weak state, according to Fijnaut and Paoli (2004) is a state that cannot enforce its monopoly of power in a meaningful way. Such states can become havens for organised criminals and terrorists whose very presence may hamper the state from growing towards stability. In such instances there is an undeniable link between the presence of organised crime and corruption in weak states. However, where the state is strong, civil unrest tends to be more threatening to the state than regular and unorganised criminal activity.

A riot could be characterised as a battle between the two sides – rioters and police – both of whom are willing to use violence for what they each regard as a good cause (King and Brearley, 1996; Waddington, 2000). This makes public order policing morally ambiguous, as it cannot a priori be assumed that the police are in the right and the protesters in the wrong. The policing of riots and mass disturbances represents a situation where one of the dilemmas of police services across the globe becomes most pertinent. Whom do the police serve? In totalitarian regimes, the police will normally serve the interests of those in power. Any public-order disturbances will be dealt with swiftly and harshly without too much concern over civil-liberty issues. The scenes at Tiananmen Square in Beijing in 1989 were testament to that. In democracies, however, the situation is often less clear-cut. The police will have to balance the rights of the protesters (to protest peacefully) against public-order considerations.

We must examine the policing of riots and protest in a global context. Such protests include the Arab Spring that led to the overthrow of several Middle Eastern governments. They serve as a vivid example of the potency of popular protest. At the same time we have seen protests such as #Occupy (Kilibarda, in press), against the current social and economic conditions further to the global financial crisis that occurred in 2008. Other riots worth considering are those in the French *banlieus* (Jobard, in press) and also the phenomenon of *SlutWalk*. This latter protest originated in Toronto in Canada in response to public comments made by a senior police officer who argued that to avoid getting raped, women should not go out dressed like sluts. SlutWalks subsequently took place in numerous North American cities and spread to cities in Europe, Asia, and South America, causing much controversy and debate (Kapur, 2012; Valenti, 2011; O'Keeffe, 2012). Such events challenge public order policing even in the most democratic environments, whereas the Arab Spring has shown that, where circumstances are conducive, public protest can indeed play a major role in toppling even the most entrenched of governments (see also Pritchard and Pakes, in press).

Wright (2002a) has distinguished four models of public order policing, depending on how the relationship between the police, the state and the military is given shape. The first is the *civil police model*, in which the police and the military are completely separate in terms of organisation and objectives. The police deal with crime and are meant to keep the peace, whereas the role of the military is to protect the country from external aggression. Their differing roles require different types of organisation, with the military being organised along hierarchical lines with a high level of centralisation. The police on the other hand tend to be decentralised, with high levels of discretion. Wright mentions England and Wales and the Netherlands as examples of countries with a civil police model.

The second model is the *state police model*, in which the influence of the state is stronger and the police and military are separated to a lesser extent. This therefore allows for the military to get involved in public-order operations and for the police to deploy so-called paramilitary methods somewhat more readily than is possible under the civil police model. Wright defines paramilitary action as police units using military-style deployments with tactical coordination and rules of deployment. This might include the use of special equipment, such as weapons and shields. Paramilitary action is characterised additionally by a lack of the discretion normally associated with everyday policing. Wright (2002a) uses Germany and France as examples where, to an extent, the state police model is followed. In France, one of the two main forces, the *Gendarmerie Nationale*, is accountable to the Ministry of Justice. As is the case with the military, they are not allowed to be unionised (Monjardet, 1995).

The third model is the *quasi-military police model*, associated with contexts in which the state has seized a great deal of control over the police, which primarily serves its interests. Police and military are closely associated and personnel are to a considerable extent interchangeable. Most Eastern European states used to correspond to this model before the transformation following the fall of the Berlin Wall.

Finally, there is the *martial law model*, which is the stronger version of the quasi-military police model. In this case there is no separation of police and military forces. Both are under the same command and control. Wright argues that an implementation of pure martial law, in which soldiers are police officers and vice versa, does not often occur in the long term; rather, it is particularly associated with law-and-order programmes in the context of war and civil unrest. Instances, however, have been seen in Britain's colonial past, for example, while Indonesia's law-and-order programme in East Timor quite recently also corresponded relatively closely to the martial law model (Wright, 2002a).

Policing styles and crime control

Though the extent to which the police are instrumental in reducing crime can be questioned it remains one of their main responsibilities. That is so in spite of strong statements made by academics such as Bayley (1994), who argue that reducing crime is a promise that the police are simply unable to keep. Nevertheless, the police can go about their business in various ways that may not only be more or less conducive to reducing crime, but also to increasing public confidence and maintaining public order. These can be termed policing styles, and I shall discuss here community policing, zero tolerance policing, policy transfer / policy diffusion, police corruption and private policing. The assumptions underlying these styles differ considerably with regard to the type of crimes to be targeted, the types of communities in which they fit, and the nature of the relationship between police and local communities. Certain contexts are no doubt better suited to certain styles than others, which makes them useful territory for comparative analysis.

Community policing

The principles of community policing can be identified as follows. First, it relies on the consent and support of local communities: policing by consent. It requires regular interactions between the police and the public with regard to what policing priorities should be, and how the police should go about tackling those priorities. The police should be aware of their community's particular characteristics and preferences and be sensitive to them.

Community policing requires a localised police force. Only locally established units are able to maintain links with communities so that they can respond to local needs properly. The nature of community policing is that the police need to ask the locals what they want from them and that should inform their policy-making, and thus they engage the community in taking joint responsibility for social control within that community. Alderson (1979) calls this a 'social contract' between police and community.

Japan is perhaps the best example of successful community policing. Japanese policing is traditionally characterised by the police and local communities working closely together (Leishman, 2007). It is a tradition for local police officers to spend a relatively large amount of their time dealing with respectable members of the community instead of chasing suspects (Bayley, 1991) and there is considerable emphasis on this non-law-enforcement aspect of their work. In comparing US and Japanese policing traditions, consider Bayley's distinction: 'An American policeman is like a fireman – he responds when he must. A Japanese policeman is more like a postman – he has a daily round of low-key activities that relate him to the lives of the people among whom he works' (Bayley, 1991: 86).

In order to serve local communities properly, the Japanese have low-level police posts called *koban*. They are a mix between a police station and a post of general assistance. The scope of general assistance is wide. *Koban* officers advise on addresses, lend out umbrellas, may act as a lost and found office, and often run various community activities. Such activities might involve the production and distribution of local newsletters and the running of classes in self-defence or sports for locals (Leishman, 1999). A normal sized *koban* employs about a dozen officers. The unit is typically housed in a two-story building, recognisable by the traditional red lamp. *Koban* officers typically do not drive around in patrol cars, but are often on foot. This encourages frequent interactions with the community, where issues of crime are not necessarily to the fore. Apart from many daily informal contacts with members of the community, the *koban* also administer surveys. Twice each year, uniformed officers visit every home in their area and ask the residents various questions. Most people seem to be willing to answer such questions and to provide useful background information as well.

It has been argued that the *koban* system of policing helps to explain the famously low crime rate in Japan (Reichel, 1999). It must also be appreciated that this system emerged apparently naturally in Japan, and that it seems to fit the country's social fabric very well. Much is made of Japan's special cultural character. For example, the country is ethnically very homogeneous, as well as inclusive though there are exceptions, such as the historically outcast *burakumin* (Upham, 1987). Apart from ethnic homogeneity, there is a supposed unity in social norms. Japanese culture places considerable value on the importance of harmony. This is certainly conducive to a community-oriented policing style (Castberg, 1990).

Leishman (1999), however, has argued that Western observers have perhaps been too keen to uncritically accept the *koban* model of policing as the reason why Japan's crime rate has been so low. There is no doubt that crime has risen considerably since the 1980s and that the community-oriented style of policing is now seeking to adapt itself to a changing society. Changing family and work patterns and increased social mobility and levels of anonymity have arguably led to a slackening of the social cohesion on which traditional policing strongly relies. It has led to the rise of popular punitivism and a general decline in faith in the police (Ellis and Hamai, 2006). Reform measures aimed at enhancing levels of communication with the community have resulted in the establishment of Koban Liaison Councils. Additionally, measures are taken in an attempt to raise the profile of *koban* policing and to make community policing more attractive to young officers who might find the battles against terrorism and organised crime more exciting career prospects (Leishman, 1999).

Despite these more recent developments, the friendliness and harmony associated with Japanese policing has generated a widespread appeal. It is therefore not surprising that the example has been followed in other countries. One of these is the city-state of Singapore. In order to serve its multicultural society of various Asian communities, a total of 91 neighbourhood police posts were introduced in 1981 at the expense of other police units, such as the motor patrol. These posts are very much modelled after the Japanese *koban* stations and are claimed to be successful too (Fairchild and Dammer, 2001). The success of community policing in Singapore is of interest because of the diversity of its population. Whereas the population in Japan is quite homogeneous, in Singapore the opposite is the case. It could, however, be argued that perhaps both cultures share a lower level of individualism than we find more commonly in Western societies. A further reason why community policing is interesting to consider in Singapore is due to the highly authoritative style of government. Policing certainly prioritises order over justice and tends to take a dim view of various types of disorder such as to do with litter and noise, for which hefty penalties can be imposed. At the same time, however, there is a great deal of responsibilisation at work, affording citizens and business a role in crime prevention and disaster management. In addition, the Singapore police are highly professional and extremely well educated. Singapore perhaps defies categorisation: community policing in an authoritarian state (Bayley, 1985; Ganapathy, 2005).

England and Wales are considered to be good examples of community policing in the Western world. Community-policing elements are, for instance, embodied in the Crime and Disorder Act 1998. It arranges for the administration of crime surveys to establish local priorities with regard to crime and disorder. The English tradition of high levels of discretion and decentralisation of the police service also fit a community-oriented policing style. Community policing is also in operation, albeit sometimes seemingly in disguise, in Sweden, Norway and the Netherlands. When introduced in Western societies it often means that a shift is made towards either more local efforts on crime prevention, a reprioritisation of non-emergency services, increased public accountability or a decentralisation of decision-making on policing (Skolnick and Bayley, 1988).

Criticisms levelled at community policing tend to focus on the role of the community. Community policing might assume too great a degree of harmony within communities. Many communities are, in fact, utterly divided among variables such as class or race. In such situations, the police might be unduly influenced by those sections of the community that do actively engage in communication with the authorities at the expense of those who choose not to. That might lead to unequal policing, which might deteriorate into unfair policing.

The second point of caution relates to perceptions of the police and of their role. Police officers seem to receive a great deal of respect in Japan, and *koban* officers are generally proud of their neighbourhood and the work they do. Needless to say, in many countries around the globe this is not quite the case. Lack of trust between police and citizens will make effective community policing almost impossible. Finally, community policing does not sit easily with an authoritarian police-role orientation. When the police serve the interests of the state rather than those of the community, then community policing as a concept seems rather pointless.

Zero tolerance policing

Zero tolerance policing is a generic term for a policing style that is proactive, confident and assertive (Hopkins Burke, 1998). While American theorist James Q. Wilson described the viewpoints that were subsequently to be labelled as 'zero tolerance' policing, not all of its proponents have actually adopted the term. It is fair to say that the term 'zero tolerance' has found a life of its own, and it is applied freely to many an initiative in criminal justice that might well be rather remote to the original idea.

Wilson and Kelling's (1982) so-called broken-windows theory underpins the zero tolerance philosophy. If the first broken window in a building is not repaired then people will assume that no one cares. That lowers the threshold for others to also break windows. More and more windows will be broken and soon the building will have no windows at all. A quick reaction to the first broken window is therefore imperative: it needs to be fixed as soon as possible. That is the idea behind zero tolerance policing, and it is in opposition to the notion that when crime is rife, the police should focus on only the most serious crimes. Zero tolerance policing is about making an effort to tackle minor crimes and misdemeanours. In that way a sense of law and order can be regained and that will serve as a deterrent with regard to more serious crimes. Signs of improvement on the law-and-order front will allow the local community to gain confidence in the police as well as in the community itself (Wilson and Kelling, 1982).

In the philosophy of zero tolerance policing, its relation to the community rests on a different footing from community policing. Whereas in the Japanese example, communities care and communicate, Wilson and Kelling (1982) describe the American experience as one in which communities can be careless and cynical. An experimental study by Zimbardo in 1969 seems to prove the point they made. Two cars were left without licence plates and with their hoods raised, one in the Bronx, New York City, and one in Palo Alto, California. The car in the Bronx was attacked by vandals within ten minutes. First of all a family – father, mother and a son – removed the radiator and the battery. Within 24 hours, virtually anything of value had disappeared. Then random destruction took place. The car in Palo Alto, on the other hand, was left untouched for more than a week. Then Zimbardo himself decided to do a bit of damage to it. That led to an avalanche of vandalism. Within hours the car was utterly destroyed. Vandalism does seem to beget vandalism.

Zero tolerance policing has been particularly successful in New York City. Under the leadership of Mayor Giuliani and Police Commissioner Bratton, a policing style with zero tolerance features was introduced with the main objective of claiming back the streets. A particular focus was on the so-called 'quality of life' crimes. These include graffiti, begging, illegal vending, street-level drug dealing and street prostitution. These offences were pursued to regain and demonstrate control of the streets. Bratton had previously been chief of the New York Transit Police and there embarked on a 'quality of life' policing programme, which saw large numbers of arrests for fare evasion (Bratton, 1997).

During the initial period of zero tolerance policing between 1993 and 1996 arrests for misdemeanours rose by 40 per cent and arrests for minor drug offences rose by 97 per cent. By way of contrast, arrests for more serious offences (felonies) rose only by 5 per cent during the same period. Interestingly, the number of reported incidents of serious crimes went down spectacularly as they fell by 44 per cent. There was a 60 per cent drop in murders, a 12 per cent drop in rapes, a 48 per cent drop in robberies and a 46 per cent drop in burglaries (Dwyer, 2001). It appeared to be a case of 'take care of the pennies and the pounds (or dollars) will take care of themselves'. It also must be noted however, that the size of the New York City police force was increased with an injection of 7,000 extra police officers on top of the 30,000 already there.

Despite protests from various interest groups, who complained about police heavy-handedness in particular against the homeless and mental health patients out on the streets (e.g., Barr, 2001) it seems that the zero tolerance approach has been a success. Although other major cities have seen reductions in crime in the same time period, the New York City data are quite remarkable. Equally remarkable is the way in which the NYPD collects crime data, and uses them to devise localised crime-fighting strategies. Crime statistics are collected with rigour and precision. Local police chiefs are held accountable for their local statistics in so-called CompStat meetings. If in a particular area reductions in crime are not achieved, questions will be asked.

The success of zero tolerance policing might tell us something about the communities to which it is applied. In order for it to be successful, it would seem that the situation before zero tolerance must be quite desperate. When a neighbourhood is struck by fear; when people do not dare to leave their houses after dark and are afraid to be alone on the streets then something drastic might be called for. In such communities a zero tolerance approach might be the best or perhaps the only answer.

Compare this to the communities described in the Japanese model. They are almost opposites. In Japanese communities, characterised by cohesion and openness, zero tolerance policing would probably destroy more than it ever could repair. It is for this reason that zero tolerance policing might well be successful in certain contexts only. These contextual factors will probably include a poor situation to begin with, so that there is little, if anything, to lose in terms of the relation between community and police. The second requirement is likely to be a strong financial commitment, so that the police can afford to be consistent and convincing in their attack on all crimes, big and small.

Zero tolerance policing in Australia

In Chapter 2 I explained the focused comparison as a method of conducting comparative research, that is, looking at a phenomenon in one context and then considering its applicability in another set of circumstances. Zero tolerance serves as a good example for such a comparison, given that its success might depend very much on the community to which it is applied and the way in which it is implemented. Because of the reported success of the technique in New York City and the fact that this success has been well advertised, combined with the fact that New York City is quite an attractive travel destination, the NYPD has enjoyed countless visits from police officers and policy-makers from all over the world. Those seeking to claim back the streets in their own communities have looked for ideas on how to achieve similar success in their domestic jurisdictions. Some of those visitors came from Australia.

Australia is a federal state. It has one police force for each of its six states as well as for the Northern Territory. There is also a Commonwealth agency known as the Australian Federal Police, which provides police services for the Australian Capital Territory and is involved in preventing and investigating crimes committed against the Commonwealth. Consequently, there are eight separate police forces.

Obviously, the introduction of zero tolerance policing in one of Australia's major cities would be a different issue from, for instance, rural Tasmania or the vast and thinly populated Northern Territory with a high proportion of Aboriginal citizens. Wadham (1998) has identified five issues in relation to zero tolerance policing from a civil liberties standpoint, which will help focus our comparison. Zero tolerance enforcement involves a prioritisation of what are minor crimes but major nuisances; it inevitably shifts resources away from other types of crimes. Second, it focuses on street crime, at the possible expense of crimes such as fraud or domestic violence. The third issue is that zero-tolerance emphasises criminalisation: whereas community-policing strategies would focus on problem-solving, zero tolerance policing would instead focus on making arrests, with the likely result of more people ending up with a criminal record. Fourth, there is the issue of discrimination: it tends to be the poor and socially excluded and sometimes particular minority groups, who are out on the streets more often and who are disproportionately associated with crime; the marginalisation of these minority groups might be amplified by employing zero tolerance techniques. Finally, the issue of accountability must be mentioned: with the potentially dramatic impact this policing style might have, public accountability is vital.

One of the acknowledged challenges to Australian criminal justice lies in its treatment of its indigenous population, which has a troubled history of over

200 years. This population consists of Aboriginals and the Torres Strait Islander population. The following quotation provides a cutting summary of the problems involved in policing Australia's indigenous population:

> Most of the conflict with Aboriginals arises from police endeavours to enforce street offences legislation. That legislation arguably seeks to impose on Aboriginals the views of the European culture about the appropriate use of public space. While sections of the Aboriginal population have adopted the values of the dominant community, in many places they are frequently challenged by groups of Aboriginals who do not conform to dominant ideas about public drinking, noisiness, language, dress and general decorum. It is thus the constant effort of police to subordinate to the standards of the white society Aboriginal conduct which reflects cultural differences. No doubt police seldom think of their role as maintaining the subordination of Aboriginal people, nor are they the only institution in Australian society that act to do so. Indeed, it is often the relationship with other institutions that is crucial, as for example, with local government or hospitals or the media or hotel owners or schools. Nevertheless, the routine nature of much of police involvement with Aboriginal people means that their day to day practices act to entrench the subordination of Aboriginal people and with it, racist attitudes in the dominant society.
>
> (Wootten, 1991: 287)

Given this state of affairs it is not surprising that the indigenous population is overrepresented in the criminal justice system. The rate of imprisonment for indigenous adult persons is about 11 times the rate of the general population. Nationally, the reason for being placed in police custody for 31 per cent of indigenous people is intoxication in public. Nearly half (48.2 per cent) of all people throughout Australia placed in police cells for public-order offences are Aboriginal or Torres Strait Islander, which is an enormous overrepresentation. Twenty-six per cent of all deaths in custody involve indigenous people (Carcach and McDonald, 1997; see also, Australian Bureau of Statistics, 2006).

Any policing strategy that increases arrest rates for these types of offence is likely to therefore have a dramatic and discriminatory effect on the Aboriginal and Torres Strait Islander people. This increase will flow throughout the criminal justice system, with increases in court appearances, imprisonment and possibly deaths in custody. These sensitivities involving the indigenous population provide for a strong argument against the introduction of zero tolerance policing in Australia. You could say that whereas what needed to be fixed in New York City was a general state of lawlessness, in Australia it is rather the treatment by the criminal justice system and society at large of the indigenous population: zero tolerance policing provides no answer to that.

Policy transfer and policy diffusion

Generally policy transfer in policing is not as easy as it may seem. We must also appreciate that it is also not always clear what form it takes. It can be in the form of a direct transfer of policies or arrangements but more often policies or arrangements are moulded to fit the local context. On other occasions, the transfer is of ideas: generalised notions of how to give shape to criminal justice processes. Jones and Newburn (2007) distinguish the transfer of policy ideas, symbols and rhetoric from the transfer of policy content or the transfer of policy instruments. They argue that *policy transfer* refers to the conscious transportation of ideas, or policies, whereas *policy diffusion* is the spread of criminal justice orientations in a way that does not involve conscious shopping around for ideas. The United States have been a potent source for policy diffusion in criminal justice arrangements as well as for policy transfer. Zero tolerance is one such notion; another is the 'three strikes and you're out' orientation against offenders (Jones and Newburn, 2007). The point is that such ideas can spread due to policy-makers consciously deciding to adopt such ideas as they seem to work elsewhere, but also much more insidiously, penal notions can spread through mass media and other means to inform policy-making in a different way. This occurs via less tractable transfer of notions that fit certain agendas, or simply the *Zeitgeist* and popular mood in the country at issue.

Policing corruption

There is no doubt that police corruption is a major issue in many countries (Punch, 2009). Earlier in the chapter we discussed police officers as violence workers using an example from Brazil. Police corruption may be defined as: 'The misuse of authority by a police officer in a manner designed to produce personal gain for the officer or for others' (Goldstein, 1977: 188). Nigeria, for instance has been described as an example where corruption is deeply ingrained within the organisation that is resistant to change although efforts are being made to improve that state of affairs (Aremu et al., 2009). Although police corruption might occur anywhere in police organisations there are certain danger areas. Many of these have to do with undercover policing (see Newburn, 1999).

Punch (1985) distinguishes four forms of corruption. They are: straightforward corruption, which is action (or inaction) for a reward; strategic corruption, where a police officer actively stimulates crime and extorts money or goods; combative corruption, where the police use illegal or unethical means to strengthen their case; and finally corruption as perverting justice, where the motivation is either revenge or avoiding prosecution.

Strategies against corruption can be classified as either internal or external. Internal controls rest within the police. External controls rely on other bodies. Both the UK's and USA's anti-corruption strategies are dominated by internal controls. They take the form of codes of ethics, integrity testing and internal–affairs departments. UK police corruption is said to be 'under control', but that does not mean that it is non–existent. In 1999 there were over 100 police officers facing charges of dishonesty (Wright, 2002b). More recently, the Leveson Report (2012) did not make pretty reading for the UK police either. In situations where corruption is feared to be more widespread and deeply ingrained within police culture, there often is a need for external control bodies with sufficient powers and resources to overcome it.

A compelling example of successful external control is to be found in Hong Kong. Hong Kong is a special administrative region of the People's Republic of China with an estimated population of 6.7 million. It was under British rule from 1842 until 1997. On 1 July 1997, Britain handed Hong Kong back to China and it was agreed that the capitalist economic system of Hong Kong would be maintained for another 50 years. In order to ensure this within the socialist system of the People's Republic, Hong Kong enjoys high levels of autonomy, which is why it is sensible to regard Hong Kong as a separate entity for comparative criminal justice purposes.

While crime in general is perhaps not very high on Hong Kong's agenda the fight against corruption has taken centre stage since the 1990s (Wing Lo, 2000). A separate office is in charge of fighting government corruption. The Independent Commission Against Corruption (ICAC) was set up in 1994, and has a staff of more than 1,200. That makes it one of the largest dedicated anti-corruption bodies in the world (see www.icac.org.hk). The ICAC was initially given rather wide-ranging investigative powers. Subsequently, the reviewing role of the judiciary has been enhanced to curtail the Commission's use of arrest and detention, and an independent complaints commission has been established as well.

The ICAC's size and powers show the preoccupation Hong Kong has with corruption, which was said to be rife at the time of its instigation. The Commission, effectively a separate police force, has been hailed a success, and the fact that the relative extent of non-anonymous reporting of corruption has increased is taken is as a sign of public confidence. What is more, the Commission claims to have eradicated large-scale police corruption, so that what remains tends to be isolated cases. That said, the number of reports of corruption to the ICAC has recently been on the rise. Reports overall were up 23 per cent from 2008 to 2009, with those of governmental corruption increasing by 35 per cent (ICAC, 2009). Over the course of the life of the ICAC, governmental corruption seems to have declined overall, whereas corruption in the private sector takes up more and more of the Commission's time. Over the years the ICAC's caseload has shifted from corruption in the public to corruption in the private sector. The ICAC utilises a so-called three-pronged approach. The first tier is effective enforcement. The second is education and prevention, while the third is to do with community relations. International cooperation in combating fraud and other forms of organised crime is high on the agenda as well (ICAC, 2009).

The example set by Hong Kong has been followed elsewhere. Similar commissions exist, for instance, in Australia, South Korea, Mauritius and Fiji.

They tend to be characterised by an investment in the investigation of corruption, often coupled with an increase in sentencing powers against crimes of corruption (Urquhart, 1998).

Corruption is thought to influence virtually every social sphere in the Baltic state of Lithuania (Pakstaitis, 2002), even though there are reports to suggest that the level of corruption is perhaps not as high compared to other states of the former Soviet Union (see Vaitiekus, 2001). The battle against corruption is a recurrent theme in the development of the criminal justice system, which is undergoing change after change since Lithuania gained its independence in 1990. There has been an emphasis on specialised internal controls, and a new police body called the Special Investigations Service was established in 1997. In the newly written Criminal Code several forms of corruption are specified under the heading of crimes against the civil service. The code specifies passive bribery (acceptance of a bribe), active bribery (paying a bribe), abuse of office, illegal participation of a public official in commercial activities, exceeding of official powers, non-performance of official duties and forgery in office. They all carry prison sentences. Over the recent five years however, only some 50 to 60 people were convicted for any of these offences (Pakstaitis, 2002). This number is tiny compared to the assumed widespread level of corruption. According to a survey, about one in three individuals in Lithuania recently paid a bribe to a government official (Vaitiekus, 2001). Juska and Johnstone (2004) continue to warn of the entanglement of the state in corruption, highlighted by the scandal that forced President Paksas out of office due to corruption and alleged links to organised crime in 2004.

Several reasons for corruption being woven into the fabric of society are given by Pakstaitis (2002). The first relates to the formation of a new civil service since gaining independence: poorly qualified people, brought up in a communist-style civil service, were required to give shape to a civil service with new aims and objectives and a new service-oriented culture. This continues to prove a challenge. Second, the transitional period was, and continues to be, characterised by economic strain: salaries of civil servants are low, and the police service is no exception. Additionally, there is the wider historical and cultural legacy of the Soviet era. During Soviet times, abuse of office was a fact of life and almost a symbol of status: those in powerful positions were often expected to abuse their offices in order to help friends and family (see Shelley, 1999, on the colonial legacy of the Soviet era).

It remains instilled into the minds of many Lithuanians that if you want to receive proper service from any authority the best way to achieve that is by paying extra via a bribe. It is probably at this level where the fight against corruption will be won or lost. While top-down initiatives are necessary, the main battlefield will be in the minds of those used to small-time corruption and who regard it not so much as an evil but rather as an inevitable inconvenience of life. As long as corruption is regarded as a useful tool for a state official to supplement wages, and a handy means to fast-track any official procedure, new anti-corruption legislation will probably struggle to have an impact (see also, Dobryninas, 2005).

The situation is even worse in Kenya: the average Kenyan bribes the police 4.5 times per month, and 95 per cent of police interactions with the public involve a bribe. This ridicules the notion of a 'free' state police and demonstrates that the notion of 'buying security' is not restricted to private firms (Baker and Scheye, 2007). Whether you buy security of the police or from the police is of course a different question. The prowess of the police in West and sub-Saharan Africa is greatly limited by resources, both in personnel (see Table 4.3) and in equipment. As pay is low, the reality is that bribes sustain many police officer's families.

Where the police are unable to offer security, it is common for private business to step in. The growth of the private security sector in Kenya is indeed connected to the erosion of state capacities and services that began in the late 1980s and continued throughout the 1990s. During this period of economic decline, state expenditure and investment were significantly reduced. The ability of government and municipal institutions to deliver law and order services deteriorated; corruption and financial mismanagement were on the increase. During that phase private security expanded massively. The exact number of private security companies in Kenya is unknown but estimates vary from 400 to 2,000. The majority are small to medium-sized. Guarding is provided by most companies and clients include industries, bank, government agencies and international organisations. The sector is thought to employ about 48,000 people. G4S, the multinational security provider employs no less than 10,000 people in Kenya. There are no formal requirements for training, vetting or professional standards. Pay is low. Guards are unarmed and there is no doubt that their work is dangerous. Although there are no national statistics, sources within the sector estimate that within greater Nairobi and greater Mombasa combined, between five and ten security guards are killed each month. It is a case of guards armed with a baton and a whistle versus criminals with machetes and guns. One leading company lost 15 guards in 10 months (Abrahamsen and Williams, 2006). With a lack of standards, poor pay and a lack of regulatory framework, corruption will be a big issue for these private security firms to tackle.

Table 4.3 Police ratios in five African countries (per 100,000 population)

Country	Number
Sierra Leone	163
Nigeria	85
Kenya	84
Guinea Bissau	41
DR Congo	23

Source: Baker and Scheye, 2007.

It is generally accepted that there is no foolproof corruption fix. Wright (2002b), however, has argued that the following points carry a certain degree of universality which may inform policy-making against it.

- There is a link between police corruption and the prevailing social, economic and cultural conditions;
- There are at least two levels of corruption, namely low-level mooching and a more serious level, which tends to be related to drugs and vice;
- Recruitment and selection and human resource management are of crucial importance;
- Integrity testing and monitoring of 'at risk' individuals is necessary;
- Defusing corruption involves breaking the code of silence while maintaining the team ethos.

Tackling widespread corruption thus might require substantial changes to police education, training and police culture and management. As the case of Lithuania shows, public perceptions of corruption will have to change along with it.

Whether private or public, centralised or decentralised, overt or covert, strategies and arrangements conducive to securing ethical policing are increasingly necessary. Ethical policing is seen to be the way out of the conundrum of the moral ambiguity of policing identified by Waddington (2000) and the point made by Bayley (1994) and Wright (2002a) that police effectiveness is not to be found in the reduction of crime rates. Neyroud and Beckley (2001) argue that policing should be guided by four ethical principles.

The first is legality. Police officers should uphold and comply with the law. The legality requirement places a burden on the law-making process as well. Laws should be transparent and accessible and created in a democratically accountable way through parliament. The second principle relates to proportionality. Police officers should ensure that any action is proportionate to the legitimate aim pursued. It should be considered whether a less intrusive or coercive action is available to achieve the same end and the decision-making concerning such actions should be fair and transparent.

The third guiding principle is that of necessity. This principle particularly relates to the use of force by the police. The test whether a pressing social need is being addressed must be considered. In a broader sense, adherence to this principle aims to ensure that the police are tolerant and broadminded. Finally, the fourth principle is accountability. This is often taken to mean external accountability, such as civilian involvement in complaints procedures and independent investigations into serious police wrong-doing.

The rise of private policing

As we saw in the case of Kenya, policing is not necessarily always the job of the police. Particularly in private or quasi-private spaces, such as nightclubs and shopping centres the policing function is often performed by the private security sector. Private security personnel do not have police powers but play important roles in maintaining public order and crime prevention. The private-security industry consists of an eclectic range of sectors offering services and products. Button (1999) has divided them into:

- The manned guarding sector. This includes in-house guarding, door supervision and bodyguard style services;
- Private-sector detention services such as private or perhaps more precisely, contracted-out prisons;
- Professional security services, such as private investigators;
- Security storage and destruction services;
- Security products such as the designers, producers, installers and maintainers of security equipment such as alarm systems or closed circuit television systems;
- Marginal sectors in which we include gamekeepers.

One thing to notice about the private-security industry is its rapidly increasing size (Button 2007). Within the European Union, there were over 1 million people working in the security industry in 2007. The number of police across the European Union at that point was in the order of 1.5 million. This shows that the private sector is not some marginal enterprise that criminology can safely ignore. In fact, as Table 4.4 shows, there are a handful of nations in the EU where the private security sector comfortably outweighs the police. It is interesting to note that the private sector seems relatively strongly in Eastern European nations such as Hungary and Poland whereas the sector seems smallest in Southern European countries such as Spain or Italy.

The scale of the private-security sector urges us to rethink the very nature of policing and accordingly the role of the state in maintaining law and order in society (see also Jones and Newburn, 1998, 2006; Johnston, 2000; Button 2002). Traditional notions of policing are increasingly superseded by complex and changeable arrangements for the provision of both surveillance and security. Various actors play a role in this, such as government (both local and national), the private sector but also non-governmental organisations and the voluntary sector. They are not organised in strict hierarchical structures but in networks and nodes (Johnston and Shearing, 2003). Policing has become embedded within broader networks of security and intelligence and in fact, the precise distinctions that once existed between public and private are in some places no longer applicable (Gill, 2006). These nodes and networks have become important areas of comparative study with Jones and Newburn's edited book on plural policing a good example (Jones and Newburn, 2006). The question therefore has shifted from identifying core tasks for the police to identifying what role the traditional police have to play within this emerging security and surveillance landscape: should we leave it to private enterprise or does the provision of security remain a crucial public function?

Table 4.4 Size, order and ranking of the private security industry in a number of EU countries

	Population	Police	Security	Security/Police ratio
Hungary	10,000,000	40,000	80,000	2.00
Poland	38,600,000	103,309	200,000	1.94
Ireland	3,900,000	12,000	20,000	1.67
Luxembourg	462,000	1,573	2,200	1.40
Estonia	1,400,000	3,600	4,900	1.36
United Kingdom	60,270,000	141,398	150,000	1.06
Slovakia	5,400,000	21,500	20,839	0.97
France	60,400,000	145,000	117,000	0.81
Finland	5,200,000	7,500	6,000	0.80
Germany	82,500,000	250,000	170,000	0.68
Netherlands	16,300,000	49,000	30,000	0.61
Portugal	10,500,000	46,000	28,000	0.61
Slovenia	2,000,000	7,500	4,500	0.60
Czech Republic	10,200,000	47,400	28,101	0.59
Sweden	9,000,000	18,000	10,000	0.56
Greece	10,700,000	49,900	25,000	0.50
Cyprus	776,000	3,000	1,500	0.50
Lithuania	3,600,000	20,000	10,000	0.50
Latvia	2,300,000	10,600	5,000	0.47
Belgium	10,300,000	39,000	18,321	0.47
Spain	40,280,000	193,450	89,449	0.46
Malta	397,000	1,800	700	0.39
Denmark	5,400,000	14,000	5,250	0.38
Italy	58,100,000	240,114	55,000	0.23
Austria	8,200,000	30,000	6,790	0.23
European Union	456,185,000	1,495,644	1,088,550	0.73

Source: Button, 2007.

Conclusion

Diversity characterises police origins and their role in various countries. That diversity is particularly apparent in the way police forces are organised. Taking one dimension, police forces can be more or less centralised. The US police service is particularly decentralised, for example. A US state may have dozens of forces: for each county and for bigger municipalities as well as for the state as a whole; and there are at least 63 supra-state forces, such as the Federal Bureau of Investigation (FBI) and the Drug Enforcement Agency (DEA) (Ebbe, 2000a). Diversity is also the name of the game in Europe's police organisations, to which the following quotation is a testament:

> Parts of the EC have single forces, organised nationally, for example, Denmark, Greece, Ireland and Luxembourg. Germany has a system in which responsibilities are divided between state and federal levels. Belgium has three forces, with conflicts over jurisdiction and competence. Portugal has several, whilst Italy has five separate, but mutually integrated, police

organisations. France has two highly centralised forces, whilst Spain has two national ones. In the UK there are 52 semi-autonomous forces, and in the Netherlands a new system has recently been established of 25 regional forces and one new national force. There is no basic uniformity or pattern to the organisation of European police forces.

(Benyon et al., 1994: 48)

It is therefore suitable to focus on policing functions over police organisational structures despite the fact that there is plenty of diversity as to the policing function as well (Mawby, 1999, 2000). Comparative research helps us gain a deeper understanding of the various types of relationship that exist between the police, other state organisations involved with security and surveillance, the private sector and the people. It illustrates that policing may constitute both a promise and a threat, depending on the nature of these relations – to be protected from crime and disorder or more generally 'looked after' by benign servants of the people, or, on the other hand to be singled out for persecution, to be harassed or oppressed, or even tortured, or murdered.

Further reading

Haberfeld, M.R. and Cerrah, I. (Eds) (2008) *Comparative policing: The struggle for democratization.* London: Sage.
Hinton, M.S. and Newburn, T. (Eds) (2008) *Policing developing democracies.* London: Routledge.
Jones, T. and Newburn, T. (Eds) (2006) *Plural policing: A comparative example.* London: Routledge.

Study questions

1 Why are case studies and focused comparisons suitable methods for considering comparative policing?
2 Why does comparing police numbers at a national level obscure important local differences?
3 What does the rise of private policing tell us about modern governance of crime and security?

Chapter 5

Global cops?

Transnational and global policing

International policing might seem quite a new phenomenon. While it is true that international policing has changed radically over the last 20 years and no doubt expanded enormously further due to the events of September 11, 2001, we must not forget that international policing in fact has a long history. Efforts against smuggling and piracy for instance are centuries old and there was a fair amount of international policing against the global slave trade once it was officially abolished as well (Deflem, 2002). We can certainly discern some of its origins in the eighteenth century.

An assumption that is persistent but not necessarily correct is that international policing is nothing but the inevitable and appropriate response to international crime. Andreas and Nadelmann (2006) argue that this explanation is a 'mantra of law enforcement officials across the globe' (p. 7) but it 'explains too little and obscures too much' (p. v). Andreas (2011) is particularly convincing in his description of rather apocalyptic imageries of organised crime. He quotes Naim (2005) and also Williams who refers to transnational organised crime as the 'HIV virus of the modern state' (Williams, 2003: 165). Such sentiments no matter how colourfully expressed tend to neglect the fact that much international policing relates to 'new' crimes, such as drug trafficking. While these are clearly offences with a strong transnational element, they only became the focus of international policing efforts due to their criminalisation by some but initially by no means all countries. Andreas and Nadelmann argue that we must not marginalise the role of criminalisation in international policing: drugs legislation in part creates drugs crime just like the establishment of borders creates the possibility for cross-border offences; similarly, only when states handed themselves a monopoly licence to print money did counterfeiting become established as a serious crime against the state. Thus, we cannot separate the development of international crime from criminalisation of transnational behaviour and the rise of the nation state.

In order to discuss the rise of transnational and international policing we need to locate this within the realm of comparative criminal justice. The distinction between what can be conceived of as international criminal justice and comparative criminal justice is not strict but there is a difference in emphasis. Comparative criminology (Beirne and Nelken, 1997) refers to the comparison of criminal justice arrangements in two or more cultures. International criminology is about the arrangements that either connect or transcend separate cultures. An argument could be construed that comparative criminology is becoming less relevant. As it tends to compare and contrast phenomena in distinct cultures or jurisdictions, diffuse interrelations and complications brought about by globalisation may be at risk of either being ignored or understated (Pakes, 2010). It needn't be so and international and transnational policing offers good examples of comparative research that does not simply acknowledge global processes but actively takes them into account and capitalises on them (e.g. Crawford, 2011; Nelken, 2011).

This chapter starts off by discussing transnational or cross-border policing. After that we move on to international policing. We will see that the very shape of international policing is complex and contradictory. In order to make sense of that state of affairs we need theoretical grounding. The first main concept we bring to bear is globalisation and the effect it has on both crime and crime control. We then move on to the distinction between *high policing*, which is political policing and *low policing*, as it were everyday community policing. We will discover that high policing has a long and dubious history in international policing, to do with undercover work, spying and the assassination of political adversaries.

Transnational offending requires the crossing of borders. We need to gain a deeper understanding of the nature and meaning of national borders. Borders are no longer strictly physical presences between countries. Some borders are no longer visible but others are enhanced. They can be digitised and, in the case of China, national borders are even imposed on the Internet. We cannot discuss international policing without gaining a deeper understanding of its governance. We need to understand the notion of nodal governance to make sense of the diversity in international policing. Finally we look at Security Sector Reform and the role of both public and private policing in that.

Transnational policing

It is fair to say that many early cross-border policing arrangements were more transnational than global. They tended to regulate situations in which criminals or criminal goods crossed jurisdictions. Arrangements were necessary in order to prevent investigation or policing coming to a complete stop, as police officers would normally not have any power at the other side of the border. This was as true in Europe as it was in the USA, where state jurisdictions were strictly localised.

The difficulties faced by law-enforcement bodies when a suspect flees across a national border can be immense. Officers on either side of the border might speak different languages, and might be embedded in rather different organisational and hierarchical structures. Who is to say that when making an arrest is the priority of the chasing officers this will also be the case for their colleagues across the border? It is even conceivable that the crime for which the suspect is being chased is only a minor misdemeanour in the neighbouring country, or perhaps not even a crime at all. In short, in the absence of any pre-emptive agreements, police officers either side of a border may have much negotiating to do before any action can take place. It is therefore useful to have agreements that deal with acute situations, and it pays off to coordinate and harmonise efforts at a higher level.

Traditional transnational police cooperation was involved with individual suspects crossing borders, and focused on transferring offenders back to the jurisdictions of their crimes. The challenges posed by modern transnational crime are of a different nature altogether. Many contemporary transnational crime problems are associated with the process of globalisation. Factors that have led to an increase in the forms and incidence of transnational offending include the increased mobility of people and the reduction in the cost of international travel, the move towards a free global market as furthered by neo-liberal governments, increased technological sophistication and access to the Internet. Cyber-crime is particularly facilitated by the latter development.

In order to analyse these cooperative developments, Benyon et al. (1994) suggested the following thematic structuring of cooperative activities. The highest or *macro* level of cooperation relates to the harmonisation of national legislation and regulations. Agreements at this level require conventions and treaties signed by governments, as they involve issues of state sovereignty (Den Boer and Walker, 1993). One such area involves agreements that grant police forces operational powers across borders. Such powers would obviously solve many of the problems identified above.

The intermediate, or *meso*, level is concerned with operational structures, practices and procedures. The issues identified at this level are common databases, and mutual access to intelligence information. Much of it relates to speaking the same tongue, quite literally so in terms of languages, but it also concerns information systems' ability to communicate with one another and the identification of common terminologies for offence types and judicial procedures. Given that there are 80 separate police forces across Europe, with different origins, structures and legislative frameworks, the meso level of cooperation contains much scope for potential mishap.

The *micro* level relates to the investigation of specific offences. This is the traditional level of police cooperation, which is invoked when a particular offender, after the commission of a crime in one jurisdiction, travels to another. This chapter will mainly discuss arrangements at the macro level such as Europol, and at the meso level, such as Interpol. We then look specifically to the USA and propose global prohibition regimes as the source of the globalisation of the war on drugs and on terror.

Transnational policing may have found its origins in cooperation between neighbouring countries but the world has significantly moved on, with policing operations occurring all over the world, some through bi-lateral agreements between states, and others through global forums such as the United Nations. Bowling and Sheptycki (2012) discuss a socio-spatial typology for transnational policing. They go from *global* (including Interpol, the International Criminal Court and UNPOL, the United Nations Police) to *regional* (e.g. Europol, and the Association of Caribbean Police Commissioners), to *national* (e.g., national agencies such as the FBI or the German *BundesKriminalAmt* (BKA) who work with international partners), to *glocal*, local agencies but with many transnational links, such as drug squads, counter terrorism units and cybercrime units. The latter are interesting as they highlight that local policing is now carried out with global awareness. This is not only true for these specialist agencies: any officer in a major city will be frequently reminded of how globalisation has shaped their working environment.

'High' and 'low' policing

Another important aim of international policing was to keep tabs on dissidents and political enemies abroad. Brodeur (1982) refers to 'political policing' as 'high policing' and the policing of everyday offences as 'low policing' (see also Brodeur, 2007). Europe has a rich and chequered tradition of 'high policing' where the police, sometimes alongside (or in competition with) secret services, spied on citizens, in particular political opponents. The beginning of the twentieth century, particularly, saw a rise of 'high policing' in Europe. It is important to appreciate the nature and operation of high policing. First, it is targeted against 'enemies of the state': dissidents, alleged terrorists, coup plotters and would-be assassins of royalty.

High policing is not focused on bringing criminals to justice. It is more about gathering intelligence and disrupting plots and other activities. Arrest and prosecution are options that can be chosen but often the public nature of criminal trials sits uneasily with the secret nature of the work. This is exacerbated by the fact that much high policing activity is extra-legal. It can vary from intrusive acts such as unauthorised telephone tapping to torture and murder. Over time in the twentieth century state power has been curtailed. More recently however, typical high policing activities are back in vogue, as part of a war on drugs or on terrorism. Where transnational policing is high policing it is immediately controversial: we cannot regard that as simply the proper response to transnational crime: it is, rather, state bodies embroiled in unsavoury activity in order to take out or otherwise neutralise enemy activity.

International policing institutions

Another important development for the growth of international policing was the establishment of specialist investigative bodies. International policing frequently used to rely on *ad hoc* liaison between national police bodies. Policing in many countries is extremely fragmented with police organisations consisting of anywhere between two or over a thousand police bodies. If you need to speak to the relevant organisation regarding a transnational policing matter who should you contact? The establishment of bodies such as Scotland Yard or national police agencies greatly facilitated that process and that subsequently led to the establishment of *Interpol*.

Established in 1923 Interpol is one of the oldest organised bodies in international police cooperation. Its mission is to facilitate the investigation of transnational and international crimes between member countries by the mutual exchange of information between police agencies. Its headquarters is in Lyon, France. Interpol is best known for its International Notices of Wanted Offenders which are spread via Interpol to police forces across the globe. An important information system is the so-called Automated Search Facility. This database contains information on crimes and criminals, including stolen vehicles, counterfeit currencies, fingerprints and stolen passports. It consists of hundreds of thousands of pieces of data (see www.interpol.int).

Although Interpol is a global affair it is said to be predominantly European in practice, with European countries the most frequent providers and consumers of information (Benyon et al., 1994). It has been argued, however, that Interpol's role in enhancing transnational policing is limited. That is because Interpol's remit has traditionally been interpreted in a restrictive fashion. Article 3 of its constitution forbids Interpol from undertaking activities of a political, military, religious or racial character (Benyon et al., 1993), which has limited its involvement in, for example, activities against Nazi war criminals and terrorist activity. However, a resolution adopted in 1984 changed the interpretation of Article 3, so that terrorist activity is now seen to fall under Interpol's remit. Another constraint on Interpol's impact has been the fact that it deals particularly with ongoing investigations and rather less with policy-making on a transnational level. It is therefore less likely to serve as an impetus for change on levels of policy or legislation. Interpol may well remain largely a 'clearing house' for enquiries (Benyon et al., 1993).

The next push in Europe regarding international police cooperation came as part of a larger programme of European integration. The Council of Europe (see box in Chapter 9) has been influential since the 1950s in making arrangements for transnational policing efforts such as extradition and other forms of mutual assistance. In the meantime, however, other countries made local arrangements that went beyond what was set out by the Council of Europe. The Netherlands and Belgium already had relatively far-reaching agreements together with Luxembourg, while the Nordic countries had made arrangements independently as well.

Europol is altogether more ambitious than Interpol. Europol is the European Law Enforcement Organisation which aims at improving the effectiveness and cooperation of the competent authorities in the European Union member states in preventing and combating terrorism, unlawful drug trafficking and other serious forms of international organised crime. Europol supports the law enforcement activities of the member states mainly against:

- illicit drug trafficking;
- illicit immigration networks;
- terrorism;
- forgery of money (counterfeiting of the Euro) and other means of payment;
- trafficking in human beings (including child pornography);
- illicit vehicle trafficking;
- money laundering.

An issue that currently is hotly debated is the so-called European Arrest Warrant (EAW). The European Arrest Warrant is meant to simplify and speed up arrests of suspects who are abroad but within the EU and facilitate their transfer to the jurisdiction where they are set to be prosecuted. Two elements of the EAW in particular facilitate this. The first is that the judge who can order the transfer of the individual should not consider the evidence in the case but only focus on whether the warrant is properly served, whether it concerns the right suspect and whether certain exceptions do not apply. In addition, classic extradition is a process that is part judicial, part diplomatic. The latter element is removed from the proceedings so that they can be hurried along more effectively. However, civil liberty issues have been raised, as has the fact that the EAW seems a step towards a Europeanisation of policing and a threat to sovereignty (see De Sousa Santos (2010) for a comparative study involving Italy, the Netherlands, Portugal and Spain; and Spencer (2013) for a human rights oriented critique). Another development concerns Joint Investigation Teams. It is very apparent that where Interpol is global yet limited, Europol is local but within the region far more far reaching.

Looking at various developments that occur seemingly side by side, international cooperation did not come about as part of a grand design. Rather there were various strands that sometimes were mutually supportive and at other times only served to muddy the waters. The platforms on which police officers in Europe engaged with each other in more or less formal ways were many. There is the European Capital Chiefs of Police Conference, and also the Cross Channel Conference that involves members from Belgium, France, Germany, the Netherlands and the UK. Today there is a plethora of forums, some tightly organised on a statutory basis and longstanding, others ad hoc, devoted to a single issue or to 'blue sky thinking'. It is a baffling landscape. In order to make sense of it we need to consider the drivers behind the growth of international policing. We need to appreciate that the European Union is a key driver on the continent. In the USA however, other forces are at work.

International policing from a US perspective

The story of international policing from the perspective of the USA is altogether different from that of Europe. Early transnational policing efforts focused, as they did elsewhere, on cross-border activity but in the twentieth century, the Cold War was a major driver for international policing. Keeping track of suspected communists and other subversive elements was a major part of both national and international policing, never more so than in the infamous McCarthy era. All this took place at a time of more common international travel by air and increased means of telecommunication so that espionage and surveillance were able to reach new heights. Soon afterwards President Nixon declared a 'war on drugs' which marked the starting point of a truly *global prohibition regime* (Andreas and Nadelmann, 2006) that continues to be with us to this day. The war on drugs has led to increased involvement of US specialist agencies such as the CIA and the FBI in international operations. In addition, the USA have gone through a phase of border strengthening which received further impetus after September 11, 2001.

Important in the perspective of the USA is the phenomenon of these so-called global prohibition regimes so that what is outlawed in the USA is in fact prohibited everywhere. Where the issue is of a transnational nature and where local legislation is seen to be inefficient, global prohibition regimes are more likely to occur. For that to happen, it is essential that hegemonic jurisdictions such as the USA and the European Union outlaw certain behaviours and apply pressure on other jurisdictions to do the same thing. The latter activity requires the work of what Andreas and Nadelmann call 'transnational moral entrepreneurs' (2006: 19). What they do can be summarised as follows:

> Often organised and linked through transnational advocacy networks, they mobilise political opinion and popular support both within their host country and abroad, they stimulate and assist in the creation of like-minded organizations in other countries, and they play an important role in elevating their objective beyond its identification with the national interests of their government; indeed their transnational efforts are often directed persuading foreign audiences (especially foreign elites) that a particular prohibition regime reflects not merely the peculiar moral code of one society but a more widely shared, even universal, moral sense.
>
> (Andreas and Nadelmann, 2006: 19)

It is such processes of mobilisation that have furthered international policing. The preoccupations of the big players on the world stage are then, over time, turned into global concerns. That process furthers international policing efforts to the heights that we experience today.

UNPOL

UNPOL is what is referred to as the United Nations Police. Police officers have been deployed in UN peacekeeping missions for decades and the scope of the role of UNPOL is expanding. Traditionally, the role of UNPOL officers (recruited from many countries) related to setting conditions for the establishment of public order (Hills, 2009), and involved the monitoring and training of local officers in conflict and post-conflict settings (such as in operations in Haiti, Kosovo or East Timor). Latterly, UN Police have become involved more integrally with direct law enforcement and the support of peacekeeping overall. But the exact nature of the deployment differs from place to place depending on local circumstances. In Kosovo, for instance, UNPOL officers had powers of arrest and detention which in many areas they do not. In 2013 some 17,000 police officers were deployed worldwide and no doubt much good work is done, in challenging places such as Haiti, the Central African Republic, Mali and Darfur, and police officers should be commended for operating in such challenging and often risky environments.

There are some flagship missions. Much was made of an all-women unit from India that was deployed in Liberia in West Africa. There was also an all-women unit in the UN Organisation Stabilisation Mission in the Democratic Republic of the Congo. This Unit consisted of women from Bangladesh (Onekalit, 2013). Their operational duties included providing training, crowd control and the protection of UN staff and materials. The first woman to lead a UN police mission has been appointed. Major General Kristin Lund of Norway took the lead of the UN police mission in Cyprus in August 2014.

Despite such good news stories, Hills (2009) provides a mixed assessment of transnational policing initiatives. On the one hand she clearly argues: 'FPUs make sense: they work. They are used for crowd control when local police are unprepared, unwilling or overwhelmed, and they have propaganda value' (p. 309). However, she also notes frequent instances of criminal misconduct. More generally an issue she identifies is that many UN police officers come from countries where police routinely use high levels of force. She therefore summarises: 'UNPOL are the equivalent of temporary, miscellaneous, civilian (although increasingly paramilitary in nature) and comparatively cheap fire-fighters, most of whom are unfamiliar with liberal style policing' (p. 308). It seems that if UNPOL were to be seen as the instrument through which transnational policing can be crafted (Goldsmith and Sheptycki, 2007) there is quite some way to go, despite the undeniable successes that there are.

Globalisation and international policing

We cannot discuss international policing in its current context without discussing the impact of globalisation. Globalisation in criminal matters is often discussed in terms of transnational crime, but the internationalisation of policing and criminal justice is obviously another feature of globalisation. Thomas Friedman wrote a book with the provocative title *The world is flat* (Friedman, 2005) which analyses globalisation, predominantly from a business perspective. The stance taken in the book is that globalisation is in the process of making the whole world a level playing field for commercial activities. Friedman discusses a number of 'flatteners' including technological developments such as the Internet and mobile technology; business developments such as *outsourcing* (separating out manufacturing activities from service activities which can take place in different parts of the world) and *off-shoring* (removing manufacturing to developing countries). That said, we must not overemphasise the notion of a commercial level playing field in which people and goods move freely while seeking to maximise their profits. Instead, trade agreements are significant barriers to Friedman's rather optimistic vision.

It might be argued that globalisation is in fact a euphemism and that what we are witnessing is in fact an Americanisation of the whole world, as it were a form of economic, military and cultural re-colonialism by stealth. Globalisation is in fact a complex multifaceted phenomenon that needs to be unpicked in order to appreciate its nature and impact.

The first element is *space-time compression*. This refers to the increasing speed of communication and movement of ideas, capital and people. Local news is world news in an instant; successful recording artists score number one hits in dozens of countries at the same time. In particular the movement of cultural images is striking. From the most unexpected to the minutely orchestrated, from the events of September 11 to the inauguration of Barack Obama, we can now almost literally say that the whole world is watching. Obama was acutely aware of that given his statement, 'Our stories are singular but our destinies are shared', during his acceptance speech in Chicago in 2008. Our worlds are no longer discrete but are intimately connected and we are getting used to the fact that happenings elsewhere, even in spheres that are seemingly distant, can have an acute economic or cultural impact upon local contexts. Mobility has acquired a whole new meaning and potency. Social networking sites have meant that these networks are maintained at a distance. Our thoughts and interactions take us away from where we physically are: space-time compression has created a 'culture of elsewhere'.

The second concept to come to terms with is the *network society*. The global economy is about flows as much as it is about space. We can see this in the policing of transnational crimes such as drugs or people trafficking. Policing objectives refer to the disruption of such flows: flows of information, money and people. Aas (2007) describes how this process has come about at the same time as the rise of *neo-liberalism*, the notion that the world of trade and commerce should require little state intervention, viewed as it is (or, perhaps, as it *was* prior to the global financial crisis) as the vehicle for economic prosperity.

Globalisation and neo-liberalism challenge the traditional conception of the state. The 'demise of the nation state', unable to stop the tide of globalisation is a frequently heard expression. In the world of policing that is epitomised by the rise of private security, much of which is carried out by multinational firms. At the same time however, there is a strong desire within many nation states to flex their muscles and show strength in relation to matters of crime and justice, seemingly following popular demand.

G4S: global private security

G4S is the company that came into existence further to a merger of Group 4 Falck with Securicor in 2004. G4S is big business. It has operations in 100 countries, has 570,000 employees and a turnover of £4.5 billion. G4S has a lot of business in the developing world. It has more employees in Asia than in Europe or North America, and almost 100,000 employees in Africa. In DR Congo almost 10,000 people are employed by G4S. The services provided include manned security and security systems, and clients include public authorities, businesses, international organisations, embassies and NGOs. In Nigeria the workforce is smaller, in the order of 5,400, but the operations are quite wide ranging and include Alarm and Armed Response, Security Risk Consultants, Emergency Rescue and Patrol Boats, Integrated Pipeline Security for the oil industry, CCTV Cameras and Control Rooms, Mobile Armed Reaction and Patrol Units, Unmanned Aircraft for Patrolling, Airport Security and the provision of trained drivers. G4S may be the biggest multinational security firm, but there are many more that operate in developing and transitional countries. The range of activities is wide and the turnover is very high indeed. Multinational businesses have clout; in our thinking about international policing and security they cannot be overlooked.

Globalisation has had consequences for criminal conduct. Passas has discussed these in terms of criminogenic asymmetries: global inequalities that breed crime. The main global asymmetry is between the wealthy, consumerist and highly regulated North (particularly Western Europe and North America) and the poorer and less regulated South. Passas (1998) has argued that such asymmetries are criminogenic for three reasons. In the first place, they generate or enhance the demand for illegal goods and services. Second, they generate incentives for particular actors to engage in illegal transactions; and third, these asymmetries reduce the ability for authorities to control such activities.

Passas has used the example of the dumping of toxic waste. Legislation regarding toxic waste tends to be underdeveloped in many developing countries. This provides for a solution to evading the cost of disposing of toxic waste in the more industrialised countries. It brings about the practice of companies in richer countries paying money to third parties to dispose of toxic waste in poorer countries. It evades regulation and saves a good deal of corporate money (Passas, 1998). Transnational criminal activity thrives on such differences in regulations among countries and regions, and differences in the rigour with which they are enforced.

Passas' notion of criminogenic asymmetries highlights the fact that globalisation is not necessarily a global leveller. Instead, there are global winners, such as multinational business and Western consumers. Set against those are the billions who fail to profit or only profit marginally. Friedman emphasises the role of information technology in producing a flatter earth. It is no doubt true that information and communication technology have greatly facilitated international trade. However it is a sobering thought that Internet broadband is rather unevenly distributed across the world. Many sub-Saharan African states do not register in the figures at all: only South Africa, Sudan, Senegal and Gabon make it on to the list, with household broadband penetration running from 1.79 per cent in South Africa to just 0.05 per cent in Sudan (a mere 3,000). North African states fare slightly better with Morocco scoring 6.78 per cent penetration with 418,000 users, and Egypt at 1.55 per cent or 240,000. Many African states are now looking to mobile phone companies to provide access to the Internet. In 2004, less than one in ten citizens in developing countries had a mobile phone. Today it is close to 80 per cent in developed nations. Mobile phone technology represents an area of substantial social change. It was only in the mid-1990s that less than 5 per cent of people in the Western world owned a mobile phone (International Telecommunication Union, 2007). Thus, against global winners we must set large groups of clearly identifiable global 'have nots'. These asymmetries feed demand for transnational crime. Fear about global movements and economic and environmental disturbances will prompt organisations to take measures against it, which again may create criminal flows and law enforcement counter-flows. In a 'runaway world' (Giddens, 2002) such movements and counter-movements will be increasingly swift and dramatic. International crime and international policing both need to be situated in that ever changing landscape.

The European Union

The crux of the European Union is that member states have given up some of their sovereignty and handed that over to the Union. The idea is that the states share the same goals so that a common pursuit of them would suit all member states. The Union's principal objectives are to:

- Establish European citizenship. It aims to protect fundamental human rights and civil liberties;
- Ensure freedom, security and justice. That involves police and judicial cooperation, such as via Interpol and Europol;

- Promote economic and social progress. The introduction of the Euro is a good example of this as are policies to benefit the poorer regions within the Union;
- Assert Europe's role in the world. This is performed by formulating joint policies on economy and trade, as well as on combating terrorism and on issues of justice and home affairs.

The Union was initiated in 1950. Six countries (Belgium, Germany, France, Italy, Luxembourg and the Netherlands) took part from the very beginning. Today, after several further waves of entry (1973: Denmark, Ireland and the United Kingdom; 1981: Greece; 1986: Spain and Portugal; 1995: Austria, Finland and Sweden; 2004: Cyprus, the Czech Republic, Estonia, Hungary, Latvia, Lithuania, Malta, Poland, Slovakia and Slovenia; 2007: Romania and Bulgaria; 2013: Croatia) the EU has 28 member states.

The legal process underlying European legislation is complex. Ideally, legislation is passed by broad consent, but the more the Union grows the more difficult consensus will be to achieve on any issue of substance. Unanimous votes are necessary in certain vital areas, while it is specified that in other areas a qualified majority will do. This works by giving the more influential countries more votes than others in the Council of the European Union.

The European Union consists of a number of institutions. The European Parliament consists of Members of the European Parliament (MEPs), who are directly elected by Europe's citizens. It has 766 seats, with the larger countries having more seats than smaller countries. The United Kingdom has 73 seats. Only Germany has more, with 99 seats. Luxembourg and Malta, on the other hand, have only 6. The Council of the European Union is the Union's main decision-making body. It is made up of ministers from the 28 member states, with responsibility for the policy area under discussion at a given meeting: foreign affairs, agriculture, industry, transport and so on.

The European Commission drafts legislation, and is a driving force behind their implementation, ensuring it comes into force in the member states. (There are other EU bodies with which we are not concerned here because they do not operate in the field of criminal justice. These include the European Court of Auditors and the European Central Bank.)

The management of these issues in the context of a dramatic enlargement in the years to come will be a big challenge for the Union. The desire to achieve consensus on the main issues runs the risk of becoming a factor that will increase sluggishness and inertia in decision-making, while not adding to its transparency.

A number of European treaties are of importance to the criminal justice area. The Maastricht Treaty (1992) regulates three areas of cooperation among European Union member states. The first pillar relates to economic cooperation; the second pillar to a common foreign and security policy; and the third to cooperation with regard to justice and home affairs. One of the achievements on the justice and home affairs front was the establishment of Europol (see Fijnaut, 1993). The Amsterdam Treaty in 1997 further enhanced the level of cooperation, as did the 1999 Tampere Treaty.

The DEA goes global

The US Drug Enforcement Agency was established in 1973 through a merger of already established anti-drug enforcement agencies. It is a federal agency initially primarily aimed at the enforcement of anti-drugs legislation. However, the international activities of the Agency have taken off in the new millennium. The DEA has no less than 86 Foreign Offices in 67 countries all over the world, the highest density of which are in Middle and Latin America. The Agency deploys over 5,000 Special Agents.

A pivotal event for the DEA was the Oklahoma bombing in 1995 for which Timothy McVeigh was convicted. It killed two of its employees and it highlighted the home-grown terrorist threat faced by the Agency. Furthermore the Agency is acutely aware of the importance of the drugs trade to the financing of terrorist activity. That nexus has served as further impetus for the spreading of DEA activities abroad.

The DEA can be argued to have been a vehicle through which the *Americanisation* of drugs policing has been achieved. The DEA has certainly influenced the policing of drugs across the globe. This is performed on the one hand by other police forces taking on operations and tactics initially deployed by the DEA. This particularly includes undercover policing. In addition, many countries have enacted legislation to either allow or add legitimacy to such operations (Andreas and Nadelmann, 2006) and allow for the DEA example to be followed legally. The active role of the DEA as 'proponent, example, tutor, and lobbyist' (Andreas and Nadelmann, 2006: 131), in other words as *moral entrepreneur* is also apparent.

To exemplify its increasingly global reach, since 2005 there are so-called FAST teams (Foreign Advisory and Support Teams) in Afghanistan who provide guidance and conduct bilateral investigations that will identify, target and disrupt illicit drug trafficking organisations. Interestingly, these teams are actually funded by the US Department of Defence, which provides a hint at another important development: the mixing of military and policing orientations and tactics in the area of international policing.

> The evolution of the DEA highlights a key transition in law enforcement. It started out as a federal agency, exclusively concerned with drugs, but has increasingly become both international and multifaceted. The link with terrorism, summed up by the phrase 'terrorists and drugs criminals drink from the same well' has further pushed the Agency's international agenda. As a consequence, the DEA is much concerned with money laundering and exploring and disrupting the links between drugs, organised crime and terrorism wherever they occur in the world.

The nature and the policing of borders

Aas (2005) notes the contradictory meaning assigned to borders: more fluid than ever and to a large extent digitised rather than physical, and probably more porous than before but at the same time of tremendous symbolic importance. The symbolism of the wall erected between Israel and Palestine is immense, while the physical border between Mexico and the USA also successfully intends to intimidate. Many borders in the world are physically and symbolically strengthened. At the same time, however, we see the virtual disappearance of borders within the so-called Schengen Area in Europe. The seeming abandonment of borders within the 25 (in 2014) Schengen countries is compensated for by the establishment of what is called Fortress Europe: a strengthening of the outer borders and an increased criminalisation of illegal entry. There is no doubt that that policy has led to harrowing scenes on ships carrying illegal immigrants from North Africa (Weber and Pickering, 2011).

Pellerin (2005) argues that borders serve a multitude of functions. First, borders serve to differentiate. That is particularly true for Fortress Europe. The borders on the outside of the European Union are meant to exclude, in particular asylum seekers and illegal immigrants. But borders also demarcate wage differentials, taxation, social and economic policies, and so on. Thus, borders are a way of both signalling and perpetuating difference. Second, we can view borders as regulators and organisers of internal space: they define inland space or homeland. Finally, borders are a space of power. States rely on old-fashioned mechanisms of authorities (such as the army and treaties) but also utilise new means such as private agencies and information technology. We might even go as far as to say that borders are everywhere (Lyon, 2005). Borders can be portable: ID cards might carry information to exclude individuals anywhere, as if they showed their passport at border control. Borders, you could say, are also virtual and contained in databases. Illegal immigrants can be arrested away from borders, at any point: they may have scaled the physical border, but cannot shake off the virtual border as easily. This highlights the multifaceted nature of both the border and the varieties of ways and means in which borders are enforced.

The Great Firewall of China

With the Internet largely uncompromised by either national borders or national systems of governance and cybercrime notoriously difficult to police, there is an approach that we could call the high policing of the Internet on a strictly national basis. It is referred to outside China as the Great Firewall of China, with obvious reference to both Internet security and the Great Wall of China built from the fifth century onwards to protect the northern border of the Chinese empire. It refers to the practice of keeping the Internet free from content that is considered subversive. It is a deep reaching form of Internet censorship aimed at controlling both foreign and domestic content.

This is, in fact, called the Golden Shield Project in China and is implemented by the Ministry of Public Security. It deploys a 'cyberpolice' of about 30,000 individuals and disrupts the flow of information in various ways. It can prosecute Internet Service Providers and block certain websites, while social networking sites, dating sites and current issue sites are scanned for keywords. Overly sexual content is quickly erased and so are references to 'Tiananmen Square', the site of pro-democracy protests in 1989, subdued by the military with the loss of many lives; 'Free Tibet', the region in western China that seeks independence; or 'Dalai Lama' the head of Tibet's government in exile.

However, the censorship does seem to be applied in rather an *ad hoc* fashion. The BBC (itself subject to a ban) refers to it as a game of cat and mouse between the government and its people, with individuals finding ways of circumventing the censor machinery and the cyberpolice seeking to counter those (Taylor, 2006). Fallows (2008) calls it 'crude, slapdash, and surprisingly easy to breach', but it highly effective nevertheless, not least because strong censorship invites self-censorship. In addition the insecurities involving the nature and extent of China's Internet 'big brother' will deter many individuals from casually surfing for what might be perceived to be inflammatory material.

It was hoped that the 2008 Beijing Olympic Games would provide leverage for democratic reform in China not least in the area of freedom of speech on the Internet. A tug of war developed between the International Olympic Committee and the Chinese authorities regarding Internet access in the Olympic Village (Fowler, 2008). Although initially there was agreement that it would be unlimited, some degree of censorship was in fact imposed and, controversially, agreed with the IOC (Reporters without Borders, 2008). Since the IOC was not able to rid the Olympic Village of censorship, the Olympics did not turn out to be a watershed event for Chinese freedom of speech.

The nodal governance of international policing

We have seen that international policing is not a clearly delineated system of organisations that work together in a structured fashion. Instead the current state of affairs is decidedly murky. The ensuing multilateralisation and pluralisation that was already discernable in policing within a national context is much more apparent in an international context. In order to gain a deeper understanding of that landscape we need to understand the notion of nodal governance. It shifts away from the notion that policing and security are given shape and controlled by the traditional agencies. That is simply no longer the case. We saw above that the International Olympic Committee (IOC) ended up playing a role (however briefly) in challenging the way the Chinese are governed. It is worth a moment's pause to consider the extraordinariness of that situation. The IOC is not an organisation that can claim such powers and neither may it possess the will to assume such a role at all. However, due to the position in which it found itself, it was judged to have a certain amount of leverage with the Chinese government. That made it a 'node' of governance: a place of power, if you will. These nodes are changeable. With the Beijng Olympics been and gone, behind us, any power that the IOC may have had in regulating the Internet has vanished.

Nodes highlight a critical feature of power. The old-fashioned notion was that power resides with the sovereign state and its subdivisions. It is much more complicated than that. In fact, nodes like the IOC are seats of power, as are private enterprise and international organisations. The way power is exercised is equally varied. The use of force is highly visible but the moral entrepreneurs we discussed earlier often use more insidious means. On occasion the state works with other nodes in partnership but at other times there is direct competition (Johnston and Shearing, 2003). The main point is that the nation state is not where inquiry on power and governance should start and end (Shearing and Wood, 2003). This is particularly true in international policing, where private security interests and those of arms manufacturers have considerable leverage.

Security Sector Reform

Security Sector Reform refers to a process of reform that takes place in post-conflict areas or nations in transition. It is often part of a wider process which goes far beyond police organisations. Where countries emerge from conflict, it is not uncommon for the security sector (including police, army, paramilitary forces, courts, prison and private security) to be in disarray or worse, part of the problem. In transitional countries it might be appropriate to reform police and other organisations away from a dictatorial to a community-oriented way of operating.

Security Sector Reform tends to take place as part of a wider drive to make peace sustainable and allow a process of democratisation to be initiated and take hold. It tends to include reform of the military, the police and intelligence services as well as the judiciary. In addition more immediate safety concerns need to be addressed such as the availability of small arms and light weapons and the sweeping of mines (Hänggi and Bryden, 2005). The police may be either an agent of, or a target of security sector reform. Police organisations may assist reform in a donor capacity to facilitate capacity building; at the same time however, local police organisations may be subjected to reorganisation efforts.

In Liberia an extensive security sector reform programme is taking place following a protracted civil war. In 2004 initial initiatives were made by UN Peacekeeping Forces in the area. The International Crisis Group (ICG) reports that the progress is uneven. Army reform entailing complete disbanding of existing forces has made significant progress. This part of the reform has been given shape by private companies, notably DynCorp International. Private military companies are key players, emphasise the ICG. DynCorp have been subcontracted by the US government to train and vet the new military. This is an example of the state (the USA in this case) working with the private sector to create a state army. It seems to work well as long as there is state oversight of the work of private companies: both nodal governance and pluralisation in a nutshell. At the same time, police reform is not yet quite as successful. The police are still seen to be corrupt, and are recruited to a lower level than army personnel. The ICG complains of:

> basic issues of poor management, lack of equipment and dismal community relations. There also appears to be inadequate realisation that successful police reform can only be sustained if it is linked to an effective judiciary that enforces the rule of law fairly and effectively to protect individual rights and assure citizen security. This has led to the growth of vigilantism and disrespect of police.
>
> (ICG, 2009)

Abrahamsen and Williams (2006) argue that Security Sector Reform is too state-centred. By that they mean that the rebuilding of the state institutions such as the police and the judiciary overlooks the presence and potency of private security providers. After all, where the state police are in fact a producer of insecurity, as totalitarian police forces frequently are, those who can, will choose to rely on private security instead. As Abrahamsen and Williams note:

> from the guarding of private and commercial properties, the surveillance and control of shopping malls and airports, to the more extreme exclusionary patrolling of enclave or 'gated' communities, private security has become a pervasive (if varied) aspect of life across the developing world.
>
> (Abrahamsen and Williams, 2006: 3–4)

We have already seen that we must not underestimate the size of the private security sector in developing countries. 'The prevalence of private security is a striking feature of urban life in contemporary Africa, with the uniformed guards of private security companies a ubiquitous presence outside banks, commercial properties, hotels, public offices, and private residences' (Abrahamsen and

Williams, 2006: 5). This demonstrates that the void left by the regular police is quickly filled by private enterprise but obviously mainly to serve those who can afford it. Security Sector Reform needs to recognise this.

In Kenya, we saw that the number of police officers is one per 950 citizens. That is low. In contrast the private security sector may employ as many as 48,000 people. There is no model of cooperation with the regular police. It is an odd situation: police officers lack the resources but have the legitimacy to carry arms; private security have the armoured response vehicles, but can carry no weapons. A cry for 'hybrid' policing is frequently heard in Kenya, where it is felt that state police and private security should join forces to be effective. That realisation demonstrates the necessity of private security in present-day Kenya. Private security in many developing nations is not a frill to be indulged in by the rich or some marginal occupational niche. Private security is part and parcel of the security landscape. Their regulation is important and the work that they do needs to be recognised and embedded in security structures (Abrahamsen and Williams, 2006).

Conclusion

International policing is difficult to understand in isolation. It is often part of something bigger. That can be part of the war on drugs or on terror and may well be supported by military action and the governance of international bodies such as the United Nations, the World Bank or the World Health Organisation. Alternatively, it can be part of Security Sector Reform where policing can be a part of a larger security enhancing and democratisation process.

On the other hand there are typical state police initiatives to facilitate policing across borders. Interpol has long had a function of information exchange; Europol on the other hand is more about direct cross-border cooperation. Despite such efforts, there simply is no global police force, although bodies such as the US DEA might appear to take on operational responsibilities that might be reminiscent of such a global force, albeit without any semblance of global legitimacy or consent. International police cooperation is a game of cat and mouse: expedience drives the cooperation but issues of sovereignty and cultural difference and distrust of foreign police organisations serve as brakes, so that international policing initiatives tend to be stop–start, although no doubt September 11 as well as the London and Madrid bombings have removed some of the reticence about closer cooperation.

You could perhaps argue that the rise of global policing is breeding new types of police officer. Bowling and Sheptycki (2012) describe a number of 'ideal type' global cops based on the specific roles they play. The first is the 'technician', an IT savvy facilitator of knowledge and surveillance-based policing. The second is 'the diplomat', someone who speaks another country's language and knows about criminal justice and policing systems abroad who can build bridges between organisations. Then there are the 'entrepreneurs'. They sell, or look to sell products or ideas, and consider their work in relation to markets, goods and services. Next is the 'public relations expert'. This is in line with the marketisation of policing; local and global PR are important to sell and protect the service. The next type Bowling and Sheptycki dramatically call 'the legal ace': the expert on law who can creatively exploit possibilities and loopholes to facilitate policing and prosecutions is an important figure in transnational policing. Next up is the 'spy', whose role is about managing secrecy and deception, often in relation to police informants. The 'field operator' is termed the workhorse of policing. They undertake a range of operational functions. Finally, there is the 'enforcer'. The enforcer comes with a warning: they are the executioners and performers of renditions and torture (Bowling and Sheptycki, 2012: 91). Good policing becomes impossible when the enforcer role dominates, Bowling and Sheptycki argue. These types provide for a vocabulary through which to perceive and understand emerging players in global policing. They are the new 'must have' characters in policing organisations, in order to give shape to global policing (whatever its imperatives) effectively.

Although international policing by public police organisations is of increasing importance, it is perhaps overshadowed by the rapid growth of transnational private security in many parts of the world. It is less encumbered with the traditional police conundrum of whether to serve the state or the police. We must acknowledge that in many parts of the world, the public police, due to insufficient resources, corruption or public distrust, will often simply need private enterprise to complement it. Private security runs prisons, armies and perhaps controls and protects more than we tend to realise. Comparative perspectives highlight the power held by the private security industry: it is a node of governance to be reckoned with. That makes its regulation and integration into proper structures of accountability all the more important.

Further reading

Andreas, P. and Nadelmann, E. (2006) *Policing the globe: Criminalization and crime control in international relations.* New York: Oxford University Press.
Bowling, B. and Sheptycki, J. (2012) *Global policing.* London: Sage.
Pickering, S. and McCulloch, J. (Eds) (2012) *Borders and crime: Pre-crime, mobility and serious harm in an age of globalization.* London: Palgrave Macmillan.

Study questions

1 What are global prohibition regimes and what is their role in understanding global crime?
2 Consider the extent to which comparative research has focused on 'high' or on 'low' policing.
3 Can there ever be a global police force to truly 'police the globe'?

Chapter 6

Prosecution and pre-trial justice

The importance of the pre-trial stage in criminal justice proceedings can hardly be overestimated. Whatever the legal system, much of the justice process takes place prior to trial, in arrangements and practices that are less transparent than trials and often less carefully regulated.

Baldwin (1985) emphasises the caveats involved in pre-trial justice. Far-reaching decisions are often made in settings that are not public or without the suspect having legal representation. Decisions made against the defendant in this phase are often less open to review. Ironically, the same is often true for decisions that favour suspects. In many jurisdictions decisions made by the prosecuting authority that involve the termination of a case before it goes to trial are difficult to challenge. Thus, when considering both the suspects' rights and the interests of victims, the relative secrecy of pre-trial proceedings raises issues of accountability.

In fact, we only need to be reminded of Franz Kafka's (1925/1998) fictional account of *The Trial* as a description of inscrutable oppression by the system of a hapless individual who meets a tragic end. Aleksandr Solzhenitsyn's *The Gulag Archipelago* (1973) hammers home the point of ruthless state oppression in secrecy even more dramatically as it is a real account of life in Soviet labour camps in the 1950s and 1960s. It shows that at its worst the pre-trial stage is a theatre of true horror. This includes detention in secrecy without charge, exposure to inhumane conditions, torture and other forms of violence, up to disappearance and murder. This makes it most important that we devote considerable time to analysing pre-trial arrangements from a human rights perspective. It is difficult to argue with Schönteich's (2008) assertion that the use of pre-trial detention as a *de facto* sentence or as a means of coercing a confession debases notions of justice by pulling the rug from underneath the presumption of innocence.

Schönteich (2008) lists further disturbing consequences of the use of pre-trial detention. Pre-trial detention negatively affects detainees' mental health, which increases risk of self-harm and suicide. Fazel and Danesh (2002) found high rates of mental health problems in detained populations and Singleton et al. (1998) documented that rates of mental health problems among remand prisoners may be even higher than for convicted prison populations, in the UK. Schönteich also warns of overcrowding and the spread of disease, in particular tuberculosis. This is particularly the case in Russian prisons. Other impacts are on detainees' families, socially, emotionally and economically. There is no doubt that unjust use of pre-trial detention is harmful, for the detainees themselves, their families and communities and society at large.

There also is a strong historical-legal imperative to study pre-trial justice in detail. The relative importance attached to pre-trial justice differs considerably between countries with adversarial and inquisitorial legal traditions. In inquisitorial justice, examples of which we find across the European continent, great emphasis is placed on information in the case file. That case file, or *dossier*, in principle contains all the relevant information obtained in the investigative phase. It is usually available to the courts, which might base much of their decision-making on its contents, thus making the pre-trial phase crucial. Adversarial systems place greater emphasis on orally presented evidence at trial, which is seen to work as a safeguard against courts placing too much trust in police investigation as the main source of evidence (Van Koppen and Penrod, 2003).

In this chapter I will consider two main areas in relation to pre-trial justice. The first is prosecution. Who is to decide whether a case should go to trial? How are such decisions made, and who is to review the processes? When looking at overarching prosecution policies, at one end of the continuum we find systems that incorporate the *principle of legality*. This means that, in principle, any case of sufficient strength should be put before a court of law. In contrast, there are systems that embody the *principle of opportunity* where prosecutions should only be brought if they serve the public interest. In practice, this distinction has faded. In many countries where traditionally the principle of legality informed prosecution policy there are mechanisms in place to divert trivial or otherwise unsuitable cases away from court. Similarly, in systems with a policy informed by the principle of opportunity there is many a case that is forwarded as a matter of cause without much reflection about the public interest. However, use of discretion has a different footing under each principle. Under the former, discretion is used to determine not to prosecute a case; under the latter the opposite is the case (Brandts and Field, 1995; Fionda, 1995).

The second area to be considered relates to pre-trial custody. Under the presumption of innocence, pre-trial custody is the incarceration of innocent people. The practice of locking people up until the day of their trial is a business that, in the interests of justice, needs to be regulated and monitored closely. The extent to which jurisdictions make use of pre-trial custody can be indicative of how those in authority relate to their citizens. Widespread use of this measure should give rise to suspicions of an emphasis not on crime control but on controlling (segments of) the population at large. Rules and practices regarding the use of pre-trial custody are an important indicator for the 'state of justice' in any given country.

I will discuss prosecution and pre-trial custody in separate sections. That might suggest that it is appropriate or even feasible for the two to be considered in isolation but in reality it is not quite as straightforward as this. The processes of investigation, prosecution and remand are often intermingled, on the European continent often even more so than in England and Wales.

Finally, I shall discuss pre-trial diversion, the process of dealing with offending behaviour without the direct involvement of the court system. Sometimes these processes tend to be relatively informal and take place in relative obscurity. In other cases, such as New Zealand, such measures have taken centre stage, in particular with regard to youth justice. Finally, we will look at diversion mechanisms in place for defendants with mental health problems.

Prosecution

In England and Wales, prosecution was historically a matter for the police. The police would conduct their own prosecutions in the lower courts where they would present cases themselves. In higher courts the police instructed counsel (i.e. a barrister) to present the case in court. The Director of Public Prosecutions would only deal with particularly difficult or sensitive cases. The Royal Commission on Criminal Procedure produced what is colloquially known as the Philips Report in 1981. It concluded that it was undesirable for the police to both investigate and prosecute. It therefore concluded that a locally based prosecution service with some national features was needed (Philips, 1981). In 1985 the Crown Prosecution Service (CPS) was created and it came into operation in 1986. Arguably, the CPS was inspired by considerations to do with the quality of justice: investigation and prosecution should be separated in order to reduce the probability of overzealous police prosecutions. Additionally, the emergence of a national prosecution service would make it easier for national guidelines to be issued and implemented. That would help to ensure that similar cases were being dealt with in similar ways across the country.

In England and Wales the days of police prosecutions have gone but in many other countries this is not quite the case. In particular, former British colonies in which an England-and-Wales-type judicial system was introduced often still rely on police prosecutions to a large extent, such as Nigeria (Ebbe, 2000b). The Director of Public Prosecutions in Nigeria prosecutes only serious cases, such as murder, armed robbery and narcotics trafficking. There is a certain poignancy in that, as these are the very crimes for which the death penalty can be imposed. The police tend to prosecute most other cases on their own accord.

The CPS in England and Wales is a relatively new institution, squeezed between two much older and well-established bodies, the courts and the police. It is perhaps not surprising that the CPS lacked a certain amount of visibility and clout as it once was described as 'sandwiched virtually to vanishing point' (Uglow, 2002: 193), but do note that the CPS is quite differently positioned today (Lewis, 2010). In most countries on Europe's mainland the situation is rather different. In these jurisdictions the public prosecutor is by custom, by law and by practice in a much stronger position. There are not many countries where the prosecution service is as strong as in the Netherlands (Corstens, 2008), which is why I devote considerable attention to the Dutch arrangements. If you compared and contrasted arrangements in England and Wales with those in the Netherlands, that would be a very different design (see Pakes, 1999) as the differences between both jurisdictions are substantial.

Prosecution in the Netherlands

Like many other European criminal justice systems, the Dutch system has been modelled after the French. This was a case of policy transfer by coercion as it was put in place during the Napoleonic rule around 1800. There are similarities between the French and Dutch criminal justice systems throughout but they are particularly discernible as far as both prosecution services are concerned. Both organisations are large, influential and governed by the Ministry of Justice. Dutch prosecutors are magistrates and trained in a way that is very similar to the training of judges. To highlight the fact that both judges and prosecutors belong to the same corporate body, prosecutors are called 'standing magistrates' because they stand up in court to present and argue cases, whereas judges are called 'sitting magistrates'. To exemplify the strong French heritage the prosecution offices in the Netherlands are called virtually the same as those in France. The French term *Ministère Publique* is translated literally into *Openbaar Ministerie* (or OM) in the Netherlands, while their offices are called *parquet* and *parket*, respectively.

The role of the Dutch public prosecution service is to direct the investigation of criminal offences, to prosecute the perpetrators of criminal offences, and to execute the decisions rendered by the courts. It is in the first core task where the Dutch prosecution service differs most from the CPS in England and Wales. In serious cases, Dutch prosecutors can and do guide and direct police investigations. In doing so, they have the law on their side. The Dutch Code of Criminal Procedure specifies that police officers wishing to take particular investigative actions require a public prosecutor's approval before those actions can be carried out. This applies to arrests, remands in custody and in most situations also to actions such as telephone tapping, house searches and seizures. Basically, police officers cannot do too much in an investigation without a prosecutor having agreed to it and expecting to be informed about the results of that action (Fionda, 1995; Blom and Smit, 2006).

This is a system of oversight or *review*: the police carry out the investigation subject to continuous review by a public prosecution officer who is invariably a highly trained lawyer. In systems of review, prosecutors exercise a dual role. On the one hand they are partners with the police. Together they fight crime and carry out investigations. On the other hand they are the supervisors of the police and ensure that suspects' rights are respected. An investigative or examining judge oversees and reviews the behaviour of the prosecution, and might get involved directly in the more complex police investigations, so that the magistrate serves as an added layer of review on top of the prosecution service (Pakes, 1999).

The second task of the Dutch OM, the actual prosecution, is similar to that of the CPS, but there remain important differences. In the Netherlands the prosecution service decides on charges and discontinuations. It also presents all cases in court, whatever that court should be. Choice of court is also the privilege of the prosecution: defendants do not have a say, although judges in lower courts may direct cases to a higher court either because the case is deemed too complex for a single sitting judge or because the sentencing powers of the lower courts might be insufficient. Because prosecutors are physically present and argue their case in court one could say that public prosecutors in the Netherlands are their own barristers. In order to appreciate this practice, it is important to understand the nature of trials in the Netherlands and other inquisitorial systems and the role that prosecutors play in that system. I shall, however, postpone that discussion until the next chapter.

The prosecution service considers itself primarily accountable to the courts, which perhaps is not surprising given that prosecutors are part of the judiciary. This is illustrated by their rather pompous name, *Officier van Justitie*, which translates as Officer of Justice and serves as a reminder of the traditional orientation of these magistrates, in which objectivity is highly valued. They aim at achieving justice rather than necessarily at achieving convictions, at least in theory. The service is politically accountable to the Minister of Justice who is a member of government. It is worth mentioning that the service enjoys a monopoly of prosecution. Private prosecutions or prosecutions brought by other agencies cannot occur. Dutch prosecutors are the sole keepers of the key to the courts. To balance this, there is a complaint procedure open to victims and other parties against a prosecutor's decision not to prosecute a particular case.

However, the system of review does not come with a guarantee of police propriety. A 1995 Dutch parliamentary inquiry (colloquially called the Van Traa committee, after its late chairman Labour MP Maarten van Traa) revealed that in some regions of the country police officers had developed a practice of performing large-scale investigative operations using very intrusive measures without any factual, prosecutorial supervision. In order to use the information thus obtained as legal evidence, the fashion in which it was obtained was either fabricated or left unclear. Thus, instead of admitting to unauthorised telephone tapping or the 'wiring' of premises, investigating officers produced reports in which it stated that they simply could not help overhearing elaborate and self-incriminating conversations between suspects. Telephones were, strikingly, often left off the hook, windows were handily left open just when police officers walked past, and drugs happened to be placed conveniently in sight and spotted through open doors and windows. Prosecutors quite often failed to pick up on such phraseology in the dossier and the same was true for courts (see Punch, 1997; Van Traa, 1997).

Hodgson observed a similar culture in France where *Magistrats* oversee criminal investigations but within a culture of trust and *laissez-faire*. It can therefore be doubted whether such 'hands off' supervision is the most effective form of review as she documents quite harsh forms of suspect interrogation and a casual approach to suspects' and detainees' rights in France (Hodgson, 2002, 2004).

The Van Traa inquiry concluded that criminal investigation in the Netherlands was in crisis. It identified shortcomings in law in police practice and ethics and in the area of prosecution review and control of police activity. Certain prosecutors were identified as standing shoulder to shoulder with the police and becoming too immersed in the 'war against drugs', at the expense of the magistrate-like aspect of their position. Others who followed the letter of the law were left uninformed about what really went on in proactive investigations and lost track of the methods police officers covertly used. While a certain amount of trust is necessary for the system of review to work, it is relatively easy for the police to hide much of what they are doing from the prosecutors, who are hardly ever physically present when such actions occur. However, too much trust may constitute a lack of review, so that this mechanism of quality control easily becomes based on something hardly more firm than quicksand (Field et al., 1995).

Arguably, the Dutch system provides a compelling example of failure of the judicial review. However, the action taken in the Netherlands was not to abandon that system but to strengthen it. New legislation has been put into place to ensure that the prosecution service has a firmer grip on police investigations. Regulations concerning intrusive policing methods have established a review committee to authorise and monitor their use on a national basis. The other mechanism to ensure national consistency concerns the operation of guidelines, of which there are many. They are typically issued by the Board of Procurators General, the formal head of the service that is in frequent contact with the Minister of Justice. This, interestingly, is in contrast to Germany, where guidelines are regarded with suspicion as a reminder of state influence on criminal justice during the *Third Reich* (Fionda, 1995).

Lay review of prosecution: the American Grand Jury

The oversight often employed by investigative judges over prosecutors is, in some of the US states, a task for the grand jury. A grand jury is formed in a way similar to petit juries, juries that decide on guilt at trial. Such grand juries are not to be confused with federal grand juries that often serve a different function, which is typically more 'watchdog'-like: these tend to be involved in investigations to monitor the performance of government and other public agencies.

Grand juries can be as large as 23 persons, for instance in Pennsylvania (see Savitt and Gottlieb, 1983), or as small as five or seven, as is the case in Virginia and Oregon, respectively. Grand juries generally serve to bring charges, to oversee investigations or some combination of the two. One way a person can be charged is for a prosecutor to seek an indictment from a grand jury by presenting evidence to it. The jury must decide whether there is probable cause, in which case they 'return the indictment', which is also called 'returning a true bill'.

The status of state grand juries differs widely among US states. In some, they can be bypassed only with difficulty, and in other states their function is largely inconsequential. Nevertheless, one could argue that a grand jury returning indictments is the US way of controlling the power of prosecutors. Where in continental Europe this review is a matter for a judge, in many US states it is, perhaps not surprisingly, a matter for 'the people'.

It is fair to say that the Grand Jury is under pressure. Its screening function has been eroded and Dillard et al. (2003) argue that the Grand Jury has increasingly become a tool to enhance the power of government by agreeing to inappropriate prosecutions where in fact it was established in order to place a hurdle in the way of overzealous prosecutors. They advocate a scaling back of the powers and the involvement of the Grand Jury. In contrast, Washburn (2008) argues that the way forward is not to marginalise the Grand Jury but to hand it back its original function in a modern-day guise: he advocates neighbourhood Grand Juries to be the voice of communities in prosecution decision-making (see also Fairfax, 2010).

It is additionally noteworthy that a prosecutor in the US, the District Attorney, can exert considerable influence over police investigations. District Attorneys may have investigative teams attached to them and on occasion conduct special investigations. Noteworthy examples have included the Watergate allegations involving President Nixon, and the Monica Lewinsky affair during Bill Clinton's presidency (Uglow, 2002).

It is perhaps little known that Japan has Grand Jury-type institutions called Prosecutorial Review Commissions (PRC). They consist of lay people who can assess the propriety of prosecutions or non-prosecutions. The institution was in fact established by American rulers shortly after WWII, another example of policy transfer further to foreign domination. US General MacArthur saw great advantages in such as body as a check against prosecutorial freedom and as a way of engaging the public in the justice process (Fukurai, 2007). However, the considerations of PRCs are merely advisory. Similar to the American Grand Juries, their relevance is disputed and the occasions where a PRC has actually changed the course of a prosecution are relatively rare. There are, however, plans to firm up the status of the PRC so that a prosecutor can only go against its advice further to a reasoned statement as to why that is the appropriate course of action (Fukurai, 2007)

The core function of a prosecution service

Prosecution is about filtering out cases that should not go to court. That requires rules and guidelines to decide how cases should be processed once they have reached the stage of prosecution. Arrangements will often involve a certain level of discretion on behalf of the prosecuting authority. Levels of prosecutorial discretion are high in France, Belgium and the Netherlands, where the principle of opportunity holds. In these countries prosecutions are brought only if they are deemed to be in the public interest, although it is not always clearly defined what constitutes public interest, unlike in England and Wales where the relevant guidelines are a matter of public record. In other European countries the principle of legality, also known as the *ex officio* principle, is upheld (Fionda, 1995). Germany is an example (Tak, 1986). It means that prosecutions should be brought for every crime that comes to the attention of the prosecution office for which there is sufficient evidence. The former principle of opportunity fits better with the inquisitorial tradition, in which state officials enjoy greater levels of freedom to decide on the course of action they think is best. Choe undertook a comparative study on pre-trial discretion involving six countries (Choe, 2013). She found maximum police discretion (to drop cases rather than prosecute) in England and Wales and the USA. In contrast, decisions by the prosecution officers are more important in France, Germany, Japan and South Korea where the police have little (France and Japan) or virtually no discretion (Germany and South Korea). The prosecution office discontinues most cases due to insufficient evidence in the latter two countries whereas South Korea and Japan see most cases not proceeded with due to a lack of public interest. Choe's (2013) study highlights that different criminal justice systems filter cases at different points for different reasons, and that the outcome of these filters may almost resemble a 'tug of war' between police and prosecution as to where key decisions involving prosecutions could or should be made.

When discussing prosecution from a comparative perspective we find that comparing like with like is virtually impossible. Prosecution in Scotland is already rather different from that in England and Wales, whereas prosecution in most countries on the European continent is very different altogether because the relation between police and prosecution has a wholly different footing. The role of the prosecutors in court differs as well, and cannot be understood without understanding how judges, jurors and defence counsels play their part in court, which is a matter to which I shall return in the next chapter. In inquisitorial systems the usual mechanism for quality control is review. In adversarial systems the safeguard is one of independence (see also Jehle et al., 2008).

Pre-trial justice: the role of magistrates

It can be argued that the phase of pre-trial justice only starts properly when a suspect is charged and makes an appearance before a judge. An independent magistrate is usually required to ensure that a suspect's detention is appropriate. It is indicative of the severity of the measure of detention that after a few days in a great many jurisdictions a judge is required to rule on it, usually having seen the suspect and having reviewed the evidence that has accumulated up to that point. But of course that doesn't mean that this always happens. Schönteich (2008) relays the story of a visit by Rapporteur Danwka in 2000 to a police station in Banjul in the Gambia who could not find a single detainee in whose case this 72-hour time limit before judicial review was in fact adhered to.

In the USA, suspects who are arrested and kept in custody normally appear before a magistrate within 48 hours (Schmalleger, 2006). Following arrest most states require a magistrate's review in order to determine whether or not there is cause to detain the suspect. Release is subject to bail, which usually involves a monetary deposit, although there are alternatives such as conditional release and release on recognisance, which involves a defendant signing a promise not to flee from prosecution.

In the Netherlands every detained suspect is interviewed by an examining magistrate within three days of their arrest. This judge can impose remand in custody, which usually involves a suspect being transferred from a police cell to one in a remand prison. The suspect is entitled to have a defence lawyer present at their hearing. Examining magistrates need to make several assessments. First, they establish that the crime the suspect is prosecuted for is serious enough to allow remand. The general rule is that only for offences that carry at least four years' imprisonment is remand in custody a possibility. The Dutch Criminal Code specifies maximum sentences for crimes, and four years can be given for most sexual crimes, most violent crimes, and the more serious class of property crimes (Corstens, 2008).

Second, the examining magistrate must be satisfied that the evidence as put forward is sufficient to warrant custody. The required level of proof is not beyond reasonable doubt, but it has to be considerably stronger than the reasonable suspicion required for arrest. The third assessment to be made is whether certain grounds apply to necessitate custody. These would include the strong possibility of the suspect re-offending, or of the suspect evading trial or disturbing the gathering of evidence. Finally, in cases of suspects of no fixed abode in the Netherlands, the possibilities for remand in custody are somewhat widened, as they frequently are in other countries as well.

In France, a suspect can be held at a police station for interrogation and questioning for 24 hours, which can be extended to 48 hours, and in exceptional cases to 96 hours (Vogler, 1996): the system of *garde à vue*. The suspect's rights relating to *garde à vue* have recently been improved, partly because of a number of European Union rulings against France (Hodgson, 2004). Only since 1993 do suspects have the right to:

- notify a relative by phone of the arrest;
- obtain legal advice, although with limitations – it is only allowed after 24 hours of detention, and the suspect does not have the right to have his/her lawyer present during interviews;

- call for a medical investigation straight away and not, as was the case before, after the initial 24 hours have expired. Relatives can request that a suspect be seen by a doctor as well;
- be told at once in a language the suspect understands about all relevant applicable rights and the legal limitations on the duration of *garde à vue*.

Garde à vue is initiated by a senior police officer and overseen by a prosecutor who has limited powers of extension as well. Remand in custody (*détention provisoire*) can only be imposed by an examining magistrate. Only those defendants charged with a grave offence carrying a penalty of at least two years' imprisonment or one year in case of an *offense flagrante* (a serious offence) can be remanded. Remand must be justified by reasons relating to the investigative process or for reasons relating to either the protection of society, the preservation of public order or for the defendant's own security. If the offence charged carries less than five years' imprisonment and the suspect has not previously served a prison sentence of at least one year, the remand period cannot exceed six months. In more serious cases, the custody can initially be for the duration of four months, but this period is renewable and the law does not state a maximum period of custody. Suspects can, at certain times, request the examining judge to lift custody, a decision that is open to appeal at a division of the Appeals Court called the *Chambre d'Accusation*.

From an English perspective, criticisms with regard to the position of the suspect in France are easily made (Hodgson, 2002). The fact that a defence lawyer is not entitled to attend police interviews is probably the main bone of contention. Despite significant changes to the system in the 1990s, defendants' access to legal advice remains limited and over 80 per cent of those initially detained do not see a defence lawyer. The system of pre-trial custody is not uncontroversial in France itself as well, and pre-trial arrangements seem to be ever-changing, but the position of the defence seems to be improved only with a certain level of reluctance. Vogler (1996) notes that defendants do have four fundamental rights – the right to know the allegations against them; the undiluted right to silence; the right to counsel; and the right to sufficient time to prepare a defence – but Hodgson warns us that the undiluted right to silence has already been taken away again (Hodgson, 2004).

To what extent defendants will always be able to exercise these rights is a matter of debate. The consensus among French legal theorists seems to be that the immediate involvement of an independent judge is one important safeguard against police wrongdoing. The fact that all decisions affecting a suspect are reasoned, given in writing and can be appealed against is another. Third, careful regulations for the behaviour of police, prosecution and examining judge also serve as indirect empowerment of suspects, who are certainly less well equipped to fight their corner directly than their counterparts in England and Wales.

The French situation, where a suspect is not entitled to have a defence lawyer present during initial police interviews, is an easy target for criticism. It is, however not unique to France. In the Netherlands the suspect's rights are similarly limited with regard to the first police interview. The official reason is, perversely, that the presence of a defence lawyer would hinder the development of rapport between interviewer and suspect. The utility of this measure can be questioned, as it appears that most suspects in the hands of the Dutch police are happy to speak anyway. The issue periodically enters the political agenda, but change in the short term does not appear to be very likely (Corstens, 2008), although a pilot has been run to establish its feasibility (Jensma, 2008).

Despite recent proposals to restrict the role or abolish the office altogether, the *juge d'instruction* remains, for the moment at least, a pivotal figure in French criminal justice (Hodgson, 2001). In Germany in contrast, the role of investigative or examining judge has been abolished. The examining judge used to gather evidence in serious trials in a process called *Voruntersuchung* (which translates literally as 'pre-investigation'). Legislation in 1974 abolished the examining judge because the post was considered unnecessary, costly and slow.

In the Netherlands on the other hand the office of the investigative judge is alive and well. Investigative judges serve a dual role in criminal investigations. On the one hand they exercise their role as protector of the suspect's rights. Certain investigative actions are subject to an investigative judge's authorisation, including, in most circumstances, house searches. However, the law in this respect is hideously complex, with different legal frameworks coming into play depending on the objective of the search. Separate acts apply, depending on whether the police are looking for drugs, weapons, other goods or evidence, or whether the home or premises is entered in order to install technical equipment for the interception of communications.

On the other hand, the investigative judge is, in certain circumstances, the actual supervisor of the investigation. It is curious that the person who is most capable of taking coercive measures against a suspect is also the one who is trusted with their protection against any overzealous application of these measures. Only in countries where the judiciary is generally trusted and held in high esteem is such an arrangement likely to work. Its importation into the UK has, in some circles, been contemplated, but never proposed with much force (Leigh and Zedner, 1992).

The figure of the investigative judge is, from a British perspective, a bit of an oddity. The concept of an independent judge being involved with the actual criminal investigation is unknown in the UK. The concept is at odds with the notion that the independence of judges is their most important characteristic. It is in this regard noteworthy that recently in France, the role of the investigative judge has been split in two: an examining magistrate (aptly named the *juge des libertés et de la détention*) to rule on issues of custody and a *juge d'instruction* to direct police investigations (Hodgson, 2001, 2002). More recently, Hodgson (2010) has described the *juge d'instruction* as being under pressure. Proposals from 2009 suggested the abolition of the office which would result in obvious drawbacks. The *juge d'instruction* is an immovable judge. To transfer their duties to a prosecutor who is ultimately answerable to the executive is risking the independence and robustness of the system. As in the Netherlands the prosecutor is already a pivotal figure in police investigations directing police investigations and controlling the case to a large extent. The *juge d'instruction* remains an important counterbalance to that power (Hodgson, 2010; see also Harris, 2010 on how these dynamics can play out in homicide investigation in France).

Pre-trial custody in law and practice

Use of pre-trial custody is almost inevitably controversial. While no one disputes that those suspected of serious offences who are likely to re-offend should be held, pre-trial custody remains by definition, the deprivation of liberty of the innocent, or at least the not yet proven guilty. The issue of human rights is pertinent. Article 5.1 of the European Convention for Human Rights guarantees the right to liberty and security and has implications for the use of pre-trial custody. It considers pre-trial custody lawful only when it is:

> lawful arrest or detention of a person effected for the purpose of bringing him before the competent legal authority on reasonable suspicion of having committed an offence or when it is reasonably considered necessary to prevent his committing an offence or fleeing after having done so.

Article 5.5 of the European Convention for Human Rights states that, 'everyone who has been the victim of this Article shall have an enforceable right to compensation'. The extent to which, in practice, suspects are able to exercise this right is another matter, not least in England and Wales (Hucklesby, 2002).

In most Western states the rules with regard to pre-trial custody are quite specific and this level of detail should work as a safeguard against abuse. Legislation usually prescribes the crimes for which remand may be considered, those who are authorised to impose it and the kind of legal advice and legal remedies available to the suspect. While the philosophy underlying pre-trial custody might perhaps be similar across European jurisdictions, the actual practice is not. In some countries there seems to be more of a readiness to use this measure, while in others there appears to be more of a reluctance to do so. Table 6.1 lists the number of suspects in pre-trial custody per 100,000 inhabitants for 29 European jurisdictions.

The European average, based on the sample of countries given in Table 6.1, is about 38 people in pre-trial custody per 100,000 inhabitants, 1998. High-ranking are the Baltic states of Estonia, Latvia and Lithuania. Together they average close to 100 detained suspects per 100,000 inhabitants, and neighbouring Belarus also seems quite enthusiastic about incarcerating large numbers of suspects. These four countries, with Kyrgyzstan (which also has a relatively high pre-trial custody rate) are all former Soviet republics. In the former Soviet Union incapacitation, often combined with deportation, was a commonly used state strategy for dealing with criminals and dissidents. Clearly, there are regional trends in rates of pre-trial custody: in many Eastern European states, coming from a high base the rates are coming down. The exception is the Former Yugoslavia where custody rates were quite low but have risen substantially of late. In a majority of Western European states, pre-trial custody is on the rise. That includes the home nations of the UK, but also Austria, Belgium, Luxembourg and Sweden (Walmsley, 2008b, see Table 6.1).

Very low, on the other hand, ranks Finland, which is geographically very near the Baltic States. In 1998 it had a pre-trial detention rate of only 5.7 per 100,000 inhabitants, about 20 times lower than Estonia, which is only a short ferry trip away and culturally said to be not dissimilar. The Finnish rules regarding pre-trial custody do not appear to be radically different from elsewhere in Europe. Under normal circumstances, remand is only applicable when there is probable cause that the suspect committed a crime that carries at least a one-year prison sentence. Additionally, it has to be judged probable that the suspect

Table 6.1 Pre-trial custody rates in 29 European jurisdictions

Country	Rate per 100,000 population	% change 1995–2004
Austria	26.2	+35.3
Belarus	114.4	–
Belgium	35.0	+50.3
Bulgaria	18.9	−25.2
Croatia	19.4	+39.7
Cyprus	3.7	+200.0
Czech Republic	85.4	−59.1
Denmark	15.5	+33.6
England/Wales	25	+10.5
Estonia	115.1	−34.4
Finland	5.7	+34.3
Hungary	33.5	+28.8
Italy	42.5	−8.8
Kyrgyzstan	70.3	–
Latvia	88.9	−10.7
Liechtenstein	51.6	–
Lithuania	80.6	+53.4
Luxembourg	33.2	+79.4
(FYR) Macedonia	7.4	+89.9
Malta	18.4	−8.4
Moldova	48.0	−17.8
Netherlands	19.9	+86.7
Northern Ireland	26.9	+46.3
Portugal	37.0	−35.2
Scotland	19.8	+28.3
Slovakia	38.0	+58.5
Slovenia	9.8	+56.9
Sweden	11.7	+51.3
Turkey	40.2	–

Source: Walmsley, 2008b.

will flee to escape trial, seek to tamper with the evidence or influence witnesses or other parties, or continue his/her criminal activity. Only a court may remand a suspect in custody, and must do this within four days of the suspect's apprehension. The Coercive Means Act 1990 also states that a judicial chamber must rule on its renewal every two weeks (Joutsen et al., 2001).

Finland's crime rate is relatively low. But the low number of people in pre-trial custody cannot be explained away by saying that there are simply not enough 'qualified' criminals available. Additionally, the Scandinavian countries of Denmark and Sweden have pre-trial custody rates that are at least twice as high as that of Finland, but also comparable rates of people imprisoned (Walmsley, 2008a). It would thus seem that the criminal justice system in Finland is particularly successful in avoiding the incarceration of suspects. As the rules are not particularly restrictive, this seems to be a matter of practice rather than of legislation.

Pre-trial custody is an area, then, where its rules are not necessarily very predictive of the extent to which they will be used. I have used Finland as an example where the rules regarding remand in custody are perhaps relatively liberal: crimes for which one year of imprisonment can be imposed may be justifiable grounds, in comparison to the Netherlands, where crimes punishable by four years imprisonment ought, in theory, to restrict the applicability of remand in custody. However, the actual use of detention in Finland is much lower than in other countries, including the Netherlands. In comparative criminal justice, rules only mean so much. What matters is their application. Sadly though, pre-trial rates are on the rise in Finland but interestingly, they are coming down at a similar rate in Estonia. Perhaps when Estonia's Soviet days drift further into the past, Finland and Estonia's usage of detention might become increasingly similar. Foglesong (2008) notes more widely that the problems with pre-trial detention are often not of a legal but of a practical nature. That means that reform may be achieved without requiring substantive legal changes. Rather it is often a matter of monitoring that existing laws and guidelines are in fact adhered to. Foglesong records that this approach has been successful in both Nigeria and Malawi where lawyers and volunteers achieved increased compliance with pre-trial detention rules by the authorities.

The relation between law and practice is probably more nebulous in China (Lu and Miethe, 2002). The Chinese communist government in the twentieth century was slow to formulate a code of criminal procedure after assuming power: that took some 30 years. A negative result of this legislative vacuum was the development of the widespread use of detention. In the 1979 Criminal Procedure Law pre-trial custody was regulated to outlaw custody in ways and situations that were not spelt out. It failed, however, to stop extra-legal practices of detention from developing. The official phrase used for this practice was 'taking in for shelter and investigation' (Fairchild and Dammer, 2000) which was a measure originally intended to protect society's most vulnerable members. However, the way this measure was employed was as a catch-all ground for detention. Criticisms were levelled at the authorities because it was felt that this type of detention was used particularly to control and deter those whose political views and activities were not condoned by the authorities. It has been alleged that persons have been arrested and detained, sometimes for years, for their involvement in the famous Tiananmen Square demonstration in 1989.

Ruihua (2003) sums up the problems with detention in China as follows. The biggest problem is its wantonness: detention is easily imposed and legal limits are easily stretched which makes anyone, at any time, a potential target for arrest and detention, a situation that reminds us of Solzhenitsyn's *The Gulag Archipelago* (1973), which details the extraordinary use of detention and imprisonment within the Soviet Union and the extent and depth of state oppression that pre-trial detention both symbolises and facilitates. Second, detention is used as punishment and control, so that it has become an end in itself rather than a means. Ruihua (2003) also notes a widespread lack of proportionality in the application of detention; long spells may occur for those suspected of trivial offences. Fourth, prolonged detention often occurs in the absence of judicial review. Appeals to have detention lifted usually have little chance of success. Finally, there are persistent reports of widespread torture of those in detention. It can easily be seen that the above characteristics can make Chinese detention centres the difficult-to-penetrate environments where torture may become an institutionalised means of dealing with alleged subversive individuals, as we saw in Chapter 4 involving police in Brazil (Huggins, et al., 2002). An Open Society Foundations project from 2011 documents graphic instances of torture in China, Kazakhstan, Togo and Jordan. Walmsley (2008a) presents an estimate of 850,000 people held in administrative detention in China. That dwarfs levels of pre-trial custody in Europe, and provides us with a true sense of the scale of injustice that pre-trial detention can represent.

Diversion

One way of relieving overloaded criminal justice systems is by diversion. Diversion is the process by which a prosecutor (or other state official) arranges for a case not to go to court but for it to be settled in a different manner (Miers, 2001). This frequently occurs as a way of enhancing victim empowerment. Offender–victim mediations have been in place in Europe for well over 20 years. The work of Norwegian theorist Christie (1977) has been influential throughout the continent, while the family group conference legislative framework has been quite successful in New Zealand and has also served as an example for other jurisdictions (see www.restorativejustice.org for more information).

Christie's seminal article is called 'Conflicts as property' and it argues that a crime should be treated primarily as an issue between offender and victim. It puts forward the suggestion that conflicts between people have been 'stolen' by the state and reconfigured as prosecutions against lawbreakers. He argues for the return of the conflict to the parties themselves, who should aim to seek a resolution via dialogue. Initiatives to bring this about have been developed in Christie's native country of Norway.

The impetus for diversion in New Zealand had to do with an over-representation of the indigenous population, the Maori people, in the criminal justice system. It was felt that the way the system dealt with Maori youths in particular was not very successful. As a response, the Family Group Conference legislative framework was adopted in 1989. It is arguably a step toward the indigenisation of the New Zealand criminal justice system as such conferences were the traditional way of solving conflicts within Maori culture. It has been reported to be very successful (Miers, 2001) and since then such mediation schemes have been adopted all over the world. It seems that restorative justice is one of criminal justice's most package-able ideas: different variations of the restorative justice theme have been put in practice in dozens of countries. Traditionally in many of these systems there was hardly any role for victims in the criminal justice process apart from the provision of information upon which the authorities could act. In mediation the views and wishes of victims can be properly taken into account (Braithwaite, 1989).

Victim–offender mediation can occur at different stages in the criminal justice process. It may occur prior to any charge: the police may formally or informally suggest that a suspect make amends to the victim. When that succeeds, a charge may be avoided. Mediation may also operate before trial but after the suspect has been charged. The results of the mediation may help decide whether the trial should go ahead, and, if it does, the mediation results may be used during decision-making at trial. Mediation may also occur after completion of the trial, as part of a sentence or as a sentencing alternative. As this chapter is concerned with pre-trial justice, we will discuss mediation at that stage.

In many jurisdictions it is the police or prosecution who serve as gatekeepers to pre-trial mediation. In France the prosecutor refers cases to such schemes. The intended outcome of such an intervention is for the offender to take responsibility for their actions and in some way make good the damage. The result of the mediation is communicated back to the prosecutor who can, if it is successful, discontinue the case.

Similarly, in Austria the public prosecutor decides whether an offender can become involved in an offender–victim mediation scheme. The scheme cannot be invoked in the case of offences for which more than five years' imprisonment can be imposed (or ten years if the offender is a juvenile). It must also have been established that no special measures are required to prevent re-offending. When the prosecutor does not invoke the scheme and the case goes to court, the court may invoke the scheme of its own accord. This does not happen very often but might occur further to a request from either the victim or the offender (Kilchling and Loschnig-Gspandel, 2000). The prosecutor is, in effect, therefore the main but not sole key holder to the scheme. The aim is to have the offender take responsibility for their actions and make amends. This often involves a face-to-face meeting with the victim, depending on the victim's willingness to participate. Where mediation took place in the case of a juvenile offender an agreement was reached in 83 per cent of cases.

Our final European example concerns Germany (Hartmann and Kerner, 2004). German prosecutors have an option of discontinuation when the offender has voluntarily made restitution to the victim or has reached some form of reconciliation. In minor cases that would mean an end to the case. In more serious cases mediation is still an option, but it is more likely to happen alongside a prosecution. The results of the mediation are taken into account by the court. Bannenberg (2000) has noted that pre-trial mediation is used only in a relatively small percentage of cases. It is also noteworthy that regional differences are large, which is probably to do with the substantial autonomy of the *Länder*, the states of federal Germany.

It is clear that mediation has become an industry that to a significant extent relies on volunteers. Perhaps its popularity is a sign of its success. On the other side of the coin there is a concern that with the growth of mediation as a solution within criminal justice the elements of spontaneity and creativity might disappear. When properly incorporated into mainstream criminal justice it is feared that the subtlety, inventiveness and zeal might disappear and that might jeopardise the success of schemes.

The New Zealand family group conference

The family group conference is firmly embedded in the pre-trial phase in New Zealand. It involves young offenders in the age range 14–17. Most offences committed by this group are minor and are dealt with by the imposition of a police fine. Only offences that involve an arrest go to court, which means only 11 per cent of all offending youths (Morris and Maxwell, 1998). The wide intermediate range of offences is referred to a police body called the Youth Aid Section. This body sets up family group conferences, of which there are some 5,000 per year.

Typically, family group conferences are made up of: the young person who has committed the offence; members of their family and those whom the family invites; the victim(s) and/or their representative; a support person for the victim(s); a representative of the police; and the mediator or manager of the process. The manager of the process is a youth justice coordinator and is an employee of the Department of Social Welfare. The main goal of a conference is to formulate a plan about how best to deal with the offender. There are three components in this process. The first is to ensure that the offender actually did commit the offence: if the offender denies guilt at the conference, the case will normally go to court. The second involves the sharing of information to do with the offence, the offender, the victim and other relevant circumstances. After that the professionals and the victim leave the family and the young person to discuss privately what plans they wish to make to repair the damage and prevent further offending. When the family is ready the meeting is reconvened. A spokesperson outlines the plans to the conference. When there is agreement the conference ends.

The notion of family conferencing draws on the idea that an offender's immediate social circle is of vital importance in addressing their behaviour and in generating ideas for making amends. While it could be argued that this is one way for the state to resolve deviant behaviour without much involvement (McKenzie, 2005), others say that the natural locus for a non-adversarial fashion of addressing problem behaviour lies in the offender's support network and not in traditional courtrooms. The fact that the notion is borrowed from indigenous Maori traditions has no doubt added to its appeal among progressive law- and policy-makers in New Zealand. As in many other places, cultural sensitivity in criminal justice is of great importance.

Family conferencing has become popular across the world, most notably in New Zealand and Australia, but also in the UK, the USA and Canada. It is perhaps driven by a romantic sense of reconfiguring justice as a family or community matter. It is no surprise that such schemes have often been put into place at a time that notions of managerialism, value for money and key performance indicators have transformed many criminal justice organisations from static and bureaucratic to performance-driven businesslike organisations. The assumed purity and non-professionalism of family group conferences appeals to our sense of what local justice ought to be like. Perhaps because of that, they are not easily embedded within regular criminal justice institutions without losing some of their essence (see Umbreit and Armour, 2011, for a compelling overview).

'Mental Health' diversion

Prisons are full of individuals who suffer from mental health difficulties. This has been established by Fazel and Danesh who analysed 62 prison surveys undertaken in 12 countries (Fazel and Danesh, 2002, for the UK; see also Singleton, Meltzer and Gatward, 1998). The rates of mental illness among those on remand are even higher. Remand represents a particular time of limbo for inmates: the shock of detention may still be resonating and there is the added uncertainty as to what will happen at trial. The uncertainty and stress caused by prison and prosecution are not good for any detainee's mental health. It is therefore no surprise that many jurisdictions have established schemes that seek to avoid detention for mental health sufferers. They are often but not necessarily diversionary. In England and Wales there are over a 100 schemes with health professionals advising Magistrates' Courts on the mental health of those who appear before them (Pakes and Winstone, 2005). This allows the court to take that into account and decide on a sentence bearing the mental health needs of the defendant in mind. The USA have taken the idea a step or two further. There are over one hundred Mental Health Courts in the US (Steadman et al., 2001). They serve as a hub: where in many places mental health problems (that need not be obvious to the untrained eye) struggle to get identified and properly appraised, they take centre stage in Mental Health Courts. Therein lies their appeal, as does the recognition that mental health problems rarely come on their own. Singleton et al. (1998) found that many prisoners suffer from more than one mental health problem, and also suffer from drug and alcohol problems at the same time. Any intervention needs to take those multiple needs into account. Although there is expressed cynicism as to what they can actually achieve in a context of reducing community and in-patient psychiatric care, we can safely say that Mental Health Courts are a neat idea (but not without fierce critics, e.g. Seltzer, 2005). No wonder therefore that policy-makers from elsewhere travel to the USA to investigate Mental Health Courts. Where policy-makers travelled to New York a decade or two ago to see zero tolerance policing with their own eyes, similar journeys are now undertaken to see Mental Health Courts in action. It must be said that careful long-term evaluation studies so far are thin on the ground. It is perhaps too early to say whether they work in producing favourable outcomes such as reduced re-offending or improved health (Erickson et al., 2006). But the idea of the Mental Health Court is powerful enough to warrant importation anyway; they are now operating in Canada and other jurisdictions.

Conclusion

Suspects need protection. Much of the traditional literature on pre-trial justice is concerned with a suspect's protection against the power of the state. The main problem identified is that of the overzealous or insidious state. This doctrine is traditionally strong in the USA and the UK. Arrangements in these countries are often characterised by a certain level of rigidity in arrangements between law-enforcement bodies. Their relative independence and the separation of their powers are thought to be guarantees against the state coming down too hard on its citizens during criminal investigations. Furthermore, the role of the defence is judged to be vital in protecting suspects' rights.

These kinds of relationship between the criminal justice agencies are characterised by a higher level of interdependence on the European continent where interaction and review serve as mechanisms for control. Police, prosecution and judiciary are constantly looking over each other's shoulders to ensure that everyone abides by the rules, although, as we have seen in the case of the Netherlands, that does not always guarantee that everyone always does; trust between professionals is the glue that holds such arrangements together.

Another important aspect of pre-trial justice relates to the worldwide trend of relying on diversion, in particular for youngsters or otherwise vulnerable people. It is often felt that the traditional adversarial courtroom does not offer the best environment for a constructive dialogue with the wrongdoer. It is therefore better to seek other solutions and venues to achieve that. While New Zealand and Norway could be said to have been frontrunners in this respect, such developments now occur on a global scale. The enhanced role of the victim in criminal justice procedures has certainly facilitated this process, as has the desire to accommodate indigenous ethnic features in criminal justice arrangements. This clearly is the case in New Zealand, while Christie's writings on crime as property were informed by his knowledge about indigenous justice in Tanzania. The acclaimed success of mediation and the fact that the Council of Europe is promoting the concept of restorative justice among its member states both confirm that diversion and mediation are here to stay.

Further reading

Choe, D.H. (2013) Discretion at the pre-trial stage: A comparative study. *European journal of criminal policy and research, 20,* 1–19.
Schönteich, M. (2008) The scale and consequences of pretrial detention around the world. In: *Open Society Foundations* (Ed) Justice initiatives. London: Open Society Foundations, 11–43.
Gilliéron, G. (2014). *Public prosecutors in the United States and Europe: A comparative analysis with special focus on Switzerland, France, and Germany.* Dordrecht: Springer.

Study questions

1   What are the global issues of pre-trial justice that comparative research can help expose?
2   Describe and outline the difference between inquisitorial and adversarial systems of prosecution.
3   Why are suspects' rights in the pre-trial phase a topic of debate in so many countries?

Chapter 7

The day in court
Systems of trial

A good way of getting a sense of how justice operates is by visiting a criminal court. In virtually any developed country justice is mostly administered in dedicated court buildings that are, for the most part, publicly accessible. Before entering, it is worthwhile considering the physical structure of the building that serves as courthouse. Its architecture can be more or less inviting or intimidating. Security features could be telling. The presence and appearance of guards or caretakers might be of interest, in particular whether or not they carry arms. Other features could include fortified entrances and CCTV. As interesting are symbolic aspects of traditional courthouses, as they seek to architecturally reinforce the fact that these buildings embody the rule of law. In many countries the concept of justice is embodied in a portrayal of Lady Justice (Iustitia, the Roman Goddess of Justice), blindfolded and with a set of scales, symbolising impartiality and a fair weighing of evidence. She also carries a sword, denoting punishment. The symbolism places the court at the very heart of justice. Traditional court buildings are rarely innocuous, as they symbolise a core state function: that of doing justice. The building is there to reinforce the message that justice is done and seen to be done within its confines. It is telling that in France and other countries, a courthouse may even be termed a 'palace of justice' (see Marrani, 2009). Once inside, it is interesting to observe the spatial organisation of the court. The positioning of judges and their attire can reveal information about their role and the esteem in which they are held. The presence or absence of a jury invariably has an impact on the way in which the courtroom is designed. The relative positions of the participants can provide hints to the actual goings on at trial, in particular about the relationships between significant persons such as judge, members of the jury, the prosecuting authority and defence counsel. Although not every courtroom necessarily looks the same within one justice system, there are interesting differences between countries in how the room is laid out.

In most Crown Courts in England and Wales, the higher courts of first instance, the defendant is physically far removed from the judge. The accused sits normally in a separate niche called the dock, at the back, whereas the defence lawyer takes a more central position. In many continental European courtrooms, in contrast, the defendant is seated very close to the judge, much closer than the defence counsel. The defence counsel is often literally right behind their client. In the Netherlands, no one is closer to the judges than the prosecutor. In the course of the chapter it will become clear that these spatial relationships reflect quite closely the actual relationships between the various actors.

Courts tend to be steeped in tradition. Proceedings are typically formal and scripted. Although changes occur to accommodate modern developments, overall, tradition tends to win. That means that courtrooms and courtroom procedures are less affected by globalisation than, say policing. It is therefore an area where a more traditional comparative outlook is more appropriate. That said, we must realise that courts have been modernised in many countries: these days evidence can be given via video-link and in some countries courtroom proceedings are televised. The O.J. Simpson murder trial in California famously dominated public consciousness worldwide over the course of 1995. The Oscar Pistorius murder trial in South Africa in 2014 similarly captured the global public imagination. TV has entered the courtroom, changing it as a result. In addition, courts worldwide struggle with the use of social media, in particular by jurors (I'll discuss this later). Thus, we cannot say that late modernity is passing courts by altogether – but they are more shielded from it than other parts of the criminal justice system.

Families of trial systems

Trial systems vary enormously around the world (Vogler, 2005). Most people in the Netherlands know the adversarial trial with a jury only from TV. Similarly, many people in the USA will have difficulties in conceptualising the procedures in the more administrative Dutch courtroom. These differences are far from superficial. Justice is done in profoundly differing ways and underlying these are deeply rooted differences as to how societies are organised. In particular, the role of the state in administering justice has important repercussions for the way trials are conducted. A significant portion of this chapter is therefore devoted to looking at inquisitorial versus adversarial modes of justice.

In addition we need to understand how the trial itself is situated within the whole of the criminal justice process. It is important to realise that the differences between the two modes of trial are not just different ways of performing the same function. Inquisitorial trials are more deeply embedded within the investigative process, whereas adversarial trials constitute more of an independent platform that is more separate from police investigation. As will become clear in this chapter, trials are, as it were, the closing ceremony of the inquisitorial process, whereas they represent the *grande finale* in the adversarial process of justice. When comparing both modes of trial I shall focus on the higher courts, where the differences are most profound. In lower courts, particularly in the case of cooperative defendants who do not contest their cases, procedures are quite administrative, and probably uneventful, in any system. It is, however in the higher courts where the adversarial element in adversarial trials truly blossoms.

I will also describe trials in the Islamic legal tradition. In *Sharī'ah* law the origins of trial procedures and of the system in which they are set is again rather different and based largely on the Muslim holy book, the Qur'an. A description of so-called indigenous courts of justice is included by means of two examples, from Papua New Guinea and Alaska. From there I will look at a wider development: that of legal pluralisation. This refers to different types of justice system operating at the same time within the same jurisdiction. This is an increasingly common state of affairs in many parts of the world.

Inquisitorial trials in France

Although the French criminal justice system tends to receive a bad press in the UK, the following quotation is worth consideration:

> The importance of the post-revolutionary French penal procedural codes as models for both European and global criminal systems cannot be overemphasised. Their influence is far more pervasive and extensive than that of the Anglo-American common law and both the intellectual coherence and the practical advantages of the great Napoleonic codification of 1808 have ensured its international popularity.
>
> (Vogler, 1996: 11)

As a result of the Napoleonic domination over much of mainland Europe around 1800, most European countries have criminal justice systems that originate from and often still bear close resemblance to, the French blueprint. The French inquisitorial system of justice is the archetypical inquisitorial example. However, it should be borne in mind that although the systems in, for instance, Germany and Belgium, are similar they are by no means identical.

The principle underlying French trials is that all relevant facts will be placed before a court in order to judge the accused. This aim is achieved by conducting extensive pre-trial inquiries and by placing the onus of eliciting the evidence at trial on the judge rather than on the parties (Sheehan, 1975). Great emphasis is placed on pre-trial inquiries. They are made in private: the evidence is examined publicly only at trial. The results of the pre-trial investigations are compiled into a case file, or *dossier*. The dossier is given to the presiding judge prior to the trial. If compiled properly, the evidence at trial will closely correspond to what is contained in the dossier. This means that the trial is for the verification of that information, not necessarily for the elicitation of new facts.

We must also state from the outset that where laws and procedures in the UK and the USA are subject to continuous debate, the situation in France is no less dynamic. Legal reforms are frequently proposed but not always implemented. However, it is clear that there is not much that is considered beyond reproach and many proposals studied would in fact strike at the core of the inquisitorial justice system. This reminds us of the fact that although legal orientations may be centuries old, the actual legal practices are continuously subject to change (see Hodgson, 2010).

In France as virtually anywhere else the type of offence determines to a large extent the eventual court of trial. The French penal code distinguishes between three different types of offence. The most serious are 'crimes' (punishable by imprisonment from ten years upwards). The heaviest offences are tried before a *Cour d'Assises* (Assize Court). It sits with three professional judges, a president and two assessors, and a jury of nine members of the public, and deals with about 2,700 cases a year (Vogler, 1996). 'Délits' are the next category of offence, tried before a court called *tribunal correctionnel*. The least serious offences are so-called *contraventions* and are tried in a court termed *tribunal de police* (police court). The term 'police court' might be misleading: the police are not responsible for the prosecuting nor do they decide cases. The reasons for the name of this court are historical and it is worth mentioning that the term has been in use in England and Wales in the past as well.

Trials in the higher and lower courts in France have a rather different feel. The atmosphere in the lower courts is characterised by informality. In these *tribunals de police* the case usually develops on the basis of a relatively unscripted dialogue between the presiding judge and the defendant. The president deals with the defendant's history and personal circumstances as described in the dossier, and may ask the defendant questions for clarification. It is the judge who examines witnesses and the defendant. Both parties can have an input but that is normally performed by means of suggesting questions for the judge to ask.

Instead of being examined in a strict question-and-answer format, the defendant is usually invited to give his or her version of events with regard to the allegations, and might be interrupted more or less often by questions from the president. Defendants are never under oath, and it is uncommon for them to exercise their right to silence (Hodgson, 2004, 2010). When witnesses are called they are also dealt with in the same conversational manner. They are invited to relate their stories before specific questions are put. There is no distinct witness examination or cross-examination as such. In their closing statements, prosecutors can propose a sentence. Judgement may be given at once or reserved, but is always made in open court.

In the *Cour d'Assises* the atmosphere is more formal although procedures are not dissimilar. The main difference between the two types of court is the presence in the *Cour d'Assises* of the nine-member jury. As I will deal with juries in more detail in the next chapter a few comments will suffice here. First, the jurors and judges decide together on both guilt and sentencing. An eight-to-four majority is needed for a guilty verdict, from a blind ballot. Sentencing decisions are arrived at by majority. Jurors do have the option of asking questions at trial, either by suggestion to the president or directly.

Despite the presence of a jury the role of the president judge remains pivotal. As the president puts most of the questions to defendants and witnesses this judge is firmly in control of the happenings at trial. On top of that, the presiding judge is the only person who has had the opportunity of reading the dossier prior to the trial. Neither assessor has the case-file at his/her disposal and nor do the jurors. The system thus places a heavy burden on the presiding judges (and perhaps at the same time it marginalises the other actors). It is their duty to take all steps to discover the truth. To that end they conduct the trial to elicit all relevant information and can call additional witnesses that neither party may have brought forward. It is strongly felt that the court needs to judge the offence as much as the defendant, in order to decide extent of guilt, appropriate sentence and capacity for rehabilitation. Much debate can therefore concern the defendant's background and personal circumstances.

Closing speeches are given by both prosecution and defence, but these are followed by closing remarks from the president. The president summarises the issues to be decided and instructs the jury on the burden of proof. In order to control the president's influence on the jury, the president cannot make statements in court that might reflect an opinion on the defendant's guilt. The law does not, however, forbid the assessors from doing that. In addition, the president is allowed to comment on, for instance, the credibility of witnesses in ways that would clearly give away their sentiments about the case. If this measure is aimed at protecting the jurors from the president's opinion of the defendant's guilt before deliberation, it is one that is certainly questionable as to its effectiveness.

Adversarial trials in Crown Courts in England and Wales

Adversarial criminal justice originated in England. It has been exported, as has the French inquisitorial system, across the world. In particular in many English-speaking nations, often former British colonies, the system enjoys an enduring popularity. Adverarial trials, you could say, have many faces. They can be long winded and frequently interrupted due to legal arguments. Trials can be affected by the unavailability of witnesses or the illness of a juror. But they can also be dramatic and intense with twists and turns in the delivery of testimony though examination and cross-examination. And of course there is the moment when we hold our breath when the jury returns to announce its verdict. The adversarial trial is therefore the poster boy of justice: it contains all the ingredients that capture our imagination.

To use the archetypical example of adversarial justice, in England and Wales the trial procedure in Crown Courts is as follows. Initially, the indictment is read out, and the accused confirms their plea of not guilty. Subsequently, the jury is sworn in, after which the prosecution opens its case. It proceeds by calling witnesses, who are positioned in the witness box: the witnesses for the prosecution. Each witness is initially examined by the prosecuting barrister. Subsequently, each prosecution witness can be cross-examined by the defence lawyer. It is in these cross-examinations that much of the drama in adversarial courtrooms is to be found, as the questioning can be intense and confrontational. After cross-examination the prosecution has the chance of re-examining the witness. This procedure is followed for each prosecution witness, after which the prosecution closes its case. This phase often takes several days to complete.

Next it is the defence's turn to call witnesses to support its case. The defence witnesses are examined initially by the defence lawyer and cross-examined by the prosecution, after which a re-examination can be conducted by the defence counsel. Prior to their appearance in court, witnesses for both parties have been put under oath by an usher. During examinations in chief (prosecution or defence) witnesses cannot be asked leading questions; the witness may only be guided. During cross-examination, leading questions are allowed and frequently used. Witnesses are expected to give 'evidence of fact' and not offer opinions (although expert witnesses constitute an exception to this rule). Additionally, they are not allowed to offer hearsay evidence: that means that they cannot testify as to statements made by others. It is a testament to the principle of immediacy that if the evidence of another person should be of relevance then that person should testify in person. However, there are exceptions to this rule as well.

When the examination of witnesses has been completed, the prosecution addresses the jury in its closing speech and the defence does the same. Subsequently, the judge sums up the facts of the case and may direct the jury on points of law regarding the charges and with regard to the issue of proof. The summing up of the facts can also be quite lengthy and should not in any way be leading. Perceived violations of this principle are frequently cited as reasons for appeal. The jury finally retires to reach a verdict in private.

There is a great deal of etiquette involved in participating in or even attending a Crown Court trial. Any attempt to interrupt proceedings may be considered contempt of court, and offences under the Contempt of Court Act 1981 carry prison sentences. The fact that judges and barristers wear traditional wigs adds to the sense of decorum and an atmosphere in which irreverence is out of place. Rising to greet the judge and bowing to the judge are common practices.

The atmosphere in US courtrooms is similar, but there are procedural differences. Examinations have been said to be more rigorous in American courtrooms. Another important difference is that judges in the USA do not sum up the facts. Their role is somewhat more restricted and umpire-like, whereas judges in England and Wales can be, and regularly are, somewhat more dominant. Arguably, therefore, the US mode of trial is more truly adversarial than its English archetypical counterpart.

Adversarial and inquisitorial justice in theory and practice

A number of differences between the system of England and Wales and that of France are readily apparent. I will elaborate on some of these because they help us to appreciate the core differences between the French inquisitorial tradition and the English adversarial way of conducting trials. Some key differences are the role of confessions and pleas, rules of evidence, and appeals and so-called reasoned verdicts.

In France, defendants do not usually plead (Hodgson, 2010). Because they are regarded more as the subjects of investigation such a declaration is not required. In England and Wales, defendants are seen as parties in the conflict. Their plea implies their factual or tactical approach to the case, an aspect deemed unnecessary in the inquisitorial philosophy in which there are usually no separate procedures for suspects who do not challenge the facts or the charge. The inquisitorial court will always examine the evidence at trial regardless of the stance of the accused. The onus on proving guilt lies with the prosecutor. This is most important in the pre-trial phase, when the prosecution is heavily involved with the investigative process. As the judge is the primary fact-finder at trial, the role of the prosecutor is more limited at this stage. The prosecution's closing statement, in which they recommend a sentence, is nevertheless known to be influential.

Confessions made during the pre-trial phase may be regarded with caution, especially when made during police investigation (when a defence lawyer may not always have been present) and subsequently retracted (Hodgson, 2004). However, French courts have great freedom in weighing the value of a confession: it may be enough for a conviction, but it may also be discarded.

Rules of evidence in France, as well as in other inquisitorial systems, tend to be minimal. The courts are trusted with the experience and reasoning powers to judge any evidence on merit. That removes the need for protecting participants from evidence that might be irrelevant, improperly obtained or biased. Courts should be able to decide that for themselves and ignore such evidence if necessary. In principle all evidence should be presented at trial. This honours the *principle of immediacy*, which is upheld in France, but only in principle. Much of the evidence is merely mentioned, particularly if it is undisputed. Hearsay evidence is not admitted, but it is in other European countries. Even evidence that resulted from improper investigative actions can be admitted. It is up to the courts to decide how to weigh it.

Because of the reliance on case files, inquisitorial trials tend to be shorter, especially in the case of confessing and cooperative defendants. Also, particularly when cases are decided by judges instead of jurors, there is a lack of courtroom drama because there is not a jury to convince but seasoned professionals who know the prosecutors in their area often rather well. It makes courtroom interactions much more routine, and for those from an Anglo-Saxon perspective, rather underwhelming, although exceptions to this have been documented (e.g. Pakes, 2007c).

With the exception of cases decided by a jury in the assize court, appeals are open to both the defence and the prosecution. Appeals receive a full new hearing at the appellate court. An appeal by the defendant alone cannot lead to the imposition of a more severe penalty than was awarded at the first instance (Vogler, 1996).

Whereas juries are often strictly forbidden to explain their verdicts, judges in inquisitorial systems are often required by law to do so. These explanations often include the evidence they use as the basis for their verdict, and the reasons why competing items of evidence are rejected. Both prosecution and defence can scrutinise these reasons, and use them as a basis for appeals. Two doubts can be raised about the usefulness of offering these reasons. First, one cannot be certain that the reasons listed are the actual ones that swung the court's decision. Second, it is perhaps unlikely that the court will phrase their reasons such as to provide the parties with ammunition for appeals. Wagenaar et al. (1993) are rather sceptical about the actual practice of reasoned verdicts in the Netherlands. They argue that verdicts rarely contain more than standard formulations, such as 'given the evidence presented', and do not illuminate the court's decision-making at all, and therefore are hardly an effective means of enhancing the court's accountability.

There is great deal of legal-historical writing about the source of the differences between inquisitorial and adversarial systems (Damaska, 1986; Pakes, 2007c). The core difference between the two systems can be understood in terms of the role that the state traditionally plays in different societies. In inquisitorial settings the traditional role of the state is prominent. We therefore speak of an active state. Active states are associated with a strong state involvement in the provision of education, health care and social welfare. Strong and active states tend to rely, by necessity, on higher levels of taxation as well.

Active states also tend to take responsibility for dispensing criminal justice. The traditional view is that it is up to the state to investigate both the crime and the accused so that justice can be done. The impartiality of the investigators and the court should guarantee that this process is carried out properly. The role of the defence is more limited: it is rather the prosecution with the investigative judge and the court who are supposed to ensure that the suspect's rights are respected. They do that by respecting them themselves and by keeping a close eye on police activities. This does however reduce the role and status of the defence.

In adversarial systems the basic premise is that the state should not be relied on to the same extent. The role of the state in adversarial systems is limited and is therefore associated with societies in which the state is smaller and more passive. The passive state does not provide for the dispensation of justice but rather provides a platform for conflict resolution. At trial, both prosecution and defence are supposed to present the case to the best of their abilities and an independent body, be it judge or jury, decides the result after having heard both sides of the argument.

The kind of welfare state established in many Western societies in the second half of the twentieth century has obscured this relation between the state and the mode of trial. In England and Wales the state at present certainly cannot pass for 'minimal' or passive. However, we have to bear in mind that modes of trial and the influence of the powers that be over courts, judges and juries has been shaped over centuries, whereas the phenomenon of the inclusive 'cradle to grave' welfare state is historically a relative novelty. The assumption that adversarial systems flourish as a response to a malevolent state, whereas inquisitorial justice fits a society in which the state is regarded as a strong and benevolent force, is still valid.

Although it is often left unsaid, inquisitorial systems are often associated by their opponents with the sinister operations of a state-run inquisition, persecuting its citizens and in which the 'truth' is found by means of torture and otherwise coerced confessions (Jörg et al., 1995). It is certainly appropriate to say that adversarial systems have blossomed in response to a societal distrust in the state and its powers. This is especially true for the USA. When state officials cannot be trusted it makes sense to leave the administration of justice to 'the people', a jury of one's peers. Ordinary people are trusted more easily than state officials with a vested interest in maintaining power. All the state needs to provide is a stage: a platform where an assessment of the suspect's guilt can take place in a rule-governed fashion. Those ideas form the basis of adversarial justice. This makes adversarial justice, arguably, literally revolutionary, as it is the result of wresting crucial power away from the state. In inquisitorial systems, on the other hand, the state is associated with objectivity and fatherly wisdom. When such sentiments are prevalent it makes sense to leave the dispensation of justice in its lap. Juries would be seen to be less important, and, as the state represents the investigating as well as the adjudicating body, there equally is no need to discount the information gathered prior to trial.

The difference between the role of the prosecution service in adversarial and inquisitorial systems is, in practice, often subtle but theoretically important: the prosecution in the adversarial system is geared more towards proving the defendant guilty (Hodgson, 2010). It is the defence whose task is to advocate innocence. Therefore the role of defence counsel in adversarial systems is more prominent. In inquisitorial systems, however, the prosecution should aim to find the truth, and therefore takes on part of the function that, in adversarial systems, is left to the defence. Hodgson (2001) correspondingly found that in France the profession of defence lawyer is held in less esteem than it is in England and Wales. As is the case in the Netherlands, defence lawyers do not enjoy the same legal standing and are less well paid and trained. The right to have a defence lawyer is generally accepted, but their role is widely seen to be relatively inconsequential to the case and its outcome.

Both systems have been accused of neglecting the defendant in proceedings, of 'taking the conflict away from victim and offender' where it initially arose. In adversarial systems a trial may easily be completed with hardly any contribution from the defendant. The battle is being fought between legally qualified actors, who argue over rules that often have little to do with the defendant or the charge. The defendant is, in a sense, removed from the actual conflict. This removal is also apparent in the spatial lay-out of the English Crown Court, in which the defendants are usually positioned further away from the judge than their representatives.

In inquisitorial systems the defendants, regardless of whether they protest their innocence or not, will normally contribute to proceedings. They are asked questions about the crime and their criminal record, and are free to speak for themselves. However, the defendant is more the subject of investigation than an actual party and the dossier normally has answered all questions anyway. Thus, the fact that defendants in inquisitorial trials often sit in a more central position does not make them more powerful actors. Cynics would say that their close proximity is primarily to allow the judges to have a good look at the defendant, and not for defendants to have equal ability to scrutinise and influence proceedings in their trial.

It is worth an extra moment of reflection about what it means for a panel of judges to have access to the case-file before the defendant appears before them in court. Through its contents the court will usually know what the defendant has said to the arresting police officers and what was found during a house search. The judges will be aware of whether defendants changed their story, and to what extent statements of possible accomplices or witnesses differ. Judges will have noted whether the investigative judge (after all, a colleague) felt that there was enough evidence for pre-trial custody, and what the suspect's attitude and level of cooperation has been throughout the pre-trial process.

Controversially, the court will also have taken note of the defendant's criminal record. In adversarial systems it is often forbidden to mention or discuss any previous crimes the defendant may have committed. In most inquisitorial systems this is often done as a matter of course. It is evidence of the fact that the inquisitorial process comprises to a larger extent an investigation into the suspect's character over and beyond the crime at issue.

Trials in the Islamic legal tradition

The third influential legal tradition is Islamic law. It is prevalent in the Middle East, and informs some or all of the legal system in countries such as Saudi Arabia and Iran. The principal source of Islamic law is the Muslim holy book, the Qur'an. The Sharī'ah is the body of rules of conduct revealed by God (Allah) to his prophet Mohammed whereby the people are directed to lead their life. According to the Muslim faith, the angel Gabriel called Mohammed to be a prophet. Mohammed preached about the need to replace old tribal customs, which drew heavily on blood revenge. Instead he preached for brotherhood among all people of the Muslim faith.

A number of features of Islamic law are worth noting. Its most important characteristic is its strong religious basis. While amplified by Islamic legal scholars, the source of the law is divine revelation. It has universal validity for

Muslims even if not officially recognised by the state. Because of its divine status it is relatively inflexible as room for interpretation is limited. Although other sources of law exist, such as the actions and words of Mohammed and the consensus of high-standing Islamic legal scholars, its strong basis in religion sets Islamic law apart from other legal traditions. While adversarial and inquisitorial justice systems are to an extent informed by Christian values, the connection between religion and law is nowhere near as strong as it is in the Islamic tradition (Fairchild and Dammer, 2001; Pakes, 2007c; Rezeai, 2002).

In some countries, Islamic law forms part of the legal system. In a minority of countries, it forms the basis for all law, often with only minor exceptions. In Saudi Arabia, for instance, Islamic law underlies the whole of the justice system, although Fairchild and Dammer note that 'certain concessions are made to modern exigencies of trade, banking (Islamic law does not allow the payment of interest), and industry' (Fairchild and Dammer, 2001: 61).

Foreign influences on the Japanese criminal justice system

The early history of Japan is characterised by a great deal of isolationism. Only after Japan opened up to the West for trading in the middle of the nineteenth century was the door opened for influence in the criminal justice arena as well. The French Napoleonic Code was translated into Japanese and it proved influential.

A French scholar was asked to draft a penal code and a code of criminal procedure, which came into effect in 1880. The latter code of criminal procedure was heavily inquisitorial. The preliminary inquiry rather than the trial was trusted to provide the courts with the relevant facts. The code gave substantial discretion to the judge in questioning the accused and witnesses at trial, and a jury was incorporated into the system only by the introduction of the Jury Act in 1928 (Nakayama, 1987).

Following Japan's surrender at the end of World War II a new code of criminal procedure was drafted by Japanese legal scholars, together with officials from the Allied forces. It came into force in 1949. The new system made a substantial shift towards a more adversarial fashion of proceeding. However, the jury system had never become popular following its earlier introduction and, further to its suspension during World War II, was not reintroduced. In the new code, the independence of the prosecution and the judiciary was given a stronger footing and the preliminary inquiry was abolished. The jury however, has made a comeback of sorts, as we will see later.

Western influences at various stages, and for different reasons, have left Japan with a criminal justice system that is truly mixed. Although there are adversarial elements, the long absence of a jury and the central position taken by the prosecution are clear remnants of the older inquisitorial tradition. However, trials are more important than they tend to be in other inquisitorial countries, and they are of a slightly different form. Trials are not necessarily full-time events, as they are in England and Wales or the USA. Rather, they may proceed over a longer period with only one or two sittings per week. True to the inquisitorial tradition, the evidence presented before trial tends to be influential (although defence counsel can object to it being used). Traditionally, much weight is given to confessions, and their value is not only evidential. Confessions are also viewed as the start of the reconciliatory process, which for centuries formed an important ingredient in the maintenance of social control. The Japanese example of the evolution of a criminal justice system is typical of those in many parts of the world: they evolve under the influence of domestic traditions and foreign domination, and notably lack any master plan (Takayanagi, 1963; Castberg, 1990; Leishman, 1999; Ellis and Hamai, 2006).

In substantive Sharī'ah law a distinction is made between crimes against God and private wrongdoings against other people. Crimes against God are called *hudud* crimes. They include defamation, denunciation of Islam and also certain sexual offences such as sodomy and adultery. In case of crimes against God, it is for the state to initiate proceedings against a suspect. Penalties in case of *hudud* crimes tend to be fixed. The offences are quintessentially anti–Islam and because of that there is little room for manoeuvring. They *must* be dealt with in a certain way. Private wrongdoings are called *quesas* crimes and here the situation is different. In such crimes a private party, such as the victim or their family, must initiate the case, and there is an emphasis on offender–victim negotiation. *Quesas* crimes may, however, also attract severe sentences as they can be serious crimes. Murder, for instance, is a *quesas* crime: not so much a crime against God, Islam and the community of believers, but rather a crime against a private individual. In such cases, there may be scope for negotiation between the victim (or their family) and the offender. There certainly is a place in Islamic law for negotiation and restitution as a means for expressing forgiveness and charity. Alternatively, this practice allows for the 'buying off' of victims and their relatives, akin to blood money, which could allow the wealthy and powerful to atone for such crimes without suffering meaningfully as a result of punishment. Many crimes against God, on the other hand, risk the death penalty or the amputation of limbs (Souryal, 1987). Finally, there are *tazirat* offences: minor crimes of discretionary punishment (see Ghodsi, 2004).

In procedural law, a number of elements are worth noting. Putting aside confessions, witness statements are all important. In the absence of confessions Islamic law seeks the truth by statements made by reliable people. The burden of proof is on the accuser. Proof-taking occurs by calling reputable witnesses. In most Islamic courts evidence from a male witness counts heavier than from a female witness and in some jurisdictions women hardly appear at all as witnesses.

Lying under oath is considered a serious wrongdoing, with severe legal and religious consequences. However, the oath works rather differently from the way it does in Western jurisdictions. Witnesses speak freely in court, and it is assumed that not everything that is being said is necessarily truthful. It is up to the judge to deduce who speaks the truth or not. The stakes become much higher when the evidence in a case is not decisive. One party may then challenge the other to take an oath in support of their assertions. The idea is that lying under oath is unthinkable, so that the party who is prepared to maintain their allegations under oath comes out as the winner. The rationale is simple: one may bend the truth in dealing with other people in everyday life but not under holy oath. The final decision about who should take the oath first rests with the *Qadi*, the judge (Pakes, 2007c).

Saudi Arabia has adopted Islamic law since the beginnings of the modern state, in 1926. The territory of Saudi Arabia, which is mostly uninhabited desert, contains the holy cities of Mecca and Medina. The government has not disseminated a penal code or a code of criminal procedure and few laws exist separately in published form, most being contained in religious writings. According to official figures, the crime rate in Saudi Arabia is very low. While there are the problems of counting and compiling statistics (the Arabic calendar year is shorter than that of the Western Gregorian calendar, for example), it seems that rates of murder, rape and robbery are very low, even compared to other Arab countries. Souryal et al. (1994) claim that Islamic law, with its strict punishments, has been instrumental in establishing a rather peaceful society.

To what extent these figures are reliable is open to debate. While in certain jurisdictions it is often relatively easy to obtain figures with regard to the criminal justice process, in Islamic criminal justice systems this often is not the case. One reason might be to do with the fact that in criminal justice systems on a more pragmatic footing, performance figures are vital for monitoring that performance. In the Islamic tradition, in which the doctrine is dogmatic rather than pragmatic, such information would be less necessary. Where policy-making is less at issue policy information is less likely to be readily available (see also Crystal, 2001, on criminal justice in the Middle Eastern region).

Wardak (2005) in fact argues that the low crime rate in Saudi Arabia must be explained by reference to five systems of social control of which the Sharī'ah legal system is only one. The first is the extended family, the most important agency of social control in Saudi Arabia. The second is the school. It plays an important part in socialising youngsters into Saudi society. The third is the mosque, which plays, apart from its religious role, also a social and community role. In fact much social and community life revolves around the Mosque. The fourth is an institution called Motwwa'in. It is quite an autonomous body with a wide religious and cultural remit and is sometimes referred to as a 'moral' or 'decency' enforcement force. Vogel (2003) argues that these forces have rather a fundamentalist reputation and enjoy a position of little accountability. The fifth is the traditional legal system: given this context alongside the other four, we should perhaps not ascribe too much prowess to the legal institutions alone.

The unbearable shortness of Dutch trials

Trials in England and Wales tend to take days or even weeks. In contrast, trials in the Netherlands tend to take only minutes or hours. Straightforward trials of burglary, drink-driving or common assault take no more than half an hour from start to finish. More complicated cases may take several hours to one day, and only the most dramatic cases take more than a day in court to be completed. So-called 'mega-cases' are cases that take more than two days in court. They comprise a tiny proportion of all cases. For those familiar with trials in England and Wales this must sound almost farcical. How can justice be done in, for instance, a rape case with a defendant who denies his guilt, when his 'day in court' is not even a day, but rather a couple of hours?

A typical trial in the Netherlands runs as follows. At first, the presiding judge assesses the identity of the defendant, if present, and reminds the defendant of his/her right to silence. The prosecutor then rises to read the indictment. Subsequently, the presiding judge questions the defendant. However, since the judges will normally have read the case-file beforehand, usually little new information comes to light. After questioning by the judge, the prosecutor and defence lawyer may ask questions. Occasionally, but not usually, witnesses are called to appear at trial. Again, it is the judge who is the principal fact-finder although both prosecution and defence can pose questions to witnesses, as can defendants themselves.

When the questioning is completed the prosecution presents its closing argument, which comprises a sentence recommendation. Following this *requisitoir* it is the turn of the defence lawyer to make the final statement on behalf of the defendant, although defendants are entitled to speak for themselves. The defendant always has the last word.

Such a trial procedure is, as inquisitorial trials go, not out of the ordinary. What is striking, however, is their short duration. In order to understand the role of the trial within the context of the whole of the criminal justice process we have to think back to the pre-trial stage. We have seen that police investigation in France and the Netherlands is, to a large extent, governed by review by the prosecution service and the magistracy. In serious cases examining judges have a great deal of involvement in ongoing police investigations. Whereas in England and Wales case-files are compiled to send to the prosecution, in the Netherlands and in countries such as France and Germany these case-files are sent to the courts.

Judges usually familiarise themselves with the contents of these dossiers. They contain summaries of witness and suspect statements, descriptions by police officers of investigative actions, the paperwork relating to coercive measures, and also the suspect's criminal record, which is usually discussed at trial (Nijboer, 1995; Corstens, 2008). The facts are established during the investigation and they do not need to be repeated. The information needs only to be verified. In the Netherlands, the dossier is not just information. Information from the dossier can be used in evidence. This can go quite far: when a defendant denies his/her guilt at trial but did confess during police investigations, that earlier confession might be taken as evidence. Obviously a court needs to explain why it considers that confession more important than the subsequent retraction, but in principle nothing stops a court from using self-incriminating statements made during the investigative stage as actual evidence on which they can base a guilty verdict. Do remember that suspects do not, as a rule, have a defence lawyer present during police interviews.

Additionally, certain investigative actions take place at the pre-trial stage so that they need not be repeated at trial. Victims are often interviewed in the pre-trial stage by an investigative judge, usually in the presence of a defence lawyer. These interviews tend to be less confrontational and traumatic than a cross-examination in a courtroom might be. A court would normally rely on the accuracy of the record of such interviews, during which both parties have had a chance to examine witnesses. Although occasionally witnesses are called into the courtroom further to a request from the defence, they would need to explain why they have left it until such a late stage to involve them. The appearance of vulnerable witnesses in particular is considered inappropriate at the trial stage.

All this means that judges are not very often taken by surprise at trial (they don't like such surprises either!) which helps to explain the routine and administrative nature of the trial process. In most cases, the trial is just a matter of wrapping things up. The battle over guilt or innocence does not start afresh in the trial itself.

Indigenous courts

Village courts were re-introduced in Papua New Guinea in 1974. These courts were established with the intention of handing the administration of justice back to the people and providing communities with a locally administered platform for conflict resolution. The country's last colonial power, Australia, had centralised criminal justice to a large extent and the village courts were a way of reversing this trend. The move responded to the sentiment that traditional Papua New Guinean communities did not easily assimilate Australian law and legal culture, so that an indigenisation of trial procedures was seen to be a positive development. On the other hand, it has been mentioned that central government also wished to exert greater control on local justice. The way this was done was not by replacing the local systems of social control but by incorporating them into more formal structures, while preserving a certain level of autonomy. Supervisory district-court magistrates were influential in making recommendations for appointments and conducting regular visits to village courts, so that any autonomy would be mediated by a certain degree of oversight from more centralised bodies.

Magistrates at village courts deal with a range of criminal and civil matters in a semi-autonomous manner. These court officials are villagers selected by the local population. Village magistrates tend to be males, between 35 and 50 years old, and relatively influential in their community. Female magistrates are few and far between. The wrongdoings dealt with are usually disturbances, fighting, abusive language and drunkenness, theft and adultery. The courts have developed an efficient, crisp interrogatory style, in which little deviation from the facts by parties or witnesses is allowed. Decisions are rendered without much delay and are usually unanimous.

This type of court does share characteristics with many courts around the world: the composition of the magistrates reminds one of England and Wales; the resulting conservatism is another feature that is widespread. On the other hand, its efficiency and effectiveness is not always paralleled in the Western world. It provides good example of 'developing' justice, in which the traditional means of achieving justice utilising trusted community members as arbitrators, combined with modern considerations involving the standardisation of procedures, produces something rather effective and suitable for the social fabric of the villages concerned (Paliwala, 1980; Fitzpatrick, 1982). With corruption a persistent problem in public life in Papua New Guinea, it has been argued that village courts work: Brison found that Kwanga village magistrates combined a rhetoric contrasting new law and tradition with a practice that included many features of local conflict resolution procedures. It seems therefore not just indigenisation in name but also in spirit: the way magistrates do justice honours and strengthens age-old traditions (Brison, 1999).

Courts in a cold climate: achieving justice for all in Alaska

Although the 2008 Republican vice-presidential candidate Sarah Palin briefly brought new levels of fame to Alaska, the US state remains a remote place. Situated west of Canada, a land surface of over 571,000 square miles (over six times the size of the Great Britain) is home to only about 626,000 people. That makes the population density just over one person per square mile. (To put that figure into context, in relatively densely populated countries this number is in the order of a few hundred.) Of these people, 69.3 per cent are White; 3.5 per cent are Black or African American; 15.6 per cent are Native American (Indian) or native Alaskan, and 4.0 per cent are of Asian origin. According to the 2000 Census, 7.6 per cent indicated a different race or more than one race. While much of the population is concentrated in the cities, such as Anchorage, there are countless remote villages and communities throughout the state. Many of those local communities consist, by and large, of native Alaskans (Alaska Justice Reform, 1996).

In a state where people are so few and far between there are challenges with regard to the provision of justice. Until the late 1980s many remote communities had become accustomed to a state of affairs that, in effect, meant a high level of self-governance. Policing functions were to a large extent administered by locals. There were usually also provisions in place to deal with minor wrongdoings. These indigenous arrangements were often extra-legal: not covered by any official law or statute.

A study of local governance including 28 villages of between 70 and 700 residents that were between 10 and 100 miles away from an urban centre, was carried out in 1995 (Alaska Justice Reform, 1996). The average native Alaskan population in these villages was approximately 82 per cent. Local government in these communities was often administered by a village council. The larger communities had a village police officer and a village public-safety officer. In spite of this, it was concluded that nearly all the communities surveyed were short of money to pay for local community safety. Most villages had established local ordinances and rules to handle undesirable behaviour. In a few cases official tribal courts had been recognised by the state, but in most villages similar operations of an extra-legal nature were in place. Most inhabitants accept their jurisdiction either voluntarily or because of social pressure. It would appear that the law exclusively applies to local residents. Misbehaving guides, fishermen and hunters were normally handed over to official law-enforcement bodies instead.

In one community surveyed, sentences imposed comprised fines and a form of community service, which might involve helping the elderly or cleaning public facilities. The administration of justice was highly informal and predominantly informed by custom. In another community, the court used a handbook comprising a set of rules and employed local, native security guards. The administration of justice was in the hands of village chiefs. Because of the fact that in this particular community it was common to walk in and out of one another's homes, no one seemed to think twice about entering homes to check on misconduct, such as the possession of alcohol, or to gather evidence. Such arrangements do not seem to be heavily informed by issues of privacy. Any form of judicial review seemed both non-existent and a non-issue. Apart from a range of lesser penalties, natives who repeatedly misbehaved could be asked to leave the village, temporarily, and in the case of recidivism, permanently. The study drew rather positive conclusions with regard to the operation of law and order in these villages:

Most of the villages in this survey have seemingly well-understood community social control methods to handle problems beyond the scope of family responsibility. These methods sometimes do not reflect the western legal system and lack articulated recognition from the Alaska Department of Public Safety, the Alaska Court System, and most other governmental organisations. The village social controls tend, however, to be confined primarily to dealing with disruptive behaviour in the community.

(Alaskan Justice Reform, 1996: 5)

It has been argued that such methods perform a useful ancillary role to the established criminal justice system. Communities who are able to resolve low-level disputes without the need for the established authorities to interfere probably help save resources. There is now increased contact between officials in formal and less formal modes of justice, which will no doubt help ensure an acceptable standard of justice that is not jeopardised by isolation.

There is also evidence that native Alaskans, in particular Yup'iks, are not always properly served by the formal criminal justice system, which they consider to be daunting and alien. This is because of differences in culture and language, but also on account of differing conceptions about what is involved in being held to account for wrongdoing (Morrow, 1993). Better education of the public, most particularly the harder-to-reach parts of the population, and an increased investment in translation and interpretation services are vital in securing some form of justice for all who live in Alaska (Shafer and Curtis, 1997).

We can note interesting similarities and differences between the Alaskan and Papua New Guinean examples of modes of justice. Both seem to be praised highly. Both seem to be operating by communal consent, and have a swiftness and directness that many Western criminal justice systems cannot achieve. Both have a rather informal feel, which will usually only enhance the quality of operations, as they are based in small communities. However, where civil liberties are at issue it is difficult to see how a firm but fair system of accountability could be incorporated.

An important difference lies in their respective genesis. The village courts in Papua New Guinea were reintroduced after colonial arrangements did not seem to fit the local context. Thus, they were instigated as a remedy. The Alaskan courts did not come into being as a response to any state-imposed bodies, but rather as a way of doing justice in the absence of formal criminal justice institutions. Both examples also show that jurisdiction can easily incorporate more than one justice system. This state of affairs is called legal pluralism.

Legal pluralism

It is still often assumed that the nation state must be home to either adversarial or inquisitorial systems as if there is a 'great divide' that places adversarial Anglo-Saxon countries in polar opposition to inquisitorial countries, many of which are on the European mainland. This is overly simplistic, as we have already seen. This inaccurate assumption of a neat divide in fact obscures two important aspects of the organisation of justice. The first is that systems can be, and frequently are, hybrid. The other is that in many countries, perhaps in particular in Asia and Africa, various systems of justice exist alongside each other. To an extent this occurs in Western countries as well where Shari'ah law, in small measures, may be in operation, alongside more established systems of justice.

The African nation of Ethiopia is a case in point. Located in the Horn of Africa, Ethiopia is home to some 93 million people making it one of the most populous African nations. It has special status in Africa as a country that successfully resisted colonisation and was the first African nation to join the League of Nations, the United Nation's predecessor. Its capital Addis Ababa is one of Africa's great cities. In a country historically plagued by poverty, famine and political unrest, sustaining a stable level of governance is an almighty challenge. The same can be said for the delivery of justice in a diverse and fraught society.

Ethiopia's constitution recognises ethno-linguistic and religious diversity (Abdo, 2011). Possibly because of that there is a great deal of legal pluralism in the country, resulting in a patchwork of various modes of justice at various levels and locations. Ethiopia's trial system is, by and large inquisitorial. There is no jury and cases are decided by a panel of judges who decide by majority. There is a right to conduct a public trial and to appeal. There also is a right to a defence lawyer but in the absence of legal aid, this is not easily implemented in reality. There is the right to rigorous defence including sufficient time to prepare a defence, and to call and question witnesses for the defence at trial. There also is the right to have proceedings undertaken in a language that the accused understands. As there are a great many languages spoken in Ethiopia, this is another challenge for the state, as it has to provide translation services where required (Blackburn and Matthews, 2011).

In addition to the state system of justice there is much room for traditional means of conflict resolution. This particularly occurs at the local level, governed by the *Kebele*, the lowest administrative unit, roughly the size of a village. It is often elder men who serve as customary mediators, and may deal with disputes ranging from land disputes, neighbourly disputes and theft, to domestic violence and sexual violence. As these forms of mediation are locally available, speedy and often free, they are particularly attractive and very frequently used. Similar forums aimed at reconciliation and compensation may occur at a regional level as well. However, Baker argues that serious concerns exist in relation to the administration of justice to women (Baker, 2013). Although public views are slowly changing on forced marriage and female genital mutilation, it seems that marriage is still regarded as an appropriate resolution between offenders and victims of rape. The extent to which women can pursue justice in a rigorous fashion under such a patriarchal system must certainly be questioned. In addition, remnants of other ancient practices remain as well. On occasion, homicides are still settled by blood money although that practice is officially outlawed (Baker, 2013).

There is further pluralism in relation to the rise of Sharīʿah justice in Ethiopia. This is in operation in particular where there are Muslim majorities or substantial Muslim minorities. It mainly operates in the areas of family law and personal disputes but may also be used in the areas of interpersonal and sexual violence. Sharīʿah resolution systems have been around since the 1940s but gained official recognition in the 1990s. They operate in parallel with the state justice system. Cases dealt with in a Sharīʿah court do not have a right of appeal in the regular courts. Transfers are also not possible. It is also interesting to note that while Sharīʿah courts apply substantive Sharīʿah law, at the same time they are bound by the state Civil Procedure Code. Finally, it requires consent by both parties for the case to be decided by a Sharīʿah court.

It seems that the Ethiopian justice system strikes a precarious balance. While it has succeeded in having a national justice system that allows the state to own and articulate justice proceedings, many disputes are solved at the local level very much in the shadow of the state justice system. These resolutions are informal and swift but are surrounded by concerns about the lack of justice that women victims receive. In addition, Sharīʿah law is in existence but compartmentalised so that it can occur alongside the state justice system, but only by consent of both parties and constrained by the requirements of mainstream civil law procedures. That way, there is, at least in principle, a state justice system that is either supported by other forms or justice, or compromised by it, depending on your point of view.

Such instances of legal pluralism are highly common, with much movement taking place in countries such as Nigeria, and also Southern Russia. In the Northwest Caucasus region in Southern Russia, the traditional mode of justice is called *adat* (customary law) and relies on reconciliation and establishing peaceful communities. In addition there is Sharīʿah law, which is more formal and institutionalised. However, due to the values and cultural strength of *adat*, Sharīʿah law became adopted in a diluted form and initially even fused into a hybrid system as many community values were commensurate with Sharīʿah law. This shows that pluralism comes in many guises and that surprising ways of either fused or co-existing legal systems can work depending on customs, values and the ethnic and religious composition of communities (Comins-Richmond, 2004).

Conclusion

There is no standard format for criminal trials. If we disregard appeals and the execution of sentences, a trial is where the prosecution of a defendant ends. In a minimal sense a trial is nothing more than a decision-making platform. It is where a decision is made about an alleged wrongdoing and then about what is to be done about the wrongdoer.

The nature of trials is, to a considerable extent, determined by the nature of the investigative phase that precedes it. The more extensive the investigation carried out under judicial supervision, the more is taken away from the trial as the all-decisive day in court. In adversarial systems, pre-trial information is usually discounted; it is only at trial that the evidence that really matters is produced. In inquisitorial systems the evidence gathered in the investigative phase is given much more weight.

Those who support the adversarial way of conducting trials often point out that it gives defence counsel the best chance to prepare and conduct a proper defence. The examination and cross-examination of witnesses in court, before a jury, is seen to be the fairest way for any defendant to be tried. It is also argued that suspects' rights are better protected by a partisan defence lawyer than by an investigative judge, who must balance these rights against the interests of the investigation. Opponents argue that adversarial trials are expensive and time-consuming affairs, and potentially traumatising for vulnerable witnesses. They argue that the involvement of the jury adds a 'hit and miss' element to the proceedings, because jury decisions are difficult to predict, and often not explained.

In this chapter I have sought to juxtapose both systems for analytical reasons. One could argue that this does not do justice to either system. In fact, there is hardly a country where the legal scholars accept their criminal justice system to be purely adversarial or inquisitorial (Vogler, 2005). The Dutch system, although quite far to the inquisitorial end of the spectrum, has been called a mixture of both, as has the German system (Huber, 1996). Legal scholars do not seem to be keen to see their system pigeonholed as part of one category or the other. The Japanese criminal justice system might, perhaps, most justifiably be called a mixture, because of the influence of European and US legal scholars in different eras.

The differences shown relate to, as we have seen, history, foreign domination and additionally differing philosophies about how justice can best be achieved. These philosophies in turn relate to how societies are organised and what role the state is given in them. Therefore, there is no easy way of judging which is better or worse. Crombag (2003) elaborates this point by arguing that adversarial and inquisitorial systems are incomparable because they seek to achieve different goals. Their ultimate goal is the same: to serve justice. However, in the methods of achieving, or at least approaching, that goal both systems settle for what Crombag calls 'proximate goals', and here is where the difference can be found. Adversarial justice's proximate goal is fair play, whereas truth via inquest is that of inquisitorial justice, and Sharī'ah law's road to justice is related to religion. Each system, therefore, has a 'different commitment to the discovery of the truth' (Damaska, 1986: 583), and there are corresponding differences as to the perceived objective of the criminal justice process. Once more, we must conclude that comparing like with like is not without obstacles, so that understanding the various systems of trial is best achieved by appreciating their internal logic in their own context.

Finally we must shift away from classic notions of countries embodying one legal tradition and one legal tradition only. In fact, in many parts of the world, the name of the game is legal pluralism, with different systems of law existing alongside each other. Sometimes they operate wholly separately and in other locations they are incorporated into dominant legal traditions. In other places they may be at odds. It is possible that countries that simply incorporate one legal system excluding everything else may become a minority as in particular informal justice and Sharīʿah justice are currently expanding into many developing and developed countries. Pluralism may therefore, over time, become the new orthodoxy.

Further reading

Terrill, R.J. (2012). *World criminal justice systems: A comparative survey*. Oxford: Newnes.
Vogler, R. (2005) *A world view on criminal justice*. Aldershot: Ashgate.
Van Koppen, P.J. and Penrod, S.D. (Eds) (2003) *Adversarial versus inquisitorial justice*. New York: Kluwer/Plenum.

Study questions

1 What is the essence of the difference of adversarial versus inquisitorial trials?
2 Would you argue that Sharīʿah law trials are more inquisitorial or more adversarial?
3 What criticisms are most frequently levelled at the inquisitorial mode of justice?

Chapter 8

Peers or patriarchs

Judicial decision-makers

Regardless of how criminal justice systems or criminal trials are organised, the ultimate decisions regarding guilt and sentencing remain in the hands of people. We can identify two schools of thought as to who those decision-makers should be. The first argues for such decisions to be left to the wisest and most experienced people in society: they would be best placed to reach a balanced judgement on the offence and the offender. This is the 'patriarch' doctrine. The other view is that such powers should be reserved for people who are as 'ordinary' as the person standing trial: people who are most similar to the offender might be best suited to judge their behaviour. This represents the 'peer' point of view. The idea of judges as arbitrators obviously corresponds to the former idea, whereas juries are associated with the latter notion of ordinary people judging the behaviour of wrongdoers.

First of all, let us turn our attention to the appointment of judges and the role that the judiciary, parliament and the electorate play in making these appointments. Later I shall make a virtual tour around Europe to see where and how the jury system is in operation. The role and powers of juries vary widely both in adversarial systems and in inquisitorial modes of justice. Where a criminal justice system incorporates the provision for jury trials to be held it is normally only the more serious offences that are tried in this way. Minor wrongdoings are usually left for a judge or a magistrate to deal with. To complicate matters, it is not necessarily all serious crimes that are eligible for jury trial. In many countries arrangements are in place to prevent the most complex or controversial crimes from being tried by jury. In some jurisdictions fraud cases are kept away from juries while in other jurisdictions terrorist offences can be tried by judges only.

Safe pairs of hands: the judiciary

The rule of law dictates that judges be independent. This means that no individual or office should be able to tell a judge how to conduct a trial or decide on a case. The legitimacy of the judiciary is further enhanced by ensuring that its members are appointed in a manner that is seen to be fair and that ensures that the judiciary is balanced with regard to certain important characteristics.

The extent to which the judiciary constitutes a fair representation of the population as a whole is a perennial issue. In many countries in the West the judiciary tends to be dominated by White, middle-aged and upper- or middle-class men. Women, minority groups as well as lower strata in society tend to be under-represented. But in comparative criminal justice there seem to be exceptions to every rule. With regard to the gender balance in the judiciary many of these exceptions occur in Eastern Europe. Data from the United Nations Economic Commission for Europe provide data for 20 European countries (see Table 8.1). It shows the United Kingdom as a nation in which the judiciary is extremely male dominated, with only one in five judges (which includes magistrates) women. Several European countries have a gender balance that is more evenly balanced or even favours women. This is particularly the case in Eastern Europe.

Although it is easy to discern an East–West divide across Europe, the question is as always what these data mean. In the Czech Republic where women make up 61.2 per cent of the judiciary the pattern is that the more senior the position the less likely the judge is to be female. The judiciary at the highest court in the land is overwhelmingly male (Osmancik, n.d.). It must also be noted that in inquisitorial systems with its short and administrative trials, the position of judge is more easily held part-time, which may make such positions more attractive to many women. In relation to the role of women in public and political life in Eastern Europe, it must also be appreciated that the judiciary constitutes an

Table 8.1 Percentage of female judges in 20 European countries in 2010

Country	% female judges
Slovenia	77.6
Romania	73.0
Croatia	67.5
Poland	63.9
Slovakia	63.8
Estonia	61.9
Czech Republic	61.2
Lithuania	57.3
Portugal	55.7
Denmark	54.6
Netherlands	52.3
Italy	43.1
Sweden	42.6
Cyprus	37.6
Moldova	33.4
Turkey	31.3
Iceland	30.8
Ireland	23.8
Armenia	21.3
United Kingdom	20.2 (2006 data)

Source: UNECE Gender Statistics Database (see http://www.unece.org).

exception when it comes to the dominance of women in the profession. Since the fall of the Berlin Wall, the number of female parliamentarians in many Eastern European countries has actually decreased (Sloat, 2004).

Gender is only one demographic factor of relevance on the composition of the judiciary. Race is obviously another, and age is a third. A further area of potential controversy is judges' political affiliation and the corresponding lack of, or perceived lack of, impartiality. Clearly, the appointment of judges can be rather a delicate matter. Judges are at the heart of the criminal justice process and the judiciary is responsible for the fair application of the law. That requires a high level of trust in the individual judges as well as in the judiciary as a whole. If you cannot trust a judge, who can you trust?

Judges can be appointed in various ways. The way these appointments work might either enhance or reduce their responsiveness to certain groups or individuals in society. The four main methods are: direct election, election by the assembly (parliament), appointment by the head of state and co-option by the judiciary.

Direct election occurs in many states in the USA (most US prosecutors are also appointed using this method). An advantage of this method is that it guarantees public support for the judge in office, at least at the time of the election. This method is also likely to increase the official's responsiveness to dominant values in the community. The downside is that impartiality might perhaps be compromised when judges find themselves unduly influenced by mood swings in public opinion and would therefore be more likely to behave in a populist fashion.

Election by the assembly is popular in some states in Latin America. While this method may also help to ensure that the judges appointed have the support of the people, political considerations may come into play through appointments because of political affiliation rather than competence (Hague et al., 1998). In Venezuela, for instance, it is argued that the political parties have great control over the appointment of judges (Salas, n.d.). Supreme Court judges are elected by Congress from a list forwarded by the president. Although a body called the Judicial Council has recently been given a role in the appointment of judges in order to depoliticise the process, in practice party politics is still regarded as a dominant factor in judicial appointments.

Spain is another example of a country in which parliament is involved with judicial appointments. As in many other countries, there are certain safeguards in place to protect the independence of the judiciary. Judges cannot be transferred from one position to another against their will. They also cannot be sacked unless via very thorough disciplinary procedures. A judicial body called the General Council of the Judiciary handles complaints against judges. There are about 1,500 complaints of various kinds each year, but very few actually result in disciplinary action (Canivell, n.d.).

Appointments by the head of state also involve the danger of political partiality. This is most common for senior judges for the highest courts. These courts often have an important role in the development of a nation's laws. In most countries judges are appointed for life, and governments usually leave their trace in the composition of the judiciary in the highest courts. The US president who appoints Supreme Court judges is a good example. It is sometimes said that these appointments are some of the more lasting influences on public policy that any president can exert. The issue most notably relevant here at present relates to abortion, which was legalised in the USA by a Supreme Court ruling (the famous Roe vs. Wade ruling of 22 January 1973). A particular configuration of Supreme Court judges may well make it more or less likely that this ruling will be overturned in the future.

Finally, option or co-option by the judiciary is a system in which judges themselves partly or completely decide who are to become their new colleagues. This way of appointing judges is probably preferable with regard to maintaining the judiciary's independence from politics, but might result in an inward-looking and out-of-touch judiciary. It is therefore the method of selection at the opposite end of the spectrum to appointing judges by direct election (Hague et al., 1998).

Thus, the danger of appointments directly from popular votes lies in the risk of producing a judiciary that is too focused on public opinion. A judiciary primarily appointed by other judges might become too resistant to change and out of touch with a changing society. It is perhaps unsurprising that judges are often therefore appointed via a hybrid system in which, at various stages, the judiciary, parliament, the head of state and/or the electorate have a say. It is also not uncommon for there to be different procedures for the appointment of senior high-court judges than for other judges. In Sri Lanka, for instance, High Court judges are appointed by the president, whereas judges in first-instance courts are appointed by a council representing the judiciary (Karunaratne, n.d.).

In authoritarian states, independence of the judiciary is usually non-existent. Judges that side with those in power are considered vital in order to enforce the law to the taste of the ruling elite. They are often called to convict defendants of such catch-all offences as 'offences against the people' or 'crimes against decency', which are common in many totalitarian states. In China, in the 1950s and 1960s, judges were selected for their party loyalty and were expected to uphold the party line in court. Hague et al. (1998) have argued that the willingness of judges to raise their heads above the parapet is often an early sign of liberalisation in such regimes, and tends to precede the final collapse of power.

Conversely when democracies are overthrown this often has severe consequences for the judiciary. Recent history shows some grim examples of this. They include Egyptian leader Nasser sacking 200 judges in one go in 1969. More recently, the former president Fujimori in Peru was known to sack judges he regarded as performing 'unsatisfactorily'. A similar purge of dozens of judges occurred in DR Congo. In Uganda, in the 1970s President Idi Amin had his Chief Justice shot dead (Hague et al., 1998). Unfortunately judges are an attractive terror target. In Colombia, following the declaration of a war on drug barons, 17 judges were killed in a few months (Fricker, 1990). In Afghanistan in 2007, four judges were kidnapped and almost two weeks later found murdered (BBC, 2007).

A well-known trick for governments seeking to evade regular courts because of the independence of the judiciary or because of the rights afforded to defendants, is to set up 'special courts'. In some areas, military courts may serve that function too as proceedings are often less open to scrutiny, with national security cited as the reason. Often in special courts, sessions are held in private and judges are more likely to be hand-picked by those in power to secure the desired outcome of trials. This occurred in Spain under General Franco in the 1970s with regard to political cases. Myanmar (Burma) is another case in point (Cheesman, 2011). This reminds us that we must be distrustful of state efforts to deal with certain groups, be they asylum seekers, alleged terrorists or others, in certain special courts under exceptional and often secretive circumstances. Often these special courts and exceptional circumstances are most in need of scrutiny in relation to suspects' rights, but that scrutiny is usually made most difficult.

Juries: an endangered species?

Juries are a remarkable entity. While criminal justice systems just about anywhere have seen an increase in professionalism, the ultimate decision-makers with regard to guilt or innocence regularly continue to be lay people. In a time when the evidence they judge is increasingly of a scientific and technical nature that is striking. The oddities of the jury system are not lost on many, including Vidmar (2001a), who describes jury service as follows:

> it brings together a small group of lay persons who are assembled on a temporary basis for the purpose of deciding whether an accused person is guilty of a criminal offence or which of two sides should prevail in a civil dispute. The jurors are conscripted and often initially reluctant to serve. They are untutored in the formal discipline of law and its logic. They hear and see confusing and contested evidence and are provided with instructions, most often only in oral form, about arcane legal concepts and sent into a room alone to decide a verdict without further help from the professional persons who developed the evidence and explained their duties.
>
> (Vidmar, 2001a: 1)

While the seemingly odd task the jury faces is widely appreciated there is equal clarity about what is perceived to be its value. Juries ensure that community values have a place within the system. They can guard against a too rigid or unfair application of laws. Juries can serve as protection against the biases of police officers, prosecution officials and judges. Juries also have the power to ensure that harsh laws are not necessarily enforced. For these reasons, the institution of the jury is seen as the embodiment of fairness and propriety (Findlay and Duff, 1988).

Juries around the world are nevertheless a somewhat endangered species. In England and Wales, there have been proposals to reduce the number of cases that are eligible to be tried before a jury (see Auld, 2001; Kirk, 2013). In other adversarial systems, such as those of the Republic of Ireland and Australia, as well as in the USA a similar trend is apparent. Jury trials are, after all, costly, time-consuming and, some say, add an unnecessary element of chance to proceedings (Hans, 2008).

Ironically, in countries without a jury system there is sometimes a trend towards introducing or reintroducing it. Both Spain and Russia introduced a jury system in the 1990s, while it is on the political agenda in other former Soviet states as well. More recently South Korea also brought in the jury (Lee, 2009). But here there also are exceptions. Particularly in Luxembourg there seems to be a widespread contentment with a jury-less criminal justice system. If this contentment is as widespread among the public, defendants and defence counsel as it is among the judiciary that would be indicative of the esteem in which the judiciary must be held.

'The lamp that shows freedom lives': the English jury

It is appropriate to start this discussion in England and Wales, where juries have been in existence for at least 800 years, although their independence became properly established after 1670. Before that, juries were commonly the victim of bullying or persecution if they did not return the verdict desired by those in power. Today, the jury is free to decide its verdict in any way it sees fit. In order to protect that freedom juries are not required to give reasons for their judgement. In fact, the Contempt of Court Act 1985 forbids them to do so. As jury decisions lack scrutiny, a jury is free to go against the law or the evidence without having to fear being held to account. Such a defiance of the law is called *jury nullification*. In order to honour the pivotal role of the jury, appeals against their decisions are difficult. Appellate proceedings are more often instigated because of the behaviour of the legal professionals in court than the fact that the jury may have been mistaken in its verdict (Lloyd-Bostock and Thomas, 2001).

Juries are, however, estimated to sit in no more than one or two per cent of all criminal trials in England and Wales (this is true in most if not all jurisdictions with a jury system). Most defendants plead guilty, which rules out a jury trial. Additionally, most crimes are minor, which also greatly reduces the chance of a trial by jury. Only the most serious offences are automatically tried before a jury in a Crown Court. There is also a class of so-called either-way offences. These offences, representing the middle range in terms of severity, can be tried by either a judge or by jury. It is the defendants' right to opt for jury trial in the case of an either-way offence. In the case of a minor offence (called a summary offence) or when the defendant chooses to be tried by a judge in case of an either-way offence, the case goes to a Magistrates' Court. In this lower type of court the case is usually tried by a panel of three lay judges.

To qualify for jury service, a person must have been a resident in the UK for at least five years since the age of 13 and be between 18 and 70 years of age. Potential jurors are chosen from the electoral register. Excluded are those who have ever been sentenced to five years or more in prison. Those who have served a sentence within the previous ten years, and those who have been placed on probation in the previous five years, as well as those currently on bail are disqualified as well. Ineligible also are people involved with the criminal justice process, such as police officers and court staff, along with the clergy and those with severe mental health problems. Others have the right to refuse to serve because of the demands of their profession. This includes Members of Parliament, medical professionals and those serving in the armed forces (Lloyd-Bostock and Thomas, 2001).

Prosecution and defence powers to exclude individual jurors before trial are limited. The reason is that that would fly in the face of random selection, which is the cornerstone of jury composition. Its advantage is the lack of intentional bias in the group of 12 people who form the jury. However, any random selection may by chance result in a jury that is imbalanced in terms of, for instance, race, gender or social status. The High Court has held that a racially balanced jury is not an automatic right, but the matter remains a sore point, especially in racially sensitive cases (Lloyd-Bostock and Thomas, 2001).

In England and Wales jurors are allowed to take notes. They can also ask questions, but they rarely do so. During deliberations they can send out questions, but this does not seem to occur regularly either. Verdicts should preferably be unanimous. However, when a jury cannot succeed in reaching a unanimous verdict, the judge can instruct that a 10–2 majority will suffice. This occurs in about 20 per cent of cases (Lloyd-Bostock and Thomas, 2001).

The relation between the judge and the jury is intricate. In principle the division of labour is very simple: matters of law are for the judge; matters of fact are for the jury. In reality, the lines of demarcation are not that easily drawn. One of the points at issue is the judge's summing up at the end of the trial. At this stage the judge will direct the jury on matters of law, but will also sum up the evidence. Here there is plenty of scope for the legal professional to influence the jury. A judge in England and Wales has considerable leeway in dispersing his or her views, much more so than US judges, who do not tend to sum up the facts. The fact that judges rule on the admissibility of evidence gives them a firm handle on the goings-on at trial. They do not decide on the facts, but they do have a grip on what evidence the jury hears in the first place.

Despite the fact that the vast majority of cases are dealt with without a jury, there is no doubt that the institution is held in high esteem in England and Wales. Attempts to reduce opportunities for jury trials for reasons of expedience are usually opposed vehemently by the judiciary as well as by other commentators. The ideological love affair with the jury is exemplified by the term 'the lamp that shows that freedom lives' coined by Lord Devlin. He argued that abolishing the jury would be the second act of any dictator, after dissolving parliament. The jury not only stands for fairness in criminal justice but seems to function as a symbol for propriety in politics and other areas of public life as well (see Findlay and Duff, 1988; Lloyd-Bostock and Thomas, 2001).

A secondary aim of jury service is to educate people about criminal justice via their participation. Most citizens are likely to be called for jury service at some point in their lives. The experience of a trial, and the subsequent deliberations and verdict, tend to make lasting impressions, for better or worse, about the justice that was done on that occasion. Jury service offers lay people the opportunity to be a part of the machinery that delivers justice. Its value therefore extends well beyond the interests of the defendant. Roberts and Hough found high levels of public support for the jury, certainly in the UK and in New Zealand (Roberts and Hough, 2009).

Recent challenges regarding the jury involve the use of social media. Jurors are instructed to base their judgement upon the evidence presented at trial but no doubt there is a temptation to 'research' the defendant through social media. There have also been instances of jurors communicating about the case on social media, and there have been examples of jurors communicating with participants in their trial as well (St. Eve and Zuckerman, 2012). These problems have been identified at least in the USA, the UK and Australia (Johnston et al., 2011). Perhaps it will be social media that force a rethink on how juries receive information at trial and come to their judgement in a fashion that is independent, well informed and not polluted by external factors.

The American jury

There is arguably no country in the world in which the jury is of more importance than the USA (Kalven and Zeisel, 1966). Because its jury system was imported from England, one might expect to find many similarities between the two systems. However, specific features of US law and culture have influenced the shape of the jury system. These include 'Americans' distrust of the judiciary, their passion for open procedures and unfettered public discourse about those procedures, their struggle to overcome racial and ethnic injustice, their commitment to adversarial adjudication, and the dual state–federal justice system' (King, 2001: 93).

In the USA the right to a trial by jury is enshrined in the constitution. The Sixth Amendment promises a jury in all criminal prosecutions. However, the US Supreme Court has held that this right can be refused in the case of petty offences for which no more than six months of imprisonment can be imposed. Another departure from the basic premise that all trials should be jury trials relates to the possibility of defendants waiving their right to one. Federal legislation since 1930 allows for defendants to be tried by a judge in a so-called bench trial, provided defendants opt for that. In many states these bench trials occur rather frequently. The US state of Massachusetts is exceptional in that it allows for the possibility of a jury trial after a defendant has been found guilty in a bench trial. This is technically not an appeal, but a two-tier system. The initial trial by judge is optional (King, 2001).

Jury arrangements vary quite widely among US states. All but four states, for example, require 12 jurors at trial (at least to begin with; jury attrition, which is a reduction in size of the jury because, for instance, of a juror falling ill, is sometimes possible). In some states note-taking is permitted, in others it is not. Normally, it is not for the judge to comment specifically on the evidence. Summing up does not occur in most states. Nevertheless, the role of the judge remains highly influential, as he/she rules on the admissibility of evidence, as is the case in England and Wales.

The differences between jury arrangements in England and Wales and those in the USA are perhaps greatest when it comes to jury selection. The Sixth Amendment states that the jury should be impartial and drawn from a previously ascertained district. That, in effect, provides little guidance. A system for the random selection of jurors from electoral lists was adopted in 1970. Nevertheless, both parties have extensive powers to exclude potential jurors. Because of that, the actual composition of the jury often turns into a battleground as if it were a trial before the actual trial itself. It is widely believed that the selection of the right 12 persons is paramount for victory or defeat at trial (Simon, 1977).

First, there is the process of *voir dire* by which both prosecution and defence can exclude a number of prospective jurors before trial without having to offer specific reasons why. The number of jurors that can be excluded can be up to 20 (Simon, 1977). Apart from that, both parties can challenge for cause, which means that jurors can be excluded for particular reasons, which need to be given and accepted by the court. The purpose of the whole exercise is to secure a composition of the jury that is satisfactory to both parties. The idea is that when both parties are satisfied, the jury is most likely to be a proper representation of the public which will consider the evidence objectively and fairly.

An important secondary objective for jury selection is to get acquainted with the prospective jurors. The counsel for both sides may use it as their first chance to sell their case to the jury. The protracted American selection process ensures pre-trial interaction between parties and jurors of an intensity that does not occur in England and Wales. That will affect the relationship both parties have with the eventual jury, which might in turn have an effect on their conduct at trial. To summarise, jury composition in the UK is largely a matter of chance; in the USA it is a matter of battle and of negotiation.

King (2001) has argued that while jury trials are relatively rare and occur in only 3–10 per cent of all felony cases, the notion of the jury is important to the nation's psyche. As is the case in England and Wales, it is felt by large sections of the population that jury trials are a fundamental human right and a prerequisite for justice. What makes juries particularly significant in the USA is the possibility for them to be involved, in most states, in decisions regarding the death penalty. Just as juries are left to themselves when reaching a judgement on guilt or innocence, the situation is essentially the same with regard to the ultimate issue of life or death.

The trial of a person charged with a capital crime (one for which the death penalty might be imposed) has two stages. The first stage is the traditional one, in which the evidence for guilt or innocence is considered. In the case of a guilty verdict, the second stage occurs, in which the same jury hears evidence concerning the appropriate sentence. The phase involving sentencing is also adversarial in nature. The prosecution will seek to prove that certain aggravating circumstances apply, whereas the defence will be looking to present evidence of mitigating factors. The jury needs to decide unanimously that aggravating circumstances apply before they can impose the death penalty.

In potential death penalty cases, the *voir dire* process centres to a large extent on the prospective jurors' attitude towards the death penalty. Prosecutors seeking the death penalty could, in the past, exclude prospective jurors who were opposed to it as a matter of principle. Nowadays however, only jurors who cannot in a particular instance apply the death penalty can be excluded for cause. Those who might sentence a defendant to death but might be reluctant to do so cannot be challenged for cause. The Supreme Court ruled that excluding anyone with a negative attitude towards the death penalty would violate the defendant's right to a fair trial and to an impartial jury under the Sixth Amendment. However, during peremptory challenges, the prosecuting party often still excludes many jurors whose attitude they find not to sufficiently favour the ultimate punishment (King, 2001).

The practice of juries imposing the death penalty is probably limited to Japan and the United States. It arguably makes sense to leave the state's heaviest weapon against its citizens ultimately in the hands of the people. However, this does not mean that the practice of the death penalty and the way in which it is imposed is necessarily just, or fair.

Juries around the British Isles

When looking around the British Isles outside the mainland of Britain, and for the moment we include in that the Channel Islands of Guernsey and Jersey, the Isle of Man in the Irish Sea as well as the Republic of Ireland and the province of Northern Ireland, we can observe quite striking local differences in jury arrangements.

As mentioned earlier, in England and Wales the jury consists invariably of 12 members, while in Scotland the number is 15. In the Republic of Ireland the jury consists of 12 members as well, but unlike in Scotland or England and Wales, the decision to render a guilty verdict must be unanimous or an 11–1 majority.

Notable in Ireland and Northern Ireland is the existence of procedures to try cases of a particularly sensitive nature without a jury. In Ireland there is the Special Criminal Court for this purpose, while in Northern Ireland so-called Diplock trials can be held in which a judge, not a jury, decides on guilt or innocence (Jackson et al., 2001).

Meanwhile, on the Isle of Man a jury of 12 persons is required for charges of treason or murder. For other crimes, a jury of seven members is sufficient. Their verdicts have to be unanimous. In the island of Jersey, off the west coast of France, any defendant in the Royal Court has the right to elect trial by jury. As is the case in England and Wales, unanimity is preferred, but 10–2 can suffice for the return of a guilty verdict. The situation on the neighbouring Isle of Guernsey is rather different again. Guernsey does not have a traditional jury system. Instead, it utilises so-called Jurats, who are prominent citizens selected by an electoral college. There are over 100 of these Jurats and seven of them are required for a criminal trial. A simple majority will do for a guilty verdict (Vidmar, 2001b).

Juries in inquisitorial systems

The adversarial courtroom is the jury's natural habitat. The adversarial process in which all evidence is orally presented at trial fits the jury model well. The inquisitorial mode of trial, in which documentary evidence is more important, is less suited to lay participation. Nevertheless, a fair amount of cross-fertilisation between adversarial and inquisitorial systems has occurred. Bench trials happen frequently in adversarial systems and similarly in inquisitorial systems there often tends to be a place for the jury. However, the role of the jury across Europe is certainly more restricted and it often involves judges and juries deciding verdicts in conjunction. We call such arrangements mixed tribunals. I shall briefly discuss jury arrangements in a number of European countries, after which I shall examine the state of affairs in Spain and Russia: both countries introduced the jury within their inquisitorial framework in the 1990s.

Regional courts in Austria hold trials by jury for serious crimes, which are defined as crimes that carry at least ten years of imprisonment. The possibility for jury trial also exists for cases that might lead to at least five years in prison. Juries deal also, as a matter of course, with crimes of a political nature, which is an arrangement enshrined in the Austrian constitution. Eight jurors decide on guilt, and in the case of a guilty verdict, sentencing is decided by judges and jury collectively (Vidmar, 2001b).

The role of the jury is very limited in Belgium. Juries only feature in the highest court, called Assize Courts. In these Assize Courts, crimes are tried before a mixed tribunal, consisting of three judges and 12 jurors. The jury was abandoned during Dutch rule, between 1815 and 1830, but following Belgium's independence it was reinstated, but only for trials involving crimes of a political nature. A majority of eight versus four is enough for a guilty verdict. However, when the majority is only seven versus five favouring guilt, the three judges may express their opinion as well and a unanimous vote from them could swing the verdict. The role of the jury has diminished over the last 50 years, and very few trials by jury are actually held. However, Article 98 of the constitution codifies the right to a trial by jury, and a change in the constitution is not very likely in the short term (Van den Wijngaert, 1993).

Trials by jury are also a rarity in Denmark, but the jury trial process has recently undergone substantial change. Previously, only serious crimes threatening the defendant with four years of imprisonment or more could be tried before a panel of three judges and 12 jurors, but since 2008 the number of jurors has been reduced to nine. In addition, in lower courts, six jurors sit together with three judges. What has remained the same is that judges and jury deliberate separately and both have to find the defendant guilty by majorities of, respectively, 2–1, and 8–4. Juries also vote on sentencing, and may rule on legal issues such as aggravating circumstances or insanity as well. To ensure parity between judges and jury, one vote from a judge counts as four jury votes. As in Belgium, the constitution guarantees the existence of the jury system, but it does not specify what crimes should be eligible for jury trial or what form the lay participation should take. Only around 60 to 100 cases per year are actually tried by jury. There is no 'hung jury' in Denmark. Where the jury cannot decide on any verdict, the defendant is acquitted. Greve comments that for some time there has been rather widespread discontent with the jury system (Greve, 1993). Jurors in Denmark are not randomly selected but appointed by a rather complicated set of processes: local authorities appoint committees who pre-select individuals from whom subsequently a set of jurors is chosen. They are appointed for four years and sit on cases, usually in the order of a few days per year. You might therefore question whether this constitutes a 'citizen's jury' in any pure sense (Leib, 2008).

Jury trials are held in the higher courts in France (*Cours d'Assises*), in a mixed tribunal setting (Leib, 2008). The panel consists of three judges and nine jurors, who deliberate together and come to a joint decision on guilt. An eight to four majority is required. As is the case in Austria, Belgium and Denmark, the jury is also involved with decisions on sentencing. The jury system in France is said to be in considerable demise (Pradel, 1993). *Cour d'Assises* trials are regularly held without the involvement of a jury. That category includes political or otherwise sensitive crimes, such as terrorist offences.

In Germany lay judges can be members of higher and lower courts. They hold the same formal position as regular judges and decide on all matters with the same vote as their professional counterparts. However, their actual position is not entirely as influential. Professional judges also have the advantage of being able to inspect the case-file beforehand. Lay judges do not have access to the dossier prior to trial. There is no lay participation in cases heard in the first instance in the High Court: this is where cases of terrorism, treason and assaults against high representatives of the state are tried. In other words cases with the most potential for political controversy are steered away from lay involvement. It is important to note that German lay members are not exactly jurors: their participation is not restricted to one trial. They are appointed for a period of time but then randomly allocated to particular cases (Kühne, 1993). The German juror (called *Schöffe*) therefore is probably a hybrid between a lay magistrate and a juror in the British understanding of those terms. Hörnle (2006: 153) asserts that:

> Germans are more inclined to let professional judges do their job ... it is easier to feel comfortable with the decisions made by people who are professionally trained. Trust in the work of the judiciary is trust in education and professional standards. The contrasting Anglo-American point of view is a symptom of a more profound underlying distrust both of lawyers and of power exercised by the state.

Lay participation occurs in mixed criminal courts in the first instance in Greece and sometimes but not regularly in appeal cases as well. Such mixed courts are presided over by one professional judge, who is accompanied by two other judges and four lay persons. As we have seen in other countries across the European continent, more complex cases do not tend to go before a jury, but the Greek constitution in fact ensures the role of the jury in criminal and political trials. Jurors in Greece must be at least 30 years old and have completed elementary school. Juries decide on guilt and also have an input on sentencing. Professional judges decide on legal matters, such as the admissibility of evidence (Mylonopoulos, 1993).

In Italy Assize Courts deal with the most severe cases, and this is where lay participation is to be found. Such trials involve two professional judges and six lay persons. They deliberate together and decide by simple majority. In cases of a tie, the defendant is acquitted. The involvement of jurors in proceedings is in demise, especially since in 1988 legislation was passed that reduced opportunities for jury trials considerably.

The Grand Duchy of Luxembourg totally abolished the jury in 1987. The reasons given did not relate to practicalities of jury trials but to the quality of justice administered by the jury system. Spielmann and Spielmann (1993) explain that there was no possibility of appeal against judgements of the Cour d'Assises, which, it was argued, violated defendants' rights. Another reason was the fact that the jury did not give reasons for its decisions, which was also considered to be unfair to defendants.

In the Netherlands the jury system, introduced in the Napoleonic era, was abolished as early as 1813, never to be seen again. Its reintroduction has long been out of the question, as the jury does not seem to be desired by either the public or the legal profession (Swart, 1993) but some feeble voices are now suggesting the introduction of some 'lay element' in judicial decision-making, possibly in the realm of sentencing (see box below).

In Norway, the jury consists of ten persons. They are drawn from a register of nominees, who tend to be respectable citizens with strong ties to the community. The first step involves the selection of 14 people from the register of nominees. These are always seven men and seven women, from whom ten are ultimately chosen. For a guilty verdict a majority of seven versus three will do. No reasons are required, and it is forbidden to disclose the distribution of the votes. Interestingly, when the presiding judge is of the opinion that the evidence favours guilt, they can order a new trial, despite a jury acquittal (Leib, 2008). Courts in the first instance tend to be mixed tribunals, whereas appeals courts embody a jury as the sole decider of guilt or innocence.

In Portugal, lay participation occurs in jury courts, consisting of three judges and four jurors. They try only the most severe crimes, carrying a penalty of at least eight years' imprisonment, including crimes against the security of the state and crimes against peace or against humanity (De Figueiredo Dias and Antunas, 1993).

New jury systems

Although the Spanish constitution guarantees popular participation in criminal proceedings, it was the 1995 Spanish Jury Law that laid down specific arrangements for jury trials (Ruiz Vadillo, 1993). The decision to forward a case to jury trial lies with the investigative judge. This is an example of the European tradition of strong judicial involvement in the pre-trial phase. The trial itself is adversarial in nature. To secure an adversarial trial, in which all the evidence is orally presented, the judge does not have access to the case-file. Jury trials are an option only in cases of certain crimes, including those committed by public officials in the exercise of their duties, crimes against persons, liberty, security and arson.

Trials begin with an opening statement from the prosecution followed by the defence's plea, and continue in true continental style with an examination of the defendant by the judge. This is followed by the questioning of witnesses, including expert witnesses, which is performed by both prosecution and defence, although the judge can ask questions after these examinations as well. While the defendant has the right not to testify, and is informed of their right to avoid self-incrimination, the vast majority of defendants do give a statement at trial. The trial ends with summations and, true to the European inquisitorial tradition, the defendant has the last word.

Initially, juries in Spain did not simply render a verdict of guilty or not guilty; rather, they are asked to answer a set of questions not unlike those that judges are supposed to answer in many European inquisitorial systems. However, that has changed and the jury can now simply return a verdict which is more in keeping with juries elsewhere. For a guilty verdict seven out of nine jurors need to agree whereas a simple majority of five versus four is enough for an acquittal, but the verdict is still accompanied by reasons supporting the verdict (Leib, 2008).

The Spanish example shows an interesting mixture of inquisitorial and adversarial elements. The role of the jury, however, must seem odd, especially for those used to the jury in England and Wales and the USA. Some of the virtues of jury decision-making are actually reversed in the Spanish structure: their verdicts are open to scrutiny, and appeals against jury decisions are possible and do happen. Thaman (2001) has argued that nowhere in mainland Europe does the requirement for juries to justify judgements go as far as in Spain.

The restrictive legal requirements surrounding jury decisions, however, did not prevent a high profile acquittal occurring in 1997. Mikel Otegi, a young Basque nationalist, stood trial for murdering two Basque police officers, but was acquitted by a jury on the grounds of diminished capacity caused by intoxication and 'uncontrollable rage provoked by alleged previous police harassment'. The verdict shocked a nation that has suffered violence from Basque nationalist terrorism for decades. The suspicion was, on the one hand, one of intimidation: jurors were suspected of being afraid of revenge against them in the event of a guilty verdict. Basque nationalists, on the other hand, would argue that the case showed the distrust in which the local community held the criminal justice system and the police in particular. Calls were made to suspend jury justice, at least in the Basque area (Thaman, 2001).

This is reminiscent of the situation in Northern Ireland, where the Troubles led to the introduction of so-called Diplock trials, in which a bench sits and rules instead of a jury. This highlights the fact that adherence to the ideal of jury justice in divided communities plagued by violence and distrust proves to be extremely difficult. Advocates of the jury system perhaps will find it heartening that even in situations such as Spain, where its role is certainly more straight-jacketed than in England and Wales, the jury still finds ways of delivering verdicts that seemingly are at odds with much of the evidence presented and against the views of those in power.

As in Spain, the jury has made a re-appearance in post-Soviet Russia. Trials by jury in Russia were common in the nineteenth century, but were abolished after the revolution of 1917. The right to trial by jury was reintroduced shortly after the collapse of the Soviet Union, in 1993. Thaman (2001) explains that while juries have been introduced, this was not accompanied by an overhaul of the pre-trial phase. In a preliminary hearing the trial judge continues to review the evidence contained in the case-file. On that basis a decision is made about whether or not a case should be committed for jury trial. Although the trial is adversarial in nature, no new evidence is presented: arguments have to be based on the contents of the dossier. The Russian mode of trial is distinctly continental European, although unlike in France for instance the examinations are usually performed by both parties. The defendant normally gives an unsworn statement, and has the last word. Thaman notes that:

For criminal justice systems that place emphasis on the presumption of innocence, the prosecution's burden of proof, and the defendant's right to remain silent, the interrogation of the defendant before any incriminating evidence has been presented to the fact finder is a lingering inquisitorial vestige.

(Thaman, 2001: 335)

A further point of note is the fact that any mention of the defendant's criminal record is forbidden. In many inquisitorial systems that record is discussed as a matter of course. To achieve some measure of equality, defendants in Russia are not allowed to present evidence of good character either. Upon coming to a judgement, a Russian jury has to answer three rather legalistic questions. They relate to whether a crime has been committed, whether the defendant was the one who committed it and whether that makes him/her guilty of the charge. Jury nullification remains a possibility, as the jury may render a not guilty verdict, even if all necessary elements for a guilty verdict are present. A conviction can be secured by a seven out of twelve majority. The jury then forwards its decision in the form of answers to set questions to the judge, who then turns that into a legal statement of guilt or otherwise. It seems that jury trials remain rare and in 2008 the Russian Parliament (*Duma*) considered steps to reduce it further (Byrne, 2008). Another disturbing feature is that jury acquittals are not terribly frequent (in the order of 15 per cent) and where they occur they can be, and frequently are, overturned on appeal (Thaman, 2007). Thaman argues that jury trials for serious offences should be mandatory (as in Spain) and warns against 'political' cases being steered away from jury justice. He also argues for a simpler verdict to be given, akin to adversarial jury justice.

Outside Europe, Japan introduced lay participation in criminal trials in 2009. The Quasi-Jury Act sets up two different panels for criminal trials. A panel of three professional and six lay assessors (*saiban-in*) is used in a contested case, while a panel of one professional and three lay judges is used in an uncontested case where the facts and issues identified by pre-trial procedure are undisputed (Fukurai, 2007). Lay assessors alongside judges decide over both verdict and sentence. These go by majority vote as long as that includes one judge and verdict and sentence can be decided in a single deliberation. The expectation is that a few thousand cases a year will be judged by such a mixed tribunal (Ambler, 2007). In a substantial proportion of those, the death penalty might be a sentencing option. That means that Japan will join the USA as a rare example of lay involvement in death penalty decisions.

Finally, let us look at the jury in Brazil. Brazil has a jury system which is guaranteed under the 1937 constitution. The right to jury trial extends to cases involving murder, infanticide, abortion and assisting suicide, and it involves seven jurors at trial. In the Brazilian scenario the jury does not deliberate. They simply vote, and a four against three majority will suffice for a verdict (Vidmar, 2001b).

The type of person society decides to put its faith in with regard to dealing with alleged wrongdoers hinges on the answer to the question of whom to trust. Where magistrates and professional judges are assigned these responsibilities there will often be an underlying conviction that seasoned specialists are best equipped to fulfil that trust. Professionals may have the knowledge and the reasoning abilities to judge each case on merit. The fact that such people are respected pillars of the community adds to their suitability for such an instrumental role in achieving social control. In communities where learned and senior members are held in high regard, it is not unlikely that they are judges, magistrates or, in the case of Guernsey, Jurats. Guernsey and Norway are examples of an intermediate solution: the principle of random selection of jurors is upheld, but the pool from which the jurors are drawn is not the population as a whole but rather a subset of people judged competent to make life-altering decisions over offenders. The typical safeguard against wrongdoing on the part of these decision-makers is by means of a requirement to render reasoned judgements in writing. Via that mechanism these individuals are held accountable in a way that juries typically are not, although Spain is a notable exception.

Systems without juries

What do Ethiopia, India, Israel, Lithuania, Luxembourg, the Netherlands and the Philippines have in common? They do not have a jury in any shape or form. Whereas in some countries the right to a jury trial is equated with fairness and central to the very concept of justice itself, other systems seem to manage perfectly well without a jury, and apparently without anyone missing it.

As discussed elsewhere in this chapter, in Luxembourg the jury was abolished only in 1987. The reasons given were the facts that appeals against jury decisions were not possible and that the jury did not have to give reasons to support its decision. It was felt that it was in the interests of justice to have defendants tried before a panel of professional judges instead. The Netherlands' acquaintance with the jury was very brief. Only in the early 1800s was a jury system incorporated, but it was generally considered to be a mistake and abolished shortly after its instigation. Its non-existence was until very recently a non-issue in Dutch politics: no one seemed to desire it. However, it now has been proposed to introduce a lay element to judicial decision-making. Interestingly that would not have to do with the verdict but with sentencing. The suggestion is indicative of dissatisfaction in certain segments of society regarding what are perceived to be too lenient sentencing practices by professional judges. In the end, the government decided against but it is significant that for the first time in almost 200 years, the government was forced to consider the introduction of some form of jury justice (NRC Handelsblad, 2007). India abolished the jury in 1960, further to a controversial jury acquittal, as it was argued that the jury was unduly influenced by external factors. It is interesting to note that those who favour its abolition frequently cite issues of the quality of justice. That is intriguing as it is invariably the quality of justice that is argued to be the very *raison d'être* for jury justice in the first place. Clearly conceptions of justice differ across the jury divide.

Article 10 of the 1948 United Nations' fundamental Declaration of Human Rights, which fed into later human rights legislation, states that 'everyone is entitled in full equality to a fair and public hearing by an independent and impartial tribunal, in the determination of his rights and obligations and of any criminal charge against him'. The key words are 'fair', 'independent' and 'impartial'. The word 'jury' is, however, not mentioned. The right to trial by jury is by no means absolute, and the right to choose when the system has a jury option is even less so.

Just as policing styles will differ depending on the communities that are being policed, so will community characteristics help understand what type of person is trusted with decisions on guilt and sentencing. Where there is distrust of official bodies, a randomly selected group of ordinary people is likely to be seen as a good alternative. Where police, prosecution or perhaps even judges cannot be relied on because of vested interests or perceived vested interests, the whole machinery of selecting and instructing a jury and presenting all the evidence in a way that is understandable to them is probably worthwhile.

Conclusion

This overview of judicial appointments and jury arrangements shows an impressive degree of diversity. In particular, the way in which different jurisdictions try to ensure a certain level of lay involvement in criminal trials is subject to immense variation. Sometimes lay participation occurs in mixed tribunals, in which both judges and jurors have to come to a verdict, sometimes together, sometimes separately. Sometimes juries decide on guilt alone, but quite often they play a role in the decision on sentencing as well. In certain countries they decide separately from the judge or judges, and elsewhere in conjunction with their professional counterparts. In some places the vote of a judge counts more heavily. There are instances where jurors do more than decide on matters of fact only, but in other places such as in Norway they can be overruled. In yet other arrangements the jury's vote is advisory only. Apart from emphasising this intriguing level of diversity, it is also worth considering a number of communalities.

First, lay participation seems to be in decline in many countries, including probably England and Wales. There seems to be a tension between ensuring lay participation for the most serious crimes and efforts to steer lay participation away from the most complex cases where jurors may have difficulties understanding the information presented to them. Jurors hardly anywhere in the world are involved with minor offences. This is why we call the jury an endangered species: highly valued, but rarely to be seen.

In countries where lay participation is very rare their involvement is often in cases where, perhaps, the state should not be trusted because of its vested interests. Belgium, for instance, reinstated the jury initially to deal with cases involving censorship and political crimes. Additionally, in Portugal, jurors are involved only in the most serious cases and those involving crimes against peace, humanity and against the security of the state. On the other hand there are several examples where the jury cannot sit on, for instance, trials for terrorist offences, in which the state is certainly bound to have a vested interest.

In countries with a more inquisitorial system the demise of the jury is often explained in terms of the quality of justice delivered. It is often said that jurors might not understand complex trials. Another reason concerns the fact that options for appeal against jury decisions are often limited. The fact that juries normally do not explain their decision is a third. In adversarial systems, in contrast, any restriction of the role of the jury tends to be inspired by pragmatic considerations. These often relate to expenditure, as jury trials are expensive.

At the same time however, the jury has been revived in places such as Spain, Russia, Japan and South Korea. That said, in Russia it is already under pressure and the institution in Spain was radically altered soon after its inception. In Japan there is the added spice of the death penalty for jury decision-making. We can probably say that although reintroduced, we cannot unequivocally say that they thrive. Another point of note is that where archaic jury systems tend to have a jury operate separately from professional judges and work towards a unanimous verdict, more recent systems are more often hybrid and work towards majority verdicts (Leib, 2008). It seems modern legislators are more concerned with the expedience of jury justice than with purity.

Despite sentiments to that effect in England and Wales and the USA, lay participation is not a fundamental requirement for justice. More fundamental is the acceptance of decision-makers as independent and impartial. The state can only serve justice by providing those decision-makers when its dependability and impartiality is generally accepted. When that is not the case, lay decision-makers serve as an invaluable protection against the state.

Further reading

Hans, V. (2008) Jury systems around the world. *Annual review of law and social science, 4*, 275–97.

Park, R.Y. (2010) The globalizing jury trial: Lessons and insights from Korea. *American journal of comparative law, 58*, 525–82.

Vidmar, N. (Ed) (2001) *World jury systems.* Oxford: Oxford University Press.

Study questions

1 In which countries has the jury been (re-)introduced and what are the common findings in these countries regarding the way the jury has been set out?
2 Why is the jury under threat in many countries?
3 Is there a case for juries to be more involved with sentencing in adversarial systems?

Chapter 9

Sentencing

Punitivity, prison and the death penalty

Consider the following quotation:

> Africans believe that an offender is a member of the community and should be corrected in the community and not outside it. The community insists on the offender paying a fine coupled with a communion feast and sacrifices to propitiate the gods, depending on the gravity of the offence. Undeniably, in Africa south of the Sahara, public offences such as incest, patricide, matricide, or desecration of a holy shrine would demand a sacrifice to appease the gods in addition to a communion feast and other communal penalties.
>
> (Ebbe, 2000a: 287)

From a Western point of view, this practice of sacrifice in order to appeal to divinity as part of a sentence is obviously outlandish. However, it tells us something essential about the sub-Saharan African orientation towards rule-breakers in their midst. In particular, the efforts not to outcast offenders are noteworthy. In Western societies there are more efforts to temporarily exile offenders from the community and send them to boot camps, prisons or other correctional centres. The extent to which offenders are 'in' or 'out' during and subsequent to punishment is a theme that pervades comparative research. Differences in sentencing practices are therefore likely to reveal meaningful information about other jurisdictions' visions of social inclusion and social control (Garland, 2001; Young, 1999). Punishment is an area almost made for comparative research.

There certainly is plenty of diversity around. There are, for example, property offences for which in Saudi Arabia you might lose a hand. In England and Wales you might lose six months or a year of your life in prison for a similar offence. In other jurisdictions you might perhaps get away with a community penalty. Different criminal justice systems certainly react differently to similar wrongdoings. The root of some of these differences lies in differing sentencing objectives. Another part of the explanation relates to differences in the perceived seriousness of offences and the perceived appropriateness of certain types of punishment. This relates to the very criminalisation of behaviours in the first place, in particular those of ambiguous morality, such as adultery, euthanasia, homosexuality and abortion.

Sentencing and sentences are perpetual sources of controversy and debate. Perhaps the main reason for that is to do with the underlying goals of punishment. In order to understand this we need to look at why certain punishments are imposed and what society aims to achieve by their imposition. The literature distinguishes between absolute and relative theories of punishment. In absolute theories, the punishment constitutes an end in and of itself. Sentences are imposed because that is the proper thing to do in response to violations of law and social order. The aim of retribution falls into this category. In the philosophy of retribution, an offender should be punished because it is deserved and therefore just: it is their 'just deserts' (Walker, 1991).

Relative theories justify punishment as a means to achieve a certain social goal. After all, punishment causes suffering and should therefore be justified by assuming that something good will come of it. The first of such aims is *individual deterrence*. It aims to ensure that the offender punished will not offend again. Another is *incarceration*, the idea simply being that an offender will be unable to commit crimes as long as he/she is off the streets (discounting for the moment the fact that the committal of crimes in prison is far from impossible). A third utilitarian aim is *rehabilitation*: offenders may be punished to give the state the opportunity to 'better' these offenders by, for instance, improving their social or professional skills. The idea is obviously that the reformed offender is less likely to re-offend after their return to society. The fourth relative aim is *general deterrence*. By punishing one offender the system aims to dissuade others from committing the same offence.

A complicating factor is that some of these sentencing goals are mutually exclusive. Incarceration, for instance is achieved easily by putting an offender in prison. However, we know that the aim of rehabilitation will be strained because the offender's subsequent integration into society is known to be difficult. In that way, sentencing poses a no-win situation to criminal justice systems: the completion of any sentence may constitute a success with regard to one objective but a failure in terms of another.

Comparative research may serve to assess how criminal justice systems deal with this sentencing conundrum. Criminal justice systems seek to strike a balance between retribution, deterrence and rehabilitation. Often in the case of young wrongdoers there is an emphasis on rehabilitation. In cases of more serious offences the element of deterrence is likely to be prioritised. The fashion in which certain sentencing goals are given priority over others is indicative of the nature of state-operated social control.

Fairness and effectiveness

Because sentences cause state-inflicted suffering issues of fairness are pertinent. What actually constitutes fair punishment is not an easy matter to define.

Sentences considered fair in one society are dismissed as anything but, in another. Additionally, perceptions of sentences have changed over time, along with changing attitudes on the value of human life, privacy and physical integrity. As far as England and Wales is concerned the practices of corporal punishment, deportations and the death penalty have disappeared. As in most Western societies, temporary or permanent confinement in prison is the dominant serious form of punishment.

While the concept of fairness has a level of elasticity to it, certain minimal standards have been formulated in international law. Quite general but influential nevertheless is the Universal Declaration of Human Rights. It was published in 1950 and it lays out certain requirements for sentencing, as it does for the ways in which defendants should be tried. Famous is the phrase contained in Article 5: 'No one shall be subjected to torture or to cruel, inhuman or degrading treatment or punishment.' However, what constitutes 'cruel, inhuman or degrading treatment' is a matter on which worldwide agreement is hard to find, although European case law has provided for certain specifications. Protocols from the Council of Europe outlaw the death penalty by any of its member states, because it is seen to be cruel. In this fashion international organisations play a significant role constraining the sentencing options that states have. The European Prison Rules, laid down by the Council of Europe (see the Council's official website, www.coe.int) are significant in this respect as are several United Nations resolutions (accessible via the United Nations website, www.un.org).

The second characteristic of sentences concerns their effectiveness. Usually, effectiveness is measured in terms of recidivism over a certain period after the completion of the sentence. We could however imagine alternative ways of establishing how effective a sentence has been. Victim satisfaction could be one of the criteria. A good sentence might be one that restores a victim's faith in the criminal justice system or in society at large. Another criterion could be of a procedural nature: perhaps the way in which the criminal justice system looks at all the evidence concerning the offence and the offender, and takes the view of all parties into account is of significance. These aspects of sentencing usually receive less consideration.

There is a wealth of research on 'what works' in sentencing. All over the world ideas have been generated, including offender–victim mediation, boot camps, day fines, short sharp shock sentences and so on. These ideas are often implemented in pilot schemes and evaluated after a certain period of operation. Under the assumption that what works in Quebec might just prove to be equally effective in Kuala Lumpur, there seems to be a certain hunger for information on effective ways of dealing with offenders. Unfortunately, it is usually far from easy simply to take an idea out of the context where it originated, implement it somewhere else and assume that it will work. Sentences are very much context-dependent.

To illustrate the importance of context, when I visited a prison in Mauritius I was told about the favourable local prison conditions. The evidence provided was that most inmates gained weight during their stay inside, and came out heavier than when they entered prison. The implication was clearly that prison took better care of those inside than they might have been able to manage for themselves in the outside world. It reminds us that sentences have to be set against the conditions that those prisoners would find themselves in outside prison. A strict prison regime in a welfare state may well feel harsher to inmates than basic prison conditions in a country that suffers from poverty.

Prisons and their comparative histories

Much of the earliest form of state-imposed social control was by means of ordering financial compensation. This practice, prevalent in the Middle Ages, involved offenders being ordered to pay a certain amount of money to the victim or their family. The motivation behind this was the need to prevent feuds. The amount of money to be paid depended on the status and position of both offender and victim. The rape of a high-status woman would require more compensation than the same offence against a victim of lower status. Similarly, a high-status offender would have to pay more towards the victim or his/her family than a wrongdoer of lower status. These levels of compensation would normally be set by rulers. Such financial penalties appear to have been preferred over corporal punishment in the early Middle Ages and were clearly aimed at preventing escalation (Barrett and Harrison, 1999).

Despite its relatively late appearance on the sentencing scene imprisonment is certainly popular in the world today. The advantages of imprisonment are obvious. Offenders are taken out of circulation, so that they will not commit crimes against the public while in prison. Victims will not have to worry about the offender for the duration of their stay in prison. Imprisonment additionally gives the state the chance of working with the offender. A major disadvantage is the cost of imprisonment. And as we will discuss later, there are serious doubts as to whether most offenders actually have been 'bettered' when they come out as compared to when they entered the prison system.

There is lively historical debate as to the birth of prisons (Hirsch, 1992). Penal historians have identified the processes to help us understand the popularity of imprisonment as a major form of punishment in the world today. Rothman (1990) analysed the rise of imprisonment in the USA during the presidency of Andrew Jackson in the 1820s and 1830s. Rothman argued that at that time crime and social deprivation began to be viewed as social problems. Before then, crime was more likely to receive corporal or in the most serious cases capital punishment. Prisons or asylums were meant to take the offender out of society with its ample opportunity for crime and other temptations. In prison inmates would be subjected to order, perform labour and get accustomed to a strictly regimented lifestyle, with plenty of time to reflect on the error of their ways. Punishment therefore shifted from inflicting pain on the body to focusing on the mind. During these Jacksonian years, imprisonment was no longer small-scale and haphazard but became part of a grand vision of social control, in which rehabilitation was the central focus (Rothman, 1990).

Foucault (1979), on the other hand, looked at the rise of the penitentiary in France before the French Revolution of 1789. In France, the king used to exercise corporal punishment in order to demonstrate and maintain his power over his citizens. Punishment was therefore highly public so as to set an example. Following public disgust over its brutality and an increased sense of repression felt by the citizenry, punishment became further removed from the public eye. Punishment shifted from public places, such as markets, to the more private surroundings of prisons. Thus, Foucault argued, the birth of the prison in France had nothing to do with any Jacksonian sense of enlightenment. Arguably, the introduction of French prisons was not to punish less but to punish better.

Other commentators, such as Garland, have emphasised the strong relation between economic cycles and rates of imprisonment. During economic booms, in which labour is abundantly available, convicted criminals are more likely to be imprisoned than when this is not the case (Garland, 1990). A further economic reason for the perpetuation of high levels of imprisonment relates to the fact that crime control has become a powerful industry, with huge employment rates, turnovers and lobby power (Christie, 1994). For that reason alone, mass imprisonment is very likely to be with us for a long time to come.

Prison dance: a YouTube classic

Prisons are closed environments. But in Cebu in the Philippines the secrecy of part of prison life was suddenly lifted by Byron Garcia, a security consultant who teaches choreographed exercise routines to inmates in Cebu's Provincial Detention and Rehabilitation Center. Footage taken shows 1,500 orange clad inmates dancing to Michael Jackson's 'Thriller' and became an instant Internet hit. Dozens of millions have seen the film on the footage-sharing website YouTube. It briefly aroused interest in life in Filipino prisons. Former Secretary of Justice José Diokno made a documentary about the dance programme and on 6 October 2007, Archbishop Ricardo Cardinal Vidal visited the establishment for the first time. In his homily, the prelate lauded the inmates for their ability to dance. However, the cardinal also wondered aloud why the daily lives of the inmates were not televised as well, such as the condition of their cells or food. 'We need to be made aware of the conditions they live in, the lack of cleanliness and food' (Awit, 2007). The reality is indeed that prisons in the Philippines are overcrowded, filthy and dangerous, with Amnesty International documenting overcrowding and use of torture to obtain confessions (Amnesty International, 2008a). The attention devoted to inmates dancing should not detract attention away from inmates suffering.

Prisoner numbers

More than 10 million people are held in penal institutions throughout the world. Most of them are concentrated in a few countries with large populations and comparatively high prison rates. In particular, the USA and the Russian Federation score high, both in absolute and relative numbers of prisoners. The number of prisoners in a jurisdiction is normally expressed as the total number of people in prison divided by the total population in that jurisdiction. Its exact measure is usually the number of detainees per 100,000 of the population. This is called the prison ratio or prison rate (Walmsley, 2013).

The United States has the highest prison population rate in the world. Walmsley found it to be 743 per 100,000. It was followed by Rwanda (595) and Russia (568). China's prison rate is not particularly high at 122 but that only consists of sentenced prisoners. That makes the figure rather unreliable as it is well known that the Chinese authorities make rather liberal use of pre-trial detention and other forms of custody. In fact, China could well be the world's biggest incarcerator as the number of 'administrative detentions' could be as high as 650,000 (Walmsley, 2013). Many states in the Caribbean have high prison rates including St Kitts and Nevis (495), US Virgin Islands (539), British Virgin Islands (468) and Grenada (423).These countries have very high prison rates but relatively small populations, so they contribute relatively little to the overall global imprisonment figure of 10.1 million.

Prison population rates vary considerably between global regions. Table 9.1 shows the median prison rate in a number of areas.

Prison populations are growing in many parts of the world; they are on the rise in 78 per cent of countries. It must, however, be kept in mind that not everyone who is, in one way or another, kept by the state is in prison. People may be held in police cells, or in other jails or remand institutions. People may also be kept in secure hospitals or mental institutions. Alternatively people may be serving their sentence in a boot camp or Borstal, while people under house arrest are not technically imprisoned but still deprived of their liberty. The way

Table 9.1 The median prison rate in a number of regions in the world

Region	Median prison rate
West Africa	47.5
Southern Africa	219
South America	175
Caribbean	357.5
South Central Asia	42
Eastern Asia	155.5
Southern & Western Europe	95.5
Central & Eastern Europe	228
Oceania	135

Source: Walmsley (2013).

in which the prison rate is calculated will depend on judgements about whether to include certain groups of people who are, in one way or another, physically constrained by the state. Another perhaps more pertinent matter is to what extent captives of the state are made visible to observers. Certainly in China but also in a good number of other countries this is a major problem.

As far as the UK is concerned, England and Wales is listed as 153, Scotland also as 153, Northern Ireland 90, Guernsey 104, Jersey 192 and the Isle of Man 121 detainees per 100,000 of the population. The Channel Isle of Sark sits 6 miles east of Guernsey. It has a total area of only 545 ha and is about 4.8 km long and 2.4 km wide at its widest point. It is a tiny place with some 600 people as permanent inhabitants to which at various times a few hundred tourists are added. Despite its diminutive size, Sark has a certain degree of independence from Guernsey as well as from the United Kingdom. There is an idiosyncratic yet lively political scene and there is a prison. It consists of two cells in which people can be held overnight. For longer detentions, individuals are transferred out to neighbouring Guernsey. This means that Sark oscillates between freedom and oppression, or a prison rate between 333 and 0. Similarly, San Marino had, in 2009, two persons imprisoned but neither was actually convicted, which leaves a prison population of zero. Prisoner numbers literally vary from a single prisoner, to millions.

Table 9.2 lists the prison rates for the countries currently in the European Union.

Within the Europe Union, the Baltic states of Estonia, Latvia and Lithuania are evidently the keenest incarcerators. In addition, countries traditionally known for their reluctance to imprison such the Netherlands are not necessarily bottom of the table. Clearly, ideas about criminal justice orientations can be dated and hence inaccurate (see, e.g., Pakes, 2004, 2007a). That said, there does seem to be somewhat of an East–West divide within the European Union with Eastern states more incarcerative and then Western states, with England and Wales an exception on the Western front and Slovenia in the East.

Table 9.2 Prison rates in the European Union

Latvia	314	Portugal	113
Lithuania	276	Italy	111
Estonia	254	Cyprus	110
Poland	218	Greece	102
Czech Republic	218	Ireland	100
Slovakia	184	Belgium	97
Hungary	165	France	96
Spain	160	Netherlands	94
England and Wales	153	Germany	85
Malta	140	Sweden	78
Luxemburg	139	Denmark	74
Romania	136	Andorra	73
Bulgaria	120	Slovenia	63
Croatia	117	Finland	59

Source: Walmsley (2013).

Female prisoners tend to make up between 2 per cent and 9 per cent of any country's prison population. There are an estimated half a million women and girls imprisoned in the world. The highest percentages of women prisoners are to be found in Hong Kong-China (22 per cent), followed by Myanmar (18 per cent), Thailand (17 per cent), Kuwait (15 per cent), Qatar and Vietnam (both 12 per cent). Female imprisonment (as a function of male imprisonment) seems relatively high in several countries in South Eastern Asia. In contrast, female imprisonment in West Africa is relatively rare (Walmsley, 2006). In real terms, the USA imprisons 183,400 women. In China that number is 71,286 but the real number of women held may be much higher as this figure fails to include those held on 'administrative detention' as mentioned before (Walmsley, 2006).

Comparing prison rates

Factors influencing prison rates are many. The extent of crime is of course the first to come to mind, although comparative research has quite comprehensively shown that the assumption that prison rates simply follow crime rates is erroneous. In the USA for instance, crime rates have gone down consistently since 1990, but the prison population remains huge and continues to grow. We have seen evidence for a global crime drop, and despite that overall global imprisonment continues to be on the rise. Crime rates and prison rates seem to lead rather independent lives. In explaining prison rates, factors such as prison capacity, public opinion, legislation, attitudes among the judiciary, policing and prosecution policies and strategies, and developments in forensic science need to be taken into account, as do alternatives to prison and the availability of the death penalty. Later in this chapter we will consider influential concepts such as punitiveness, populism and exceptionalism, in order to add a deeper level of analysis to the question of varying prison rates.

An illustration of the fact that crime levels have little to do with prison rates is provided in a focused comparison by Downes (1988). He compared prison rates after World War II in the Netherlands to those in England and Wales. Both countries saw a steady increase in crime levels between World War II and the 1970s. In England and Wales, the prison rate rose along with it, but in the Netherlands a period of lowering of prisoner numbers, or decarceration, occurred. In 1950, the prison rate in the Netherlands was actually higher than that of England and Wales: 82 per 100,000 versus 64 per 100,000 inhabitants in England and Wales. By 1957 the rates of imprisonment had converged, and from then onwards the numbers of prisoners became more and more divergent. In real numbers England and Wales experienced a doubling of its prisoners by 1975. In contrast, the Netherlands had about half as many people incarcerated by 1975 as 25 years previously.

These opposing trends in prison rates cannot be attributed to levels of crime, as these were quite similar, albeit slightly lower in the Netherlands. Downes discusses a number of other reasons as possible explanations. The first factor was differing limits of penal capacity. Unlike in England and Wales, one prisoner per cell has, for a long time, been standard practice in the Netherlands. That, in practice, means that a prison is literally full when each cell is occupied. The Dutch prison system can therefore not flexibly accommodate more prisoners than there are prison cells. To alleviate the burden on prisons, various policies were introduced to somehow try to match the number of available spaces with the number of prisoners sentenced to fill these cells. This applied equally to remand prison spaces as it did to prisons. As a result, in the 1980s prisoners frequently had to go home after sentence and wait until a prison cell became available. Similarly, a large number of suspects to be detained in pre-trial custody were simply sent home because of a lack of available cells.

Second, Downes describes a culture of tolerance in Dutch society and within the judiciary. This is evident in lower maximum penalties set by law for many offences, and a tendency among the judiciary to sentence more leniently. Long prison sentences were much less frequently imposed, and life sentences were, and still are, very rare indeed. A third factor is the so-called politics of accommodation. Accommodation stands for a non-confrontational style of political life, which seeks consensus and compromise rather than confrontation and radical shifts. The politics of accommodation was, in the Netherlands, underpinned by a social stratification, called pillarisation. This is described by Downes as follows:

> Catholics, Calvinists, secular liberals and secular radicals each form their own constituency, to which their elites are responsive, and which therefore possess by proxy a stake in the system. The major price, so to speak, for such an arrangement is that the elites, both in and outside government and Parliament, are relatively insulated from criticism, unless in exceptional circumstances.
>
> (Downes 1988: 74)

The level of horizontal stratification was remarkable. There were separate schools, radio stations, clubs and social structures for members of each pillar. Nevertheless, this segregation never led to substantial social exclusion, as all pillars were represented in parliament and had a reasonable chance of getting into government. Because of a system of proportional representation in parliament, and without any of these pillars ever getting an outright majority, governments were, and are, invariably two- or three-party coalitions. While that may cause inertia in decision-making, it has also served as a further safeguard against radical or populist changes in penal policy. Although pillarisation has disappeared, some of its associated practices, such as a focus on compromise and consensus, have endured.

These arguments undoubtedly all carry weight. Prison rates are a result of various forces at work, including political discourse and attitudes and practices within the criminal justice system. To assume that prison rates are an inevitable response to, and therefore a straightforward function of, crime rates is simply incorrect.

The punitive turn and Nordic exceptionalism

One of comparative criminology's most debated social facts is the so-called 'punitive turn'. The term (see Wacquant, 2005) describes a sustained and widespread increase in *punitivity* or *punitiveness*, and was said to have originated in the USA. Wacquant argues that prison rates in the USA were actually on a downward spiral in the 1960s and early 1970s but then suddenly and unexpectedly underwent exponential growth. Between 1975 and 2000 the prison population expanded by about 500 per cent, leading to a prison ratio of over 500 per 100,000 population, and it is higher still today. This represents a staggering level of change. Why did the American criminal justice system suddenly punish so much more?

An important feature of the punitive turn is that is seems quite unrelated to crime rates, as these failed to increase from 1980 onwards and even went down substantially from the early 1990s onwards. David Garland explains the punitive turn through emerging cultures of control (Garland, 2001). The argument is that through rises in crime from 1960 onwards, crime has become 'normal'. Governments have sought to adapt to this new normality and cope with their inability to control and prevent crime. They do that through expressive and emotional responses to crime. These may not be evidence-based or effective but do communicate to the population that they are serious about crime. Garland argues that this reaction comes with a change in tone in crime debates, one that is more vindictive and emotional. It is also associated with populism, seductive slogans and a demise of expertise so that criminal justice policy becomes ostensibly based in common sense or perceived popular perceptions. Punishment becomes more about crime control and less about rehabilitation. Although frequently ineffective, it does subscribe to its own logic so that when more severe penalties do not seem to stop crime, even harsher measures are seemingly required: that way, the punitive turn generates its own momentum. It takes on a force of its own, unconnected to rates of crime. We need to realise that under such regimes, at a societal level, levels of crime and of punishment simply fail to explain each other.

The punitive turn is often evidenced by an increase in prison rates. It is indeed an important measure but there is more. This includes net widening, that is, punitive responses to behaviour that previously escaped such responses, changes in prison conditions (such as austerity conditions and the emergence of supermax high-security prisons), and more punitive approaches to non-criminal issues, such as immigration and welfare. It can also include control measures that may be experienced as punitive post-sentence such as tags, registrations and other restrictions.

Garland argues that the punitive turn has typified crime policy in the USA first and foremost, but also the UK. Researchers have questioned whether the punitive turn has subsequently taken place elsewhere. While it is true that prison rates have risen in many countries, few if any have been the dramatic rise of imprisonment seen in the USA, the punitive turn archetype. That said, as Newburn has documented, policies, inspirations, discourses and slogans do travel and some of these, instrumental in pushing up punitivity such as 'zero tolerance' and 'three strikes and you're out', may have served as catalysts for more punitive approaches to crime elsewhere.

The punitive turn is contested as it is argued that punitivity is both ill-defined and not necessarily all that widespread (e.g. Matthews, 2005). Others point to exceptions. Canada is frequently mentioned as a country that has escaped the punitive turn, which is striking as it is the USA's northern neighbour (Meyer and O'Malley, 2005). In addition, much is made of what is referred to as Nordic exceptionalism (Pratt, 2008a, 2008b).

John Pratt travelled to Finland, Norway and Sweden and refers to them as low-imprisonment societies. Apart from low prisoner numbers he marvelled at the treatment of prisoners and the strong focus on 'normalization', that is, making life as normal as possible for inmates. He says:

> Generally speaking, in this region, it is recognized that going to prison is itself the punishment for crime; prison conditions can then approximate to life outside as far as possible, rather than being allowed to degrade and debase all within.
>
> (Pratt, 2008a: 119)

He then goes on to provide a vivid and compelling account of prison conditions and penal philosophies in the three countries. He calls Bastøy Prison in Norway the shining jewel in the Scandinavian open prison system. It is set on an Island in the Oslo Fjord. The only way to get there is by a boat which is operated by inmates. The prison houses a good hundred prisoners most of whom work in the woods or on a farm. Although perhaps an exception, its very existence provides credence to the claim that prisons are simply conceived of differently in Norway and its neighbours. Upon a recent visit to Bastøy I was told that although escapes are rare, would-be escapees are asked to please contact the prison if they ever get away: 'we'd rather know that they escaped than fearing that they drowned'. Similar stories, that place the welfare of prisoners over and above any punitive or security objectives, seem plentiful in the Nordic prison system folklore. All this does point to a radically different approach to imprisonment. Pratt's work received much criticism, not least from within the Nordic countries itself. Mathiesen (2012) has argued that Pratt's idea of consensus politics in the Nordic countries is too rosy, whereas Barker (2013) warns of the 'other face' of the Nordic state which can be cold and oppressive and which in the past gave rise to questionable practices such as forced sterilisations. All that said, the distinct nature of penal thinking in the Nordic countries cannot be dismissed.

In considering the causes of this exceptional state of affairs, Pratt and Erikson considered longstanding cultures of homogeneity and egalitarianism. This was partly due to living conditions as isolated small communities in harsh climatic conditions offering little room for social stratification. Added to that, they argue, is the role of the Lutheran protestant church that preaches frugality, offers solidarity and places an emphasis on education. This is evident in the prison system that was founded upon such principles. The adherence to the 'Philadelphia prison model' with an emphasis on solitary confinement, reflection and spiritual correction helped set structural conditions for the present-day prison system. The generous welfare state did not create these social relations but certainly helped solidify them. The welfare state is not conceptualised as a safety net with associated shame involved for those who need it, but a home, administered by a patriarchal, distant and perhaps cold, but ultimately benign, state. These forces combined have produced a system that fails to outcast prisoners, desires to keep them as a part of society and only reluctantly makes concessions relating to security or dangerousness. Pratt (2008b) wrote a paper on the future of Nordic exceptionalism, and argues that the three countries face differing threats. We only need to consider the example of the Netherlands to see that such states of affairs are not necessarily enduring or unmalleable. Indeed such exceptional states of affairs always seem under threat, which you could argue is consistent with O'Malley's notion of a 'criminology of catastrophe': the worst always seems about to happen (O'Malley, 2000).

Comparative levels of penality: a political-economical approach

Research from the last decade has allowed us to move beyond case studies to identify drivers and protective factors against any punitive turn. A good number of factors have been identified that help us understand why certain countries seem to be experiencing punitive turns while others do not. An important issue, as identified by Cavadino and Dignan (2011) is political-economic factors (Esping-Andersen, 1990). States that embrace a neoliberal approach with a reliance on market forces seem to have higher prison rates, most notably of course the USA. Countries with a conservative corporate model such as Germany, which are more communitarian, have lower rates. Countries with a stronger social democratic approach, such as the Nordic countries identified by Pratt (2008a) have lower rates still.

Lacey (2011) adds further factors such as political systems. In countries with a so-called first past the post electoral system (where one winner takes all, such as in the UK and the USA) political life tends to be more adversarial and confrontational. In systems utilising proportional representation political life tends to be more focused on achieving consensus or at least compromise. The latter can serve as insulation against penal populism. Broad coalitions may also be less swayed by the lobby power of single-issue pressure groups. She also notes the importance of the extent and status of welfare provision and the contrast between the Nordic countries with all embracing and generous welfare systems and the USA and to a lesser extent the UK where welfare is more stigmatising and less generous.

But there are still other factors at play and further differences to be explained. The role of media cannot be overlooked, nor can the public role of the judiciary, or the jury in sentencing, and levels of trust in public institutions. There is also little doubt that social divisions and public finances may be potent factors that can shape punitivity. David Nelken identifies the prevalence of tolerance as an explaining factor but notes its nebulous nature: 'Can it be irrelevant that what I call tolerance you call permissiveness, indulgence, favouritism, neglect, indifference, impunity, denial or collusion?' (Nelken, 2010: 67). Susanne Karstedt (2011) considered the broad social-cultural factors of egalitarianism and individualism. Egalitarianism refers to an emphasis on equal rights and opportunities. Individualism refers to the extent to which there is free expression and opportunity. Interestingly she found that prisoner numbers were not really explained by differences between countries along these lines. However, the *treatment* of prisoners in prison did co-vary with these variables. Egalitarian and individualistic societies seem to produce milder prison climates and settings that are more focused on rehabilitation. This reminds us that comparative penality goes far beyond numbers games, disturbing as those differences in prison rates can be. We must not forget that perhaps more important is not just how many prisoners there are, but also how these prisoners are treated. In that regard, the emergence of highly austere and no doubt debilitating conditions in supermax prisons in many countries is a phenomenon that should disturb us (Shalev, 2009; Ross, 2013).

Where Von Hofer (2003) emphasises the role of political will as a driver of prison rates, Roberts et al. (2002) explain this in terms of *penal populism*. This is aimed at gaining an understanding of a rise in both the rhetoric and practice of severe punishment at a time when public opinion has played a pivotal role in sentencing policy and reforms. Prison, they argue, is the pivotal tool of penal populism. The authors' concern is with malign penal populism: 'the promotion of policies that are electorally attractive, but unfair, ineffective and at odds with a true reading of public opinion' (Roberts et al. 2003: 5). To be precise, penal populism involves three pillars. The first is an excessive concern with the attractiveness of policies to the electorate. The second is an intentional or negligent disregard for evidence concerning the actual effect of such policies, and the third is a tendency to make simplistic assumptions regarding the nature of public opinion on matters of sentencing and punishment. The authors describe the rise of penal populism in Canada, the UK, the USA, Australia and New Zealand. For the moment we will focus on the latter country to highlight how penal populism can serve as a powerful comparative construct in explaining the global rise of imprisonment.

Pratt and Clark (2005) describe the processes that underlie the rise of penal populism in New Zealand. First, it must be noted that crime peaked in 1992 and that the country has seen a decline in crime rates since. But at the same time concern about crime has increased and it has come to dominate both parliamentary and public discourse. Pratt and Clark note the importance of extra-political forces such as victim organisations, newspapers and other groups that have become agenda setters to which governments feel compelled to respond. This process signals as well as amplifies disenchantment with the regular political and judicial processes. Garland makes an important point when he says that sentencing is no longer framed as a matter of applying the law, it is a matter of expressing loyalty to a real or an imagined community of victims (Garland 2002). Added to that is a fair bit of nostalgia, the seductive notion that life was simply much better in the olden days and that policy should aim to bring those days back. Pratt and Clark furthermore notice the emergence of a new type of 'expertise', away from the bureaucrats or scientists supporting government and towards a spurious 'common sense' that ostensibly is less cultured but more trustworthy. These forces combine to put pressure on government not to pursue its own agenda dictated by evidence and expertise, but to respond instead to a maelstrom of ideas, wants and needs on behalf of what it perceives to be 'the public'. That leads then to penal populism: harsh policies that sound appealing in the short term but that will not be successful in the long term (Pratt and Clark, 2005).

The use of imprisonment in Nigeria

Table 9.3 shows official data from the Nigerian Police Force Annual Reports. They are from 1987, and reported in Ebbe (2000b). One can see that across the board the number of prosecutions is about half the number of arrests. Three additional matters are worthy of discussion. First, it can be noted that relatively few people are prosecuted for fraud. Ebbe notes the possibility that politicians and corporate executives sometimes successfully attempt to prevent certain prosecutions from occurring. The crime of fraud might be particularly susceptible to this form of corruption.

Table 9.3 Numbers of arrests, prosecutions, discharges and imprisonments for seven offence types in Nigeria (percentages of the number of arrests, per offence, in brackets)

Offence	Arrested	Prosecuted	Discharged	Imprisoned
Assault	33,019	20,341 (61.6)	9,874 (48.5)	1,316 (6.5)
Stealing/theft	31,281	14,077 (45.0)	2,163 (15.4)	4,722 (33.5)
Rape	1,116	471 (42.2)	113 (24.0)	358 (76.0)
Armed robbery	1,012	579 (57.2)	66 (11.4)	125 (21.6)
Murder	716	441 (61.6)	38 (8.6)	147 (33.3)
Manslaughter	618	339 (54.9)	102 (30.1)	237 (69.9)
Fraud	169	60 (35.5)	22 (36.7)	38 (63.3)

Source: Ebbe (2000b).

The second issue to arise from Table 9.3 relates to the administration of assault cases. Of the over 33,000 cases where there was an arrest, only 1,316 individuals actually received a prison sentence, and almost half of all prosecutions did not end in a guilty verdict but in a discharge. This imprisonment rate is very low. This is an instance in which the perceived severity of the crime of assault helps explain the sentences imposed. Fighting has traditionally been a relatively accepted form of conflict resolution between friends. Despite the fact that these behaviours were criminalised under British colonial rule, which lasted until 1960, the practice refused to die out. Most of the time such cases do not lead to a prison sentence, as these tend to be reserved for more serious (or perceived as such) cases of assault.

Finally, the reader may observe relatively low incarceration rates for the crimes of murder and armed robbery. That is because 256 murderers (63 per cent of those convicted) received the death penalty for murder. Additionally, 388 armed robbers (75 per cent of those convicted) were sentenced to death (Ebbe, 2000b). These data show that sentences can be considered sensibly only if you also take into account the sentencing alternatives available to courts. A low rate of incarceration for assault requires an explanation wholly opposite to that for armed robbery. While the former are sent home, the latter are sent to the hangman.

The death penalty

Before discussing the practice of the death penalty we must make a number of distinctions. It is not necessarily obvious what it means for a jurisdiction to 'have' the death penalty. First, it is a fact that not everyone who is sentenced to death will actually be executed. Prisoners on death row may be pardoned or their cases may be re-opened. Their sentences might be changed into custodial ones after appeals or review processes. In the US state of Texas, for example, only about 15 per cent of all death sentences given were actually carried out between 1977 and 1993. In many US states this percentage is lower still (Bedau, 1996). Throughout the USA, many prisoners on death row are subjected to the uncertainty of not knowing if, let alone when, their execution might take place.

Another issue relates to the statutory status of the death penalty. Many countries do have the penalty in their law books but reserve it only for special circumstances, such as for particular crimes in times of war. These countries are usually still called abolitionist. Other countries have the death penalty as a sentence available to courts but have a policy in place to prevent its imposition. Such countries are called abolitionist in practice. Then, there are states in which the death penalty may be imposed, but where it is decided that, temporarily, no executions will take place. Such a state of affairs is called a *moratorium*. Finally, there are retentionist countries. In these countries there is a real chance of convicts dying for their crimes (Hood, 1996). Arguably, the strongest indicator of a commitment to abolition principles is when states have explicitly dismissed the death penalty in their constitution. Constitutions tend to be very robust pieces of legislation, which are difficult to change. A constitutional ban on the death penalty serves as an important safeguard against its reintroduction at any point in the future.

Abolitionist and retentionist countries

Amnesty International have documented that more than two-thirds of all countries have in principle or in practice abolished the death penalty. That number is on the rise with Uzbekistan and Argentina abolishing the death penalty for all crimes in 2008. Since then others such as Bolivia and Burundi have followed suit. It is very notable that Rwanda abolished the death penalty in 2007, less than 15 years after the genocide in that country. Following are lists of countries in the four categories: abolitionist for all crimes; abolitionist for ordinary crimes only (e.g. excepting the death penalty in times of war); abolitionist in practice; and retentionist. The lists (sourced from Amnesty International, 5 April 2014, see www.amnesty.org) include a few territories whose laws on the death penalty differ significantly from those of other countries within the same group. First to follow is the list of 140 countries whose laws do not provide for the death penalty for any crime:

Albania, Andorra, Angola, Argentina, Armenia, Australia, Austria, Azerbaijan, Belgium, Bhutan, Bolivia, Bosnia-Herzegovina, Bulgaria, Burundi, Cambodia, Canada, Cape Verde, Colombia, Cook Islands, Costa Rica, Côte d'Ivoire, Croatia, Cyprus, Czech Republic, Denmark, Djibouti, Dominican Republic, Ecuador, Estonia, Finland, France, Gabon, Georgia, Germany, Greece, Guinea-Bissau, Haiti, Holy See, Honduras, Hungary, Iceland, Ireland, Italy, Kiribati, Kyrgyzstan, Latvia, Liechtenstein, Lithuania, Luxembourg, Macedonia, Malta, Marshall Islands, Mauritius, Mexico, Micronesia, Moldova, Monaco, Montenegro, Mozambique, Namibia, Nepal, Netherlands, New Zealand, Nicaragua, Niue, Norway, Palau, Panama, Paraguay, Philippines, Poland, Portugal, Romania, Rwanda, Samoa, San Marino, São Tomé and Principe, Senegal, Serbia (including Kosovo), Seychelles, Slovakia, Slovenia, Solomon Islands, South Africa, Spain, Sweden, Switzerland, Timor-Leste, Togo, Turkey, Turkmenistan, Tuvalu, Ukraine, United Kingdom, Uruguay, Uzbekistan, Vanuatu, Venezuela.

The following list comprises countries whose laws provide for the death penalty only for exceptional crimes, such as crimes under military law or crimes committed in exceptional circumstances:

Brazil, Chile, El Salvador, Fiji, Israel, Kazakstan, Peru.

The 35 countries listed next retain the death penalty for ordinary crimes such as murder, but can be considered abolitionist in practice because they have not executed anyone during the past 10 years and are believed to have a policy, or established practice, of not carrying out executions. The list also includes countries that have made an international commitment not to use the death penalty:

Algeria, Benin, Brunei, Burkina Faso, Cameroon, Central African Republic, Congo (Republic of), Eritrea, Ghana, Grenada, Kenya, Laos, Liberia, Madagascar, Malawi, Maldives, Mali, Mauritania, Mongolia, Morocco, Myanmar, Nauru, Niger, Papua New Guinea, Russian Federation, Sierra Leone, South Korea, Sri Lanka, Suriname, Swaziland, Tajikistan, Tanzania, Tonga, Tunisia, Zambia.

The final list consists of 58 countries that retain the death penalty for ordinary crimes:

Afghanistan, Antigua and Barbuda, Bahamas, Bahrain, Bangladesh, Barbados, Belarus, Belize, Botswana, Chad, China, Comoros, Democratic Republic of the Congo, Cuba, Dominica, Egypt, Equatorial Guinea, Ethiopia, Gambia, Guatemala, Guinea, Guyana, India, Indonesia, Iran, Iraq, Jamaica, Japan, Jordan, Kuwait, Lebanon, Lesotho, Libya, Malaysia, Nigeria, North Korea, Oman, Pakistan, Palestinian Authority, Qatar, Saint Kitts and Nevis, Saint Lucia, Saint Vincent and the Grenadines, Saudi Arabia, Singapore, Somalia, South Sudan, Sudan, Syria, Taiwan, Thailand, Trinidad and Tobago, Uganda, United Arab Emirates, United States of America, Viet Nam, Yemen, Zimbabwe.

During 2013 at least 778 people were executed worldwide. The trend is steadily downwards: 1,252 people were executed in 24 countries in 2008 (Amnesty International, 2008b). Amnesty International recorded approximately 1,600 official executions in 1998 and this number was about twice as high back in 1981 (Amnesty International, 2001). There is, if one takes a historical perspective, a slow but definite decline in its use. There was however a spike in 2013 mainly due to increased numbers of executions in Iran and Iraq. The year 2014 might also see a spike to due to disturbing goings on in Egypt. In one mega trial no less than 683 people received a recommended death penalty by a judge in Egypt. The defendants were assumed to be involved in riots in 2013 in which a police officer died. A month earlier, another 528 received the death penalty but most of these have been amended to become prison sentences. Regardless, mega trials such as this are an affront. Organisations within Egypt, Amnesty International and the UN commissioner for Human Rights have all expressed outrage. Amnesty also notes that China may well execute many more than any other country but as this takes place in secrecy figures are not available.

Going against the global trend, China and Egypt, as well as Iran, Iraq and the United States, are increasingly becoming vestiges of brutality when it comes to the death penalty. In 1899 only three countries had abandoned the death penalty. These were Costa Rica, San Marino and Venezuela. The US state of

Michigan has in fact been quoted to be the very first jurisdiction to formally abolish the death penalty, which it did as early as 1847 (Bedau, 1996). By 1948 the number of abolitionist countries had risen to eight, and to 19 by 1978. In 1998, there were 67 countries without the death penalty. Now that number is no less than 140. Executions therefore are primarily a practice taking place in a small number of countries without democracy or much accountability in the criminal justice system. The main exception to this, as it is with other matters of punishment, is the United States.

The death penalty in the USA

The Western country where the death penalty is most widely accepted and used is evidently the USA. The death sentence can be imposed for certain federal crimes, and most, but not all, states have the death penalty on their books as well. The extent to which the death penalty is imposed in these states varies widely.

The death penalty has had a chequered history in the second half of the twentieth century. It was not in use during a period in which the Supreme Court had ruled against it on the grounds that it considered the protracted death-penalty procedure cruel and unusual punishment. This process, which tends to take years, inevitably induces great uncertainty for convicts regarding the 'if' and the 'when' of their execution. This moratorium lasted from the late 1960s until 1977. Since then, the number of executions had been on the rise for a number of years but more recently there has been a decline. In the previous chapter I explained how juries in the USA decide on capital punishment. In this chapter I shall consider the actual practice.

First, there are substantial differences among the various US states with regard to the death penalty, as there are with regard to many other aspects of criminal justice. First of all, we must remember that certain states do not have the punishment on the books at all. Abolitionist states are in a minority, as there are currently only 16 (and the District of Columbia): Alaska (1957), Connecticut (2012), Hawaii (1957), Illinois (2011), Iowa (1965), Maine (1887), Maryland (2013), Massachusetts (1984), Michigan (1846), Minnesota (1911), New Jersey (2007), New Mexico (2009), New York (2007), North Dakota (1973), Rhode Island (1984) and Vermont (1964). Most of these are midwestern or northeastern states. In some of these states efforts have been made to reintroduce the death penalty, but they have not been successful so far.

The way in which executions take place also varies between states. Many use death by lethal injection, whereas electrocution by means of the so-called electric chair is used in others. Montana, New Hampshire and Washington allow for the possibility of hanging. Idaho and Utah retain the possibility of using a firing squad to carry out executions but also use lethal injections (Bedau, 1996).

The minimum age of persons eligible for capital punishment is subject to similar variation. In 2000, 15 states had legislation in place to prevent juveniles from being eligible for the death penalty. Where specified, the threshold is often 18 years of age, as is the case in, for instance, the states of California, Ohio and Tennessee. Sixteen states have a lower minimum age. These include Georgia and Texas, where the age is 17 years; Mississippi and Oklahoma, where it is 16 years of age; while Arkansas is reported to have a statutory 14 years of age as the minimum age eligible for capital punishment (Bedau, 1996).

Clearly there is a north–south divide on the death penalty, with northern states frequently having abolished it and southern states retaining it and what is more, using it.

But what if we kill the wrong person? It turns out that since 1973, over 120 people have been released from death row with evidence of their innocence. That is a worrying number of miscarriages of justice, with potentially fatal consequences. Apart from these miscarriages of justice, a further persistent point of critique is an alleged bias in its application. It has long been held that Black defendants are more likely to receive the death penalty than White defendants. More specifically, and more worryingly, there is evidence that Black defendants convicted of a crime against a White victim are statistically most likely to be sentenced to death (see Eberhardt et al., 2006, for a particularly hard-hitting study on race and the death penalty in the USA). The data on miscarriages, as well as the data on race, provide strong ammunition for the anti-death penalty lobby (see also Bedau and Ratelet, 1987). Further evidence against it is derived from empirical studies, which demonstrate a lack of a general deterrent effect. Crime figures from abolitionist countries fail to show that abolition has harmful effects with regard to crime rates. In Canada, for example, the homicide rate per 100,000 population fell from a peak of 3.09 in 1975, the year before the abolition of the death penalty for murder, to 2.41 in 1980, and since then it has remained relatively stable. In 1993, 17 years after abolition, the homicide rate was 2.19 per 100,000 population, 27 per cent lower than in 1975 (Hood, 1996).

Reviewing the evidence on the relation between changes in the use of the death penalty and crime rates, a study prepared for the UN in 1988, and

Table 9.4 Top 10 US states that most frequently execute the death penalty

Texas	388
Virginia	98
Oklahoma	84
Missouri	66
Florida	64
North Carolina	43
Georgia	39
South Carolina	36
Alabama	35
Arkansas	27

Source: Death Penalty Information Center, 2008.

updated in 1996, stated that: 'the fact that all the evidence continues to point in the same direction is persuasive a priori evidence that countries need not fear sudden and serious changes in the curve of crime if they reduce their reliance upon the death penalty' (Hood, 1996: 187).

There is increasing discomfort with the death penalty in the USA. Mainly thanks to DNA profiling an increasing number of offenders sentenced to death are in fact found to be innocent. Since 2000 there have been about five exonerations per year (Death Penalty Information Center, 2008). Overall, fewer offenders have been put to death in recent years. The peak was 1999 with 98 executions. In contrast 2006 and 2007 saw 53 and 42 executions respectively and the trend remains downwards: 2012 saw 43 executions; in 2013 there were 39 (Death Penalty Information Center, 2014).

How the death penalty (just about) disappeared from Europe

In Europe the death penalty is becoming a thing of the past. Many Western European countries stopped carrying out executions shortly after World War II. Striking the death penalty off the books became more of a matter of urgency after 1985, when the 6th Protocol to the European Convention on Human Rights was drafted. To understand the significance of that protocol, we need to examine the body that issued it, the intergovernmental organisation called the Council of Europe. The Council of Europe should not be confused with the European Union, as the two organisations are quite distinct. The 28 European Union states, however, are all members of the Council of Europe.

The Council of Europe (see www.coe.int) was created shortly after World War II. Today, any European state can become a member of the Council of Europe provided it accepts the principle of the rule of law and guarantees human rights and fundamental freedoms to everyone under its jurisdiction. In total, 47 European states are currently members, with Belarus as a notable exception. Armenia, Azerbaijan, Bosnia-Herzegovina, Serbia and Montenegro have recently joined. The Committee of Ministers is the Council of Europe's main decision-making body. It comprises the foreign affairs ministers of all the member states, or their permanent diplomatic representatives. Its headquarters is in the *Palais de l'Europe* in Strasbourg, France. The Council of Europe established its mission as promoting the ideals of a democratic society and protecting the rights and freedoms of individuals from arbitrary interference by a state and/or its officials.

The European Convention on Human Rights is an agreement between a number of countries with the status of international law. The original members of the Convention, of which the UK was one, wrote and signed it to guarantee a number of fundamental human rights. The Convention was ratified in 1951 and it sought to set standards for the behaviour of states and the parameters of individuals' rights. Countries that sign and ratify such a document make a pledge to abide by it. Since 1951 the Convention has been added to by means of protocols.

Since 1 March 1985, the 6th Protocol to the European Convention on Human Rights and Fundamental Freedoms established the abolition of the death penalty by legal obligation under international law. With the exception of Turkey, all of the member states of the Council of Europe have now signed this Protocol. Russia is the only signatory country that is yet to ratify it. The 6th Protocol is nine articles long, but Article 1 is the one that matters most. It reads: 'The death penalty shall be abolished. No one shall be condemned to such penalty or executed.' In Article 2 the possibility for the death penalty in times of war is acknowledged:

> A State may make provision in its law for the death penalty in respect of acts committed in time of war or of imminent threat of war; such penalty shall be applied only in the instances laid down in the law and in accordance with its provisions. The State shall communicate to the Secretary General of the Council of Europe the relevant provisions of that law.

In 2002, however, a further protocol on the death penalty was drafted. This 13th Protocol effectively seeks to ban Article 2 from the 6th Protocol. Although this protocol has yet to come into force, it shows the pan-European intention of outlawing the death penalty under any circumstances.

The Council of Europe is a less well-known organisation than the European Union. In one respect it is the larger of the two with virtually all European Countries as members. Its mission is to develop throughout Europe common and democratic principles based on the European Convention on Human Rights and other reference texts on the protection of individuals. Four aims have been specified:

- to protect human rights, pluralist democracy and the rule of law;
- to promote awareness and encourage the development of Europe's cultural identity and diversity;
- to find common solutions to the challenges facing European society: such as discrimination against minorities, xenophobia, intolerance, bioethics and cloning, terrorism, trafficking in human beings, organised crime and corruption, cybercrime, violence against children;
- to consolidate democratic stability in Europe by backing political, legislative and constitutional reform.

The Council of Europe has a Secretary General but the role is not as high profile as you might expect. At present the role is performed by Norwegian Thorbjørn Jagland. Before him it was Briton Terry Davis. More important is the Committee of Ministers, the organisation's decision-making body, composed of the 47 Foreign Ministers or their Strasbourg-based deputies. Although there are other bodies within the Council of Europe, the Committee of Foreign Ministers is a key policy driving force. Within Council of Europe history, much emphasis is placed on the speech given by Winston Churchill in which he advocated a United States of Europe. Speaking not long after World War II he said: 'we must recreate the European family in a regional structure called – it may be – the United States of Europe and the first practical step will be to form a Council of Europe' (Churchill, 1946).

Zimring (2003) has observed that at present the USA and Europe are far apart in terms of both views and practice on the death penalty. He calls the retention of the death penalty in the USA an 'against-the-grain' policy. Zimring documents a widespread ambivalence towards the death penalty: a majority of the public is in favour but at the same time is distrustful of the way in which the system works. It favours retention but at the same time favours a moratorium. In short, to simply suggest that Americans are cheerleaders for the death penalty, so that elected officials have no choice but to retain it, is crude, simplistic and probably incorrect. Instead, Zimring argues, the 'saving grace' for the death penalty may have been its reframing in terms of a community-oriented tool: rather than the death penalty signifying ultimate power of the state over its citizens, the death penalty now ostensibly serves to do justice in the name of victims. In Europe in contrast the death penalty is framed as a human rights issue. Thus, the differing discourses have set Europe and the USA on decidedly different pathways and it is only very recently with the decline of the death penalty in the USA that a certain degree of convergence might be observed.

On the one hand, therefore, we see an increased reliance on evidence in policy-making in punishment. Reducing reoffending has become a mantra in criminal justice in many societies and although you can quibble over the exact strength of the evidence that supports evidence-based practice it is important to note its epistemology: research to inform practice. That said such research is dismissed by others who argue that such administrative criminological efforts merely serve to legitimate punishment and that a more radical rethink is required. That is a dominant stance within cultural criminology (e.g. Ferrell et al., 2004). They argue that the public and governments simply fail to understand crime and that technocratic approaches to punishment simply will not work. The punitive turn fed by penal populism seems to ensure that this situation persists, despite all the evidence to the contrary.

Beyond punishment: crimmigration

Crimmigration refers to the fusion of immigration law and criminal law and recognises that criminal punishment-type measures are increasingly in use within the immigration system. Prisons are re-configured as immigration detention centres for instance and a host of offences has been created to criminalise various aspects of immigration. A possible result of this (or perhaps a cause) is that immigrants and criminals are seen as of the same ilk, and hence treated similarly. Juliet Stumpf (2006, 2013) coined the term crimmigration. It is an example of a concept that labels a wide variety of state initiatives as corresponding to a single pattern and as such it focuses our gaze (Guia et al., 2012).

Both criminals and immigrants share many features in popular imagination: they are outsiders, often seen as unwanted, unproductive, undeserving and possibly dangerous. It is perhaps therefore unsurprising that the systems of control that concern both have converged. Aspects of relevance here are the many ways in which illegal immigrants can be detained and the many obligations upon employers, airline carriers and educational establishments to control and monitor foreign nationals (see Mitsilegas, 2012, for such processes in the European Union). In many countries, residing in a country without proper papers is now an offence that will not just lead to deportation but also to criminal proceedings. Deportation of criminals after the completion of their sentence is more frequently applied, even in cases where, from a human perspective, 'home' is clearly the country in which the immigrant lives (and often has done for most of their lives) rather than a country of birth or of nationality.

Originally studied in the USA, crimmigration is topic of study in the UK, the Netherlands and several other European countries, disturbed as many are that penalities are reaching further beyond convicted criminals to affect many other groups. It is also important to take on board Van der Leun and Van der Woude's (2012) point that crimmigration should not be too narrowly defined. It could also refer to a set of wider responses that may not tackle immigration per se but remains targeted to control, coerce or symbolically remove 'the other' from view. The Burqa ban, as in operation in France, could be an example of this, as would be the, in certain circles, proposed insistence to speak a specific language in public spaces. Such bans on cultural and religious expressions are in the spirit of crimmigration: to punish, control and marginalise 'the other'. Certain police practices that disproportionately focus on minorities can also be regarded as such, such as ethnic profiling (Van der Leun and Van der Woude, 2011). This carries an important conceptual point: that the notion of 'punishment' is rather restrictive as punishment carries the implication that it is further to a crime, imposed by a court and surrounded by safeguards and limitations. The concept of crimmigration shows that wider aspects of penality, such as coercion, surveillance and restrictions of rights cover a set of interrelated processes of which punishment in the classic sense is but one. Comparative criminal justice, as I have argued earlier in this book, cannot afford to take terms such as punishment for granted. The unthinking embrace of such terms may obstruct our view of other aspects that involve, or relate to, crime and justice that urgently demand our attention. We need to be questioning such grand terms, and ensuring that they do not restrict our view of social processes of coercion and control that the term in a narrow sense fails to alert us to. Crimmigration is an area of study of great relevance to comparative criminal justice.

Conclusion

We often learn about sentencing abroad by means of media reports on persons sentenced by foreign courts. It is, however, near impossible to base sweeping statements on the level of 'punitiveness' in any country on such isolated instances of sentencing. In almost every criminal justice system there is discretion available for those who do the sentencing. It is therefore certainly possible that particular individuals are being sentenced much more severely, or more leniently, than might generally be expected. It is therefore important to bear in mind that any isolated verdict is not necessarily a reflection of general practice.

In the Netherlands, murders have occasionally been punished rather leniently: when medical doctors were found to slightly overstep the guidelines laid down for legally committing euthanasia, they ran the risk of being charged with murder. If such cases led to a conviction, they would not usually lead to imprisonment. However, any assumption on the basis of this that the Dutch do not take murder very seriously is far from the truth. One nominal sentence for what technically constitutes murder does not necessarily imply a careless attitude towards human life.

Sentencing must, therefore, be viewed in the wider societal context, in which public discourse, fear of crime, perceived seriousness of offences and agreed severity of punishment combine to give shape to sentencing practices. These practices do vary significantly across countries, not only in their performance but also with regard to the philosophies that underlie them. I have discussed these orientations in terms of the fairness and the effectiveness of sentences.

The first orientation is the one that most of this chapter has focused on: that of fairness. Human rights legislation gives us a handle on discussing these matters. One can see that, historically, the death penalty is slowly but surely, though not quite everywhere, in decline, most particularly because of its perceived cruelty. But, as we have seen, definitions of cruelty have changed over time. The point remains that cruelty is, to an extent, a culturally defined concept.

The second issue is that of effectiveness of sentences. Although it is fair to say that criminal justice has moved beyond the 'nothing works' catchphrase, this is another area where clear answers are not easy to obtain. The trend seems to be that it is impossible in terms of specific types of offence to predict their effectiveness (usually measured in terms of re-offending rates), but that general guidelines can be put in operation that might ensure that any intervention will have a reasonable chance of being effective.

It is worth repeating that international agreements, such as those set out by the Council of Europe, set standards in criminal justice. Some of these pertain to sentencing, as we saw with regards to the death penalty in Europe. States that sign up to such agreements make a pledge to abide by them. In this way, democratic governments are accountable not only to the electorate but also to international bodies. Such agreements help strengthen the position of citizens across countries and are instrumental in setting minimal standards of what treatment citizens deserve to receive from the state.

From a comparative perspective it is perhaps unfortunate that as far as punishment is concerned, it is focused more on what we should condemn, rather than on what can be learned from other criminal justice systems. In many a country minimal standards of justice are not adhered to. In others, lip service is paid to human rights legislation, but behind-closed-doors violations of these rights may frequently occur. Amnesty International plays an important watchdog role in monitoring and publicising such violations, as does the Open Society Foundation.

In Western democracies there is much concern about the punitive turn. This is particularly worrying as it tends to occur without much of an evidence base or without much scrutiny of the public demand that ostensibly underlies it. From a global perspective it is decidedly strange that where crime has been going down, to the extent that the 'global crime drop' has now become a social fact within criminology, punishment continues to increase, responding as it does to very different dynamics. The issue of crimmigration is a further cause for concern as it shows that the imagery and 'solutions' of the criminal justice realm are easily transferred across to other unwanted or demonised groups. While crime is on the retreat, systems of punishment and control are only spreading wider.

Further reading

Garland, D. (2001) *The culture of control: Crime and order in contemporary society.* Chicago: University of Chicago Press.

Pratt, J., Brown, D., Brown, M., Hallsworth, S. and Morrison, W. (Eds) (2013) *The new punitiveness.* London: Routledge.

Zimring, F. (2003) *The contradictions of American capital punishment.* Oxford: Oxford University Press.

Study questions

1   Outline and summarise the case for a widespread 'punitive turn'.
2   What are the key factors identified with such a punitive turn?
3   What factors have been listed as instrumental in avoiding a punitive turn, such as for instance in Finland, Norway and Sweden?

Chapter 10

States, state crimes and genocide

Comparative criminal justice offers varied perspectives on the state. We have already discussed the role of the state in criminalisations, where we discovered that various behaviours are criminalised in some countries but not others. This is particularly evident in areas such as drugs and sexuality. We have also seen that states approach punishment very differently, both in type and in severity, and that the nature and infrastructure of states and their relationship with citizens may embody risk factors or protective factors against punitive turns. We have also considered the role of so-called weak states in relation to terrorism and drug trafficking. The role of the state and the extent to which citizens trust the machinations of those in power helps us to account for the popularity or otherwise of the jury. In short, the fashion in which states are organised has profound impacts on the way in which apparatuses of justice and control are given shape.

States may be naively thought of as unchangeable and everlasting. However, we must not forget that through the vast majority of human existence, the state did not exist and since its existence, the meaning of what a 'state' is and does has been subject to continuous change. Although there have been 'states' for thousands of years, such as the Roman Empire, the notion of the modern state was mainly further to the Treaty of Westphalia of 1648. This Treaty ended the 30-year war in an area that is present-day Germany and which at the time was an elaborate patchwork of dozens of mini states. The Westphalian Treaty codified many things including Dutch independence from Spain (through the Peace of Münster that ended the so-called 80-year war between Spain and the Dutch United Provinces) and Switzerland's independence. Important for our present purposes is the fact that it set out a new political order: one in which the nation state received unprecedented prominence.

From 1648 onwards states were the principal agents of international relations. In the resulting Westphalian doctrine states are independent and sovereign. This means that states should not interfere in other states' internal business. International relations operate on the premise that states have equal status. A later phase of nineteenth-century nationalism further bolstered this system that we still recognise today: it assumes that states are cultural and political homogeneous entities with every state the home of a 'nation', a people, a culture and a language in which being a 'national' is strongly linked to identity and belonging and a set of rights and entitlements. States are assumed to contain societies. States have thus become the units through which much of society is organised, from education, to defence, to health care. We still recognise such arrangements today.

However, at the same time it is obvious that the heyday of the Westphalian state has passed. Through supranational bodies, such as the United Nations, NATO and the European Union, and through a wide array of bilateral and international agreements, states have voluntarily given up a degree of sovereignty and independence. This is judged to be advantageous. It is clear that certain issues, such as defence, climate change and global trade are best organised at a level beyond the state. At the same time, examples where the 'one people one state' doctrine simply does not apply are, and have always been, plentiful. They are better thought of as 'imagined communities' (Anderson, 1983) rather than natural and never changing entities. This has culminated in assessments that call the Westphalian state a 'myth', and its strong version probably is. All that said, the state is and remains an important concept through which much is organised and if not organised then imagined. A sense of national identity runs deep. National rivalries, although often not all that ancient, may feel that way and be considered to be of epic proportions. National characters, heroes, languages, customs and histories are dearly held and forever deemed under threat. That way, the nation state continues to structure popular sentiments. Thus, there is a chauvinistic affinity with nationality and that may obscure our perspective on the many roles that the state plays in producing harm. Certainly when the culprit could be our own.

It is now time to examine the role of the state in the guise of perpetrator of serious wrongdoings. In criminology this perspective is relatively new. Jamieson and McEvoy refer to state crime as a 'slippery concept' (2005: 505). It comes in many shapes. Kauzlarich et al. (2003) define state crime as harmful behaviours that are committed by states upon its citizens (e.g. the Holocaust), upon citizens of another state or upon another state. A distinction is often made between wrongdoings that states commit against their own population and more expansive aggression, which is reminiscent of the Westphalian dogma that whatever a state gets up to within its borders is, crudely put, nobody else's business. Green and Ward (2000) in contrast distinguish two kinds of state crime. The first is violations of human rights. The other is state organisational deviance, which could, for instance be large-scale state corruption. Kauzlarich et al. (2003) note that powerful elites have considerable influence in shaping political discourse, ideologies and institutions so as to facilitate state crime on their behalf. Links between class, power and ideology are therefore paramount in understanding state crime.

Kauzlarich et al. (2003) argue that state crime has a number of characteristics. The first is that it generates harm, to individuals and groups. The second is that it is the product of action or inaction on behalf of the state or state agencies.

Third, these actions relate to an assigned or perceived trust in, and duty of, the state. Finally, it is committed by a governmental agency or representative and is done in the self-interest of the state. State crime accounts for many of the worst atrocities of humankind. This includes the Holocaust in World War II, other genocides, countless wars of aggression, famine, colonisation and other forms of oppression and persecution of peoples. State crime accounted for many millions of deaths in the twentieth century alone.

With that in mind it is rather baffling to consider that criminology has rather ignored state crime. Maier-Katkin et al. (2009) give two reasons for this. The first stems from the *nullum crime sine lege* (no crime without law) doctrine that has constrained criminology in a wider sense. The argument is that much state crime is or was in fact not proscribed by statute when it occurred. This highlights the problems of a discipline too closely aligned to law in the books: it poses the risk of criminology losing perspective on harmful behaviour that is not illegal. The other reason lies in the culture and sociology of the discipline: 'the safer course to academic respectability ... was to focus on agreed-upon national concerns such as violent crime, delinquency and drug abuse' (Maier-Katkin et al., 2009: 230). However it is safe to say that this state of affairs has now changed so that the study of state crime is now quite a vibrant field (e.g. Ross, 2000; Rothe et al., 2009).

Jeffrey Ross considers state crime in relation to a number of democratic countries. You could say that that is both a brave and an intriguing decision. After all, you could harbour the naive assumption that state crime is by definition the province of rogue states or dictatorships. It is also the case that in democracies with a free press, state crime is more likely to be uncovered so that the phenomenon is more accessible and less risky to research. At the same time, you would expect state crime to be not so easily committed due to democratic controls, issues of legitimacy and public accountability. Counter to that runs the idea that populations are not always terribly interested in scrutinising potential state crime in their own country. In his introduction Ross notes that state crime is rarely studied comparatively and his edited collection, considering the control of state crime in the UK, the USA, Canada, Israel, France, Italy and Japan, is a landmark study. In the countries analysed, the most frequent state crimes are: cover-ups (documented in all seven countries); corruption/bribery (in six); illegal police violence (five); illegal surveillance (four); torture (three); tax evasion by politicians (three); human rights violations (three); and military violence (three). Note that the book was published in 2000, so before September 11 2001, and the war in Iraq.

The book makes for a rather sobering read. State crimes in the UK that are discussed include the events of 'bloody Sunday' in Northern Ireland in 1972 when 13 people were killed by British soldiers, and instances of police corruption and use of violence in protest (Ross, 2000). In France, killings in public protests to do with the war in Algeria in the early 1960s are mentioned. In one such event in 1961, 200 protestors are said to have been killed. There was also state involvement in the sinking of Greenpeace's ship the *Rainbow*

Warrior in New Zealand. The vessel was there to protest against nuclear tests carried out by France in the Pacific. This makes France, Wolfreys (2000: 120) argues, the only Western democracy since World War II to have confessed to perpetrating an act of terrorism in peacetime.

There clearly is merit in considering state crime where you may expect it least, carried out by politically and socially legitimate governments, ruled by democratic consent and under scrutiny of elected parliamentarians, active civil society, grass-roots politics and an engaged and free press. As we find that all that is no guarantee against the occurrence of state crime, we can only ponder how frequently state crime occurs in other places where such safeguards are not in operation.

At this point is it important to problematise the 'state' in state crime. State crime can be outsourced, to private security or military companies and these outfits may be less open to scrutiny than traditional agencies of the state. In addition, we know that organisations beyond the state have become extremely powerful. We can think of military bonds such as NATO, the European Union but we may also need to consider other forums. The G8 is a forum for the governments of eight industrialised nations. They are Canada, France, Germany, Italy, Japan, Russia, the UK and the USA (and there is separate representation from the European Union). The G8 heads of state meet regularly and the finance ministers meet at least four times a year. Although the remit of the G8 is unclear, it is no doubt an important agenda-setting body. Of growing importance is the G20. This includes the G8 but also a number of emerging economies and represents more geographic and cultural parts of the world: Argentina, Australia, Brazil, China, India, Indonesia, Republic of Korea, Mexico, Saudi Arabia, South Africa and Turkey, while there is, again, a role for the European Union. Its outlook is primarily economic but we may also need to consider its role in both countering crime, and at the same time its criminogenic properties.

Genocide

Genocide, perhaps the worst crime of all, has traditionally been ignored by criminology. Day and Vandiver (2000) have argued that criminologists have paid scant attention to genocide because it was assumed that political science would 'own' the subject. However, Day and Vandiver note that genocide rather acutely came to feature on the criminological horizon further to two genocides in the 1990s, in the Former Yugoslavia and in Rwanda. These atrocities took place in disparate locations but in close succession and both sparked unprecedented international responses, including the establishment of International Criminal Tribunals, as I will discuss in the next chapter. It was probably in particular the former, the genocide in the Former Yugoslavia, close as it was to Western Europe, that initially prompted most interest but plenty of research has since considered the events in Rwanda as well.

Part of the literature on genocide seeks to pull genocide studies into general criminology. Day and Vandiver (2000) consider 'classic' criminological theories to establish the extent to which they may explain both events. Kelman (1973) in particular links the notions of *authorisation*, for example following orders; *routinisation*, for example for atrocities to be so widespread that this temporarily comes to represent a kind of a perverted 'norm'; and *dehumanisation*, a set of processes that allows the perpetrator to regard victims as less than human and therefore undeserving of empathy or restraint. Day and Vandiver argue that 'authorization' played a role in both conflicts in the 1990s but more profoundly so in Rwanda where the Tutsi genocide was said to be carried out in a surprisingly 'orderly' way: 'The genocide had less to do with whether ordinary Hutus believed killing their Tutsi neighbours was a good idea than with upholding standards of good citizenship, which in the spring and early summer of 1994 was to kill Tutsis in broad daylight' (Day and Vandiver, 2000: 50–1). Announcements were made, people where gathered and given instructions and the genocide proceeded in that orderly fashion. Day and Vandiver explain that in between sessions of killing compatriots many perpetrators went home for lunch to continue their murderous day's work in the afternoon. Dehumanisation certainly took place in both genocides in the 1990s but Day and Vandiver question the role of routinisation as a factor that can account for the occurrence of genocide. Although they are careful to present their findings as far from a definitive answer, their analysis does show that even seemingly extraordinary events such as genocide can be pulled into mainstream criminological thought with regular criminological theory applied. In a similar vein, Maier-Katkin et al. (2009) apply criminological theories such as strain theory and group theory to genocide and argue that a multi-level theory will be a necessity. Similarly, Neuberger (2006) has applied Milgram's obedience study and Matza's concept of neutralisation to state crime.

An important lesson that we can take from this is that social groups which may not be all that dissimilar can be construed as oppositional, such as Jews in Germany, Tutsis in Rwanda and Muslims in Bosnia. This was also at play in Darfur in Sudan from 2003. Hagan and Rymond-Richmond (2009) note a hardening of racial demarcations between Arab groups and Black African villagers prior to atrocities of genocidal proportion that took place here. During the genocide, refugees identified Arab group attackers targeting them with explicit epithets in the process of mass murder, rape, robbery and displacement (2009: 508). In Hagan and Rymond-Richmond (2008) hyper-racist quotations are provided, ascribed to Arab attackers, such as: 'You donkey you slave' and 'We going to change the color', in reference to rape so as to produce 'less Black' offspring: evidence of dehumanisation and ethnic othering in action.

In comparing events in Bosnia and Rwanda, Jamieson (1999) is seemingly more struck by difference than by similarity. That said, both atrocities did correspond to the same genocidal logic: both were planned at the highest level, and organised and coordinated by the state apparatus. They were locally executed and both re-ignited and capitalised on pre-existing ethnic or tribal fears and tensions.

In considering important differences, a feature of the Bosnian atrocities was the concentration of it at the front line of the war so that it was mainly military actors that were involved. Jamieson (1999) notes the widespread and strategic use of sexual violence. A striking feature of the Rwandan genocide was that on the ground, much of the killing was committed by regular Hutu citizens including many women, even children, certainly in a second phase subsequent to the murder of Tutsi political and intellectual leaders. During the Rwanda genocide women played a highly active role. Women were documented as cheerleaders for massacres, as enablers, such as providing petrol for fire setting and as 'finishers off', killing those victims still living with knives, machetes or sticks. She calls for a radical reorientation of notions of gender in genocide where women cannot simply be assumed to be either victims or bystanders (Jamieson, 1999).

Despite the consensus on the fact that genocide tends to require high-level organisation, there is a great deal of fascination with the role that 'normal people' in the midst of the action play. Smeulers (2002) has investigated the personal characteristics and processes involved of those at the sharp end of crimes against humanity, those that have been referred to as 'willing executioners' in the past (Goldhagen, 1996). How does an individual become involved, stay involved and at some point come to terminate their involvement? Smeulers (2002) argues that this transformation process starts with a preparation phase. Many of the perpetrators that Smeulers investigated were part of a command structure and emphasised authority as part of the context. She quotes Nazi Adolf Eichmann as saying: 'You must understand … I was a soldier. … I had orders to follow. … The order came from the Führer himself. … There was nothing to be done' (p. 4).

When the atrocities actually start perpetrators report both anguish and a sense of numbness or dissociation. A US soldier in Vietnam reported:

> That day in My Lai, I was personally responsible for killing about 25 people. Personally. Men, women. From shooting them, to cutting their throats, scalping them, to … cutting off their hands and cutting out their tongue. I did it. I just went. My mind just went. And I was not the only one that did it. A lot of other people did it. I just killed. Once I started the … training, the whole programming part of killing, it just came out. … It just came. I did not know I had it in me … I had no feelings or no emotions or no nothing. No directions. I just killed.
>
> (p. 6)

A torturer from South America said: 'I can only say that when you first start doing the job, it is hard … you hide yourself and cry, so nobody can see you.'

Subsequently, processes of rationalisation and justification kick in: 'You have to realize that you yourself have not killed anyone and that you are just an instrument of the state' said a US executioner (p. 7). In the case of prolonged engagement, habituation may occur as well as further dehumanisation of the victims. 'Yes, definitely there comes a moment when you feel nothing about what you are doing,' said a South American torturer (p. 9). A Nazi camp commander from Treblinka said:

> I think it started the day I first saw the *Totenlager* [death camp, FP] in Treblinka. … It had nothing to do with humanity – it could not have: it was a mass – a mass of rotting flesh. … I think unconsciously that started me thinking of them as cargo. … I rarely saw them as individuals. It was a huge mass. I sometimes stood on the wall and saw them in the tube. But – how can I explain it – they were naked, packed together, running, being driven with whips like … It has nothing to do with hate. They were weak: they allowed everything to happen – to be done to them. They were people with whom there was no common ground, no possibility of communication – that is how contempt is born. I could never understand how they could give in as they did.

Afterwards, perpetrators may use a variety of strategies to maintain an intact identity. One is to maintain previous justifications. Another is to regard themselves as simple cogs in a machine, void of agency and without any power to stop the atrocities from occurring. Others, however report anguish, terror and trauma (Smeulers, 2002).

Despite the evocative accounts of executioners we must not forget that genocides require top-down planning, and a social or institutional structure in which these events become possible. That makes it clear that the comparative study of genocide also requires a multi-level approach. Hiebert (2009) indeed argues that three broad categories are often invoked in explaining genocide. The first is that of individual and group agency; Smeulers' approach. The next refers to structural factors such as culture, societal cleavages, type of regime and ideology. The third refers to processes of collective identity construction such as the othering and demonisation of targeted groups. Hiebert calls for increased rigour in comparative genocide research as to how those terms are defined and applied.

A further view is that comparative study of genocide runs into ontological problems due to the intense political associations of the term. This in part stems from the deeply held view that genocide is to do with 'evil' leaders and barbaric regimes, nowhere more so than in relation to the Holocaust. This creates, Shaw (2012) argues, a 'domestic mindset': genocides are assumed to be national events and the international community is, at worst, a bystander, but never complicit. Another factor is that the literature tends to focus on responses to genocide and insufficiently on the conceptual 'production' of genocide: who calls what a genocide? After all the term was heavily contested in relation to Darfur, and Shaw (2012) notes a habit of avoiding the term while genocides are actually occurring. Instead, media and political commentators refer to terms such as 'humanitarian crisis' or 'ethnic cleansing'. This is not just word play. Instances of genocide may provide the international community with an obligation to intervene. Of course, the International Criminal Tribunals of the 1990s, for the Former Yugoslavia and Rwanda, defined genocide and so did the International Criminal Court. But still, the word genocide has power and meaning beyond these definitions in international law. The word genocide therefore, probably due to its very potency, is one that is often seemingly avoided.

Shaw (2012) places genocide research back in international relations. Rubinstein (2004) takes account of genocide in a geo-political historical fashion and identifies three phases. The first is the colonial era (mainly the eighteenth and nineteenth centuries) during which colonisers killed and displaced subdued populations. The second is the totalitarian era of the twentieth century culminating in the Holocaust. The third is the era of ethnic cleansing, a term frequently applied to events in the Former Yugoslavia in the 1990s. This is another example of the historical and political embedding of genocide, not within criminology but within politics, history and international relations. Comparative criminological research should therefore be comfortable with venturing into these fields.

Beyond comparison? A comparative criminology of genocide

It is perhaps appropriate to say that the contours of a comparative criminology of genocide have emerged. There is a certain resistance against this. An important reason is the understandable drive to consider genocides as unique events. This is perhaps most strongly articulated in relation to the Holocaust. Where a notion of uniqueness is applied to an event such as the Holocaust any comparison may be regarded as diluting the specific understanding of the uniqueness of the Holocaust. Bauman has argued that there is comfort in such exceptionalism: it places it beyond comparison as it is placed in a category of its own. Another perspective is to regard genocides as extreme events that can be understood in relation to each other and in relation to the factors and events that may have given rise to them. In that way, genocide research may not only tell us about their specific logic, but shed light on 'normal' society as well. In other words, genocides can be placed into a more regular context.

Thus, the literature on comparative genocide emphasises two separate comparative questions. The first is whether genocides are comparable at all. There is an argument that sometimes is only implicitly made that each genocide is embedded to such an extent within historical and social structures as to make them both unique and perhaps, incomprehensible. On the other hand, the work of Smeulers, and Hiebert and others shows that comparative analysis of genocides is possible. Smeulers' work draws upon testimony from various atrocities to suggest that experiences do compare across settings. The work of Jamieson also shows that we can analyse atrocities and identify different causes, processes and other particularities. The second issue is whether genocide is at all comparable to other crime. If it is, it becomes appropriate to analyse genocide through regular criminological conceptual apparatus. If it is not, the analysis of genocide requires its own language, or requires the tools of other disciplines such as history and international relations, as we saw in the work of Shaw (2012).

Woolford (2006) seems to favour the latter. He argues that classic criminological theories fail to account for genocide due to its extraordinary nature. He argues that we should be more reflective. Understanding the Rwandan genocide needs to include consideration of its colonial past and of the regional tensions that existed at the time of the genocide. He ends with an impassioned plea: we should not see genocides as simply data, as opportunities to test criminological theory. It is about responsibility. We should not consider causes in a narrow sense and nor we should we simply 'apply' criminology to genocide, or vice versa, consider genocide to discover what it tells us of our discipline:

> [H]istorical events such as genocide are not simply sources of data on which to test our hypotheses, they are potent symbolic narratives used to construct the social world. The ways in which we use these narratives have moral consequences; therefore, our responsibility is to consider how in the past our discipline has failed those who suffered the human consequences of genocide, and to re-order our discipline and society in a manner that helps to make genocide unthinkable.
>
> (Woolford, 2006: 103)

Sexual violence and crimes against humanity

Comparative research has highlighted the importance of the study of sexual violence in relation to genocide. That there is a connection between sexual violence and warfare has long been known. Sexual violence was always understood to be an outcome of warfare and the phrase 'the spoils of war' even seems to denote a sense of inevitability of looting and raping subsequent to battle: as if the opportunity to rape could be constituted as a 'reward' for the troops after victory in battle. Despite this, criminology has largely remained silent on this, at least until recently. That is amazing as rape during conflict seems frequent, and widespread. Mullins (2009) documents that during the Rwanda genocide, between 250,000 and 500,000 women were raped; between 10,000 and 60,000 Muslim and Croatian women were raped in the Former Yugoslavia in the early 1990s; and between 200,000 and 400,000 Bangladeshi women were sexually victimised by Pakistani soldiers in the 1974 conflict.

These data are staggering and because of that immediately cast doubt on the conventional explanation that sexual violence is further to a release of trauma and fear in the aftermath of combat, or regarding it simply as 'what soldiers do'. In fact it is clear that sexual violence in conflict frequently goes well beyond that. Mullins (2009) argues that rape is both a tool of terror and of population elimination, and that makes rape in fact an essential part of genocide. Looking at evidence transcripts of the Rwanda tribunal Mullins found that rape was at times state directed. The way in which campaigns of rape occurred was to humiliate women directly and whole communities through them. Other forms of sexual violence occurred such as the castration of Tutsi community leaders. The symbolic impact of that was no doubt the demonstration of the victim's powerlessness and emasculation (Mullins, 2009). Mullins' work highlights the organised nature of rape during conflict and the strategic and ideological purposes that it serves.

Wood (2010) has noted that both the extent and the form of sexual violence are highly variable between conflicts. She found that sexual violence can occur through sexual slavery, as part of ethnic cleansing or through sexualised torture or other forms. In some conflicts primarily women are targeted whereas elsewhere males are as well. Whereas rape was frequent in the Rwandan genocide, in Darfur and the Far East during World War II other conflicts saw little organised sexual violence. She makes a key distinction based on whether rape plays a strategic role or a tactical role in conflict situations. Where it is strategic (such as in Rwanda, and the Far East) the leadership regards it as beneficial and rape is likely to be systematic and widespread. Where the leadership does not think it is an effective combat strategy (for instance because sexual violence may make a subdued population more difficult to control, or because of fear of negative reporting in the world's media) rape may still occur but probably on a smaller scale and more tactically, in situations where it is judged by local leaders that sexual violence serves a particular purpose at that time, or because perpetrators are confident that their conduct will have no repercussions.

Comparative research has shown that sexual violence can be genocidal in nature. It can be a tool of oppression, terror and population decimation (there are reports of HIV positive men ordered to rape victims in more than one African conflict). It is therefore a positive development that sexual violence is increasingly recognised as such in International law, as we shall see in the next chapter.

Beyond the state: crime by global institutions

A key objective of this chapter is to come to a more sophisticated position on the state in relation to crime and justice. But we must remember that not all that is thought of as the state's business is carried out by the state. It is important to discuss the 'outsourcing' of state crime to private companies. There are a number of obvious benefits to not utilising state-recruited and -employed soldiers either through conscription or as career military personnel. Walker and Whyte (2005) argue that inevitably these, ostensibly, include arguments of effectiveness and efficiency. Another is that the private military industry is big business, certainly in the UK, so that there is an economic argument for the furtherance of private warfare. Another insidious advantage of using private armies is that it reduces political exposure should operations not go as planned.

Private contractors are likely to receive less coverage should there be any human rights abuses and governments will find it easier to blame the contractor for any wrongdoings. This is the 'dirty work' argument: states may find it convenient to have private contractors do the dirty work for them, for less money and with less reputational risk.

It is therefore no surprise that the use of private contractors in warfare is controversial. Afghan President Hamid Karzai's plan to ban all private security companies from Afghanistan in 2010, although never implemented, is a reminder of the strong feelings that private contractor involvement evokes. There is the added worry that where warfare can become a money-making exercise, that might lead to perverse incentives in relation to the commencement and sustainment of hostilities, as it would benefit the arms industry and private military companies. Clearly, careful regulation and oversight is important. However, this is easier said than done. This is not only because in the fog of war scrutiny is difficult. A further complication is that methods of military action develop fast and regulatory frameworks may be slow to catch up, such as in the case of using unmanned aircraft, *drones*, in combat zones. A further complication is the notion of business confidentiality. Whereas in many countries public bodies are more open to scrutiny, the machinations of private companies are often hidden, with the reason given that such matters are commercially sensitive. This allows for a cloak of invisibility in relation to the actual operations of these companies.

However, Tombs (2012) argues that the main reasons for a lack of accountability do not lie in the difficulties noted above. Instead, he argues that the state and the private sector are engaged in symbiotically producing global harm: corporate crimes and state crimes frequently co-occur and can facilitate each other. Part of that relationship expresses itself through inadequate regulation. Another factor is that decision-makers in government and the private sector are often closely connected. Neo-liberal governments certainly are highly market focused, furthering the idea that much, if not most, public endeavour is best carried out by leaving market forces to it. Warfare is no exception. One of the lesser discerned consequences of this are that the talk of warfare is changing. The deployment of private contractors depoliticises warfare. It is less about who is right and wrong, or about ideology or humanity, and more likely to be couched in terms of 'service provision', and 'aims and objectives'. It is the talk of combat zones as 'theatres', where 'personnel' do a 'job'. This allows a depoliticised and sanitised picture of combat to be painted: 'it is just about private companies going about their business'.

This symbiosis was heavily criticised in the Iraq war (Whyte, 2007). Whyte argues that much of Iraq's oil revenue ended up in private hands, through bribery, overcharging, embezzlement and bid-rigging. Importantly, the large scale sell out to the private sector was never sanctioned by the Iraqi people. Leander and Van Munster (2007) note the heavy involvement of private security contractors in the Darfur humanitarian crisis. They specifically note the aforementioned depoliticisation of the conflict: 'a technocratized and militarized framing of security which crowds out alternative political options and discussions about priorities' (2007: 208).

The notion of the state paving the way for a neo-liberal mode of governance is described particularly lucidly by Naomi Klein in her book *The Shock Doctrine* (Klein, 2007). She has considered the aftermath of serious crises, in South America, Asia, the Former Soviet Union and elsewhere such as following Hurricane Katrina in New Orleans in 2005. She found that serious financial or humanitarian crises are framed by decision-makers in the USA and global financial institutions as opportunities. These opportunities are for spreading neo-liberal rule, large-scale privatisation, the cutting of state spending on welfare, and the removal of what are perceived to be measures against free markets such as export restrictions, rent control and social security. This allows global companies to acquire these assets and gear them towards profit, often at the expense of national economies and the fate of the people in these crisis-ridden countries. Through Klein's study, written in a journalistic style but in essence very much a comparative project, we see how deep the symbiosis between the neo-liberal state and the global private sector runs. It is such reasons that led Friedrichs (2013) to postulate that crimes of globalisation, in particular carried out by global financial institutions (such as the International Monetary Fund (IMF) and the World Bank) should be a specific criminological project. He argues that criminology should get its definitions on international crimes clearer. He also calls for ethnographic studies not just of the inner workings of such financial institutions but also of the experiences of people in developing countries that are subjected to their programmes. All this will help turn the lens of criminology towards global harm and the actors that cause it.

In addition to this work, there are highly readable yet shocking accounts of those who have been on the inside. That includes John Perkins' *Confessions of an Economic Hit Man* (2005). The preface starts:

> Economic hit men (EHMs) are highly paid professionals who cheat countries around the world out of trillions of dollars. They funnel money from the World Bank, the U.S. Agency of International Development (USAID), and other foreign 'aid' organizations into the coffers of huge corporations and the pockets of a few wealthy families who control the planets' natural resources. Their tools include fraudulent financial reports, rigged elections, payoffs, extortion, sex and murder. They play a game as old as empire but one that has taken on new and terrifying dimensions during this time of globalization.

Perkins' first-hand account certainly should give criminology the encouragement to consider state crime beyond the state, committed by international organisations in tandem with big business and hegemonic government agencies. The work of Noam Chomsky, for example, *Profit over People* (1999) and of

Nobel prize winner and former chief economist of the World Bank Joseph Stiglitz, for example, *Globalization and its Discontents* (2002) are certainly important reads as well. They all highlight the *realpolitik* of international relations and macro-economics and paint a landscape of amoral states and agencies ruthlessly furthering their self-interest. There is plenty there for comparative studies to discover.

Conclusion

The areas of state crime, corporate crime, genocide and crimes against humanity are both daunting and haunting. But the good news is that they have become part and parcel of criminology and comparative criminal justice plays its part, in particular in considering aspects of genocide and other forms of state crime. It is probably fair to say that comparative criminal justice has not quite come to terms with financial institutions and international organisations with vague remits and little infrastructure such as the G8. That said it is good to see that the worst crimes of all are no longer beyond criminology's horizon. However, state crime remains difficult from a conceptual perspective. An indicator of this is the endless debates about the status of world leaders having been involved in big decisions about going to war. To some in the UK, Tony Blair, prime minister at the time of the Iraq war, is a war criminal who was involved in starting a war of aggression under false pretences. To others he is a global hero, a toppler of authoritarian regimes. It is without exaggeration that we can say that views about Tony Blair and probably others such as George W. Bush do not just vary between 'guilty' and 'not guilty', but in fact oscillate truly between hero and villain. This shows that the status of acts that could or could not be deemed a state crime are ferociously contested.

This push towards recognising the wrongs of states and crimes during conflict and warfare is no doubt aided by the fact that the International Criminal Court has provided agencies and statutes to globally criminalise genocide and crimes against humanity. It gives the discipline something it historically is attached to: a legal basis. To be fair, there were criminal definitions that were applied in the Military Tribunals after World War II, in Germany and Japan in the 1940s but these were left to gather dust for almost 50 years. The genocide events in the 1990s brought international criminal law statutes and two international criminal tribunals, and the International Criminal Court was established soon after. Those developments in a way brought genocide back into the criminological fold. The impressive research that has taken place over the last 15 to 20 years in a way makes it all the more incomprehensible that it was ever different.

Further reading

Ross, J.I. (2000) *Varieties of state crime and its control*. Monsey, New York: Criminal Justice Press.

Rothe, D.L., Ross, J.I., Mullins, C.W., Friedrichs, D., Michalowski, R., Barak, G., Kuazlarich, D. and Kramer, R.C. (2009) That was then, this is now, what about tomorrow? Future directions in state crime studies. *Critical criminology, 17,* 3–13.

Woolford, A. (2006) Making genocide unthinkable: Three guidelines for a critical criminology of genocide. *Critical criminology, 14,* 87–106.

Study questions

1   Why is defining state crime so problematic? What consequences does that have for comparative study?
2   Why was (comparative) criminology slow in addressing genocide as a topic of study?
3   Outline three key findings that comparative genocide studies have yielded.

Chapter 11

International criminal justice
Tribunals, statutes and prosecutions

Legislation to deal with crimes against humanity is often international in nature. In fact, criminal justice everywhere is increasingly affected by international law. International law is the system of rules that states and other bodies regard as binding in their mutual relations. However, there is no such thing as a global constitution, nor is there a universally accepted international criminal code, although the closest thing to that would be the Statute of the International Criminal Court that I will discuss later. By and large, the nature of international law is more diffuse than that. That is why it is called soft law, as opposed to the hard law of codes and constitutions. International law is used, on the one hand, to regulate how states should treat each other, and on the other hand is concerned with how states should treat their citizens. It derives from treaties, custom, accepted principles and the views of legal authorities (Hague et al., 1998).

International law impinges on criminal justice in four ways. First, international law defines states and statehood, and sovereign states remain responsible for much of the way in which criminal justice is organised. Second, international law may form part of national law: the Human Rights Act 1998 in England and Wales is a good example. The provisions in this Act were already legally binding as international law before the Act came into effect, but its incorporation into domestic law has enhanced their enforcement. The International Criminal Court Act 2001 is another example as it is the law that makes the crimes defined for the International Criminal Court in The Hague part of domestic law as well. Third, international law can apply directly against individuals: this is so in the case of the International Criminal Tribunals for the Former Yugoslavia and Rwanda, and the International Criminal Court. Finally, international agreements can set the parameters of actions by national legislators. Such agreements can set out the objectives that national governments should put into effect.

There are four sources of international law. The first comprises international conventions and treaties; the second, international customs which have been ripened into international law; the third consists of generally accepted principles of law; and fourth there are judicial decisions and judicial teachings and writings. The first source is the most important. International conventions and treaties are often drafted by diplomats and other government officials, who come together for a short period of time to produce an agreed document. When the final draft is written the delegates may sign it, and this signature carries a certain degree of weight. However, a diplomatic signature does not mean that the diplomat's country has accepted the statute, treaty or convention. For that, ratification is required: the formal agreement of the state's government to the statute. This will usually require the treaty to be formally agreed to by a parliament or other representative body, which can take considerable time. It is a fact that not every state whose diplomats sign a treaty will eventually ratify it.

Additionally, the fact that an agreement exists does not necessarily make it part of international law. For that it is important that it is widely *ratified*. That is an indication of the level of global consensus, which is important with regard to whether the content of the agreement is binding. The right not to be subjected to the death penalty, for instance, is laid down in the United Nations Second Optional Protocol for the Abolition of the Death Penalty from 1989. The operative word in the title is obviously 'optional'. It has been ratified by 76 countries as of 2014. Although that is a substantial number there are over 190 countries that could have decided to sign up, so 76 signatories is not enough for it to be considered sufficiently widespread. Thus, convicts on death row cannot claim that international law prevents the death penalty from being imposed. Any principled ban on the death penalty is not part of international law. We have, however, seen that the situation in Europe is different: the protocols to the European Convention on Human Rights do outlaw the death penalty, but only in Europe.

In international law, the United Nations (UN) is the most important legislative body. The United Nations was established on 24 October 1945 by 51 countries committed to preserving peace through international cooperation and collective security. Today, virtually every nation in the world belongs to the UN: membership totals 193 countries in 2014 and the list includes Afghanistan, Libya and Iraq. Recent additions are Switzerland, Timor-Leste and Tuvalu with South Sudan the most recent member, acquiring membership in 2011. We cannot properly understand the way in which international justice develops without understanding the importance of the United Nations and its processes. International criminal courts, such as the Tribunal for the Former Yugoslavia and the International Criminal Court have been established further to UN resolutions. In case of the latter, as we shall see, the UN Security Council plays a potentially pivotal role in its prosecution decisions.

When states become members of the United Nations, they agree to accept the obligations of the UN Charter. This is a treaty that sets out basic principles of international relations and the workings of the United Nations. According to the Charter, the United Nations has four purposes: to maintain international peace and security, to develop friendly relations among nations, to cooperate in solving international problems while promoting respect for human rights, and to be a centre for harmonising the actions of nations. The United Nations has six main organs. Five of them – the General Assembly, the Security Council, the

Economic and Social Council, the Trusteeship Council and the Secretariat – are based at UN headquarters in New York. The sixth, the International Court of Justice, is located in The Hague, the Netherlands. For our present purposes it is the General Assembly and the Security Council that are the most important.

All UN member states are represented in the General Assembly. It is a kind of parliament of nations and meets to consider the world's most pressing problems. Each member state has one vote. Decisions on important matters, such as international peace and security, admitting new members and budgetary issues are decided by two-thirds majority. Other matters are decided by simple majority. Efforts are usually made to reach decisions through consensus rather than by taking a formal vote.

The UN Charter gives the Security Council primary responsibility for maintaining international peace and security, and it may convene at any time whenever peace is threatened. Under the Charter all member states are obliged to carry out the Council's decisions. There are 15 Security Council members. Five of these, China, France, the Russian Federation, the UK and the USA, are permanent members. The other ten are elected by the General Assembly for two-year terms. Decisions of the Council require nine 'yes' votes. Except in votes on procedural questions, a decision cannot be taken if there is a 'no' vote, or veto, by a permanent member. This gives the five permanent members strong control over peace and security matters around the world, but they obviously frequently disagree, such as in the build-up to the war in Iraq in 2003.

Indeed despite the technocratic nature of these descriptions and the fact that virtually every state is a member of the United Nations, some of its decisions are intensely contested. Its role in the war in Iraq in 2003 is much debated, also within criminology (Kramer and Michalowski, 2005; Whyte, 2007). There is also much debate on the structure of the United Nations' decision-making bodies, in particular that of the Security Council where the five veto-holding members are considered to have an inappropriate stronghold over world affairs not least, as we will see, in relation to the International Criminal Court. It is argued that other forums have emerged partly because of this, such as the G8 and the G20 (Nederveen Pieterse, 2011).

Universal human rights

While human rights can be traced back to the medieval English *Magna Carta*, the United Nations Charter of Human Rights formulated soon after World War II certainly was a turning point. It led to the setting up of a commission to draft the Universal Declaration of Human Rights. This Declaration was adopted on 10 December 1948, and it was the first time that human rights were given statutory status. It was three years after the end of World War II, and in the voting the newly emerging world order was already apparent. The Soviet Union, for instance, did not vote in favour of adopting the Declaration; South Africa abstained as well. The Universal Declaration must, with hindsight, primarily be viewed as a declaration of good intentions: there was no enforcement machinery established along with it. Nevertheless, it was an influential document, perhaps not least because no state has ever been prepared to boast about a breach of it, which is of course not to say that breaching never occurred in the decades that followed (Robinson, 1999).

The rights of freedom and equality are guaranteed in Article 1. This, however, does not mean that the state can never legitimately take away its citizens' freedom. It can do so, for instance, when an independent court finds a person guilty of an offence in a way consistent with national legislation and international standards.

The Universal Declaration of Human Rights

The preamble to the Declaration asserts that if man is not to be compelled to have recourse, as a last resort, to rebellion against tyranny and oppression, the rule of law should protect his human rights. To this end, the articles of the Universal Declaration include rights to:

- Article 1 – Freedom and equality in dignity and rights;
- Article 2 – The entitlements of the Declaration without discrimination;
- Article 3 – Life, liberty and security of the person;
- Article 4 – Freedom from slavery or servitude;
- Article 5 – Freedom from torture or cruel, inhuman or degrading treatment or punishment;
- Article 6 – Recognition everywhere as a person before the law;
- Article 7 – Equality before the law without discrimination;
- Article 8 – An effective remedy for acts violating fundamental rights;
- Article 9 – Freedom from arbitrary arrest, detention or exile;
- Article 10 – Fair and public hearing by an independent and impartial tribunal;
- Article 11 – Presumption of innocence;
- Article 12 – Privacy of family, home and correspondence;
- Article 13 – Freedom of movement;
- Article 14 – Asylum from persecution;
- Article 15 – A nationality;
- Article 16 – Marriage and family;
- Article 17 – Property ownership;
- Article 18 – Freedom of thought, conscience and religion;
- Article 19 – Freedom of opinion and expression;
- Article 20 – Freedom of peaceful assembly and association;
- Article 21 – Participation in the government of one's country, to have equal access to public service in one's country and to vote in periodic and genuine elections under universal suffrage and secret ballot;

- Article 22 – Social security and economic, social and cultural rights;
- Article 23 – Work, just remuneration and equal pay for equal work; the right to form and to join trade unions for the protection of his interests;
- Article 24 – Rest and leisure;
- Article 25 – An adequate standard of living and the protection of children;
- Article 26 – Education;
- Article 27– Participation in the cultural life of the community.

(United Nations, 1995: 23–7,
see http://www.un.org/en/documents/udhr/)

Article 3 specifies the right to life. However, we have seen that that does not make the death penalty necessarily illegal. Even this most fundamental right is a qualified one: it can be watered down, since there are circumstances under which the state may lawfully take the life of a citizen. Article 4 reads: 'no one shall be held in slavery or servitude; slavery and the slave trade shall be prohibited in all their forms'. This right is absolute: slavery is never permitted, and any state that engages in it is in violation of international law.

The box below lists some of the rights guaranteed in the European Convention on Human Rights. Although in content it is not dissimilar to the Universal Declaration of Human Rights, there are important differences. The most important difference is in practice: it is better observed (Merrills and Robertson, 2001). One reason for this is that the group of nations that subscribed to it is smaller in number and perhaps more homogeneous, as they are the member states of the Council of Europe. The more important reason is that this Convention (with its additional protocols) comes with a court of law to enforce it. The European Court of Human Rights in Strasbourg, France, is the venue where citizens in Europe can seek justice if they feel that human rights are violated by any member state within the Council of Europe. This is important: the European Court of Human Rights can override national legislation and national legislations have been changed as a result.

Excerpts from the European Convention on Human Rights

- Article 1 – Obligation to respect human rights;
- Article 2 – Right to life;
- Article 3 – Prohibition of torture;
- Article 4 – Prohibition of slavery and forced labour;
- Article 5 – Right to liberty and security;
- Article 6 – Right to a fair trial;

- Article 7 – No punishment without law;
- Article 8 – Right to respect for private and family life;
- Article 9 – Freedom of thought, conscience and religion;
- Article 10 – Freedom of expression;
- Article 11 – Freedom of assembly and association;
- Article 12 – Right to marry;
- Article 13 – Right to an effective remedy;
- Article 14 – Prohibition of discrimination;
- Article 15 – Derogation in time of emergency.

(see conventions.coe.int for this,
and all other, Council of Europe conventions)

Article 2 (the right to life) is the first article to specify a particular human right in the European Convention. Article 3 specifies the right to not be subject to torture or to cruel, inhuman or degrading treatment or punishment. Torture is defined as the intentional infliction of severe pain or suffering, whether physical or mental, by or with the consent of a public official, although it specifically excludes suffering attendant on the imposition of lawful punishments (Robinson, 1999). The fact that the torture must be carried out under the auspices of the state is important. Human rights particularly seek to protect citizens from the state and not from the wrongdoing of private citizens.

Important for comparative criminal justice purposes is Article 6, which secures the right to a fair and public trial by an independent and impartial tribunal for any criminal charge. It also enshrines the principle that the courts shall presume that anyone charged with a criminal offence is innocent until proved guilty. Minimum rights are specified in relation to being informed of the charge, being given time to prepare a defence, the right to legal representation, the right to call witnesses and the right to have the services of an interpreter.

Other rights include the right to marry and to be regarded as a family, the right to free movement, the right to freedom of opinion and expression and the right to privacy. This right to privacy requires explanation. Article 8 prohibits arbitrary interference with privacy, home or correspondence by state officials. Nevertheless, this right to privacy can also not be said to be absolute. After all, there might be legitimate reasons why the state would want to intercept citizens' mail, tap their telephones or enter their homes. Such reasons might involve a suspicion that a person has committed offences or might be planning a coup or a terrorist attack.

The current position, reinforced by the European Court of Human Rights, is that countries can invade the privacy of their citizens for law-enforcement purposes only if certain conditions are met. States must ensure that there is a procedure of prior authorisation (typically by a judge) in place, which law-enforcement officers must follow. Such a procedure is designed to safeguard against arbitrary or overzealous interference of state officials in the lives of citizens (Wright, 2002b).

Apart from citizens, states and non-governmental organisations may all seek access to the European Court. They can do this only when all routes to seek redress under the national legislation have been exhausted. That process will usually take years, so that the road to Strasbourg can be exasperating. Citizens who win their cases often get compensation. Apart from exerting an effect in individual cases, national laws have been known to be amended after the European Court has ruled that the application of that law violated a suspect's human rights.

The European Court consists of as many judges as the Council of Europe has member states. This does not mean that every member state is represented by one judge. There can be several judges from one country, and each judge is supposed to sit independently and not represent his/her country. The Court consists of four chambers and the judicial process is public and adversarial. Judgements are made by majority vote. Dissenting opinions can be added to the reasoned verdict. All final judgements of the Court are binding on the member states involved.

War-crimes tribunals

In the 1990s a pressing need for so-called war-crimes tribunals was identified after almost 50 years of stagnation in the furtherance of international criminal law. The atrocities on a scale not seen on the European continent since World War II that took place from 1991 in the territories of the Former Yugoslavia brought the resolution that the prosecution of individuals responsible should be part of the peace process. At the same time, the world was shocked by the eruption of violence and mass murder in the African state of Rwanda in 1994. A very similar tribunal was set up to deal with those responsible for these acts. Both the International Criminal Tribunal for the Former Yugoslavia (ICTY) and the International Criminal Tribunal for Rwanda (ICTR) were *ad hoc*: they were instigated for specific purposes and with narrowly defined jurisdictions. They were also meant to be temporary. Apart from discussing both present day tribunals we will also look their predecessors. These are the post-World War II tribunals in Nuremberg and Tokyo.

Military tribunals after World War II

After the end of World War II the allied powers France, the Soviet Union, the United Kingdom and the United States convened in London to decide on how to bring high-ranking Nazi war criminals to justice. On 8 August 1945 they signed the so-called London Agreement, which laid out the Statute of the Nuremberg International Tribunal and a set of guiding principles for the trial that was to be conducted. The allied powers nominated four judges, one from each country, and similarly four prosecutors. Defendants could be charged with one or more counts of three crimes: Crimes against Peace – mainly initiation of a war of aggression; War Crimes, which included murder or ill-treatment of prisoners of war or plundering of property; and Crimes against Humanity – inhumane acts committed against any civilian population.

In Nuremberg, the city of the Nazi party's headquarters, there were 22 defendants (Smeulers et al., 2013). They included Rudolf Hess, Hitler's deputy, Hermann Goering, commander-in-chief of the Nazi Air Force, and Albert Speer, the minister of armaments and war production. They were all tried together in one mega-trial after each defendant had pleaded not guilty. The trial lasted 11 months in 1945/1946 and was conducted by eight judges. There were three acquittals; 11 defendants received the death penalty. Eight others were given prison sentences. (Yale University runs a research project on the Nuremburg Trial. See www.yale.edu\lawweb\avalon\imt for a wealth of documentation.)

The so-called Tokyo Charter was drafted in Potsdam, near Berlin, in July 1945. It set out the constitution, jurisdiction and functions of the International Military Tribunal for the Far East, or, in short, the Tokyo Tribunal. Unlike the Nuremberg Statute this document was not the result of combined efforts by the Allied powers, but drafted exclusively by US officials. They decided that the bench should be composed of nine judges, and during the trial two judges were added. They did not come exclusively from victors' countries, but included representation from the Philippines and the Netherlands. The one prosecutor was American.

In the Tokyo trial there were 28 defendants, including the prime minister, the minister of foreign affairs, as well as several diplomats and high-ranking military figures. All pleaded not guilty. Nevertheless, all were found guilty on majority verdicts (either 9–2 or 8–3). One indictment was withdrawn. Seven defendants were sentenced to death. Others received prison sentences, ranging from seven years to life (Smeulers et al., 2013).

Both tribunals were landmark events in the history of international law. Never before were individuals accused and convicted of war crimes on the basis of individual or command responsibility. Nevertheless, both were subjected to severe criticism both at the time and by later generations. First, there is the legal issue of introducing legislation and applying it retrospectively. After-the-fact legislation is generally considered shaky, although the actions of the Japanese and German aggressors were widely considered criminal at the time anyway. The fact that what they did was not illegal in their native countries at the time was, probably appropriately, not given much weight.

Second, there was the distinct feeling that the tribunals were primarily about the winners of the war judging the conduct of those who were on the losing side. Various characteristics of both tribunals suggest this. The prosecutors and judges in Nuremberg were exclusively of victor countries. This was not the case in Tokyo, but here the statute was drafted exclusively by American officials. The suspicion that the USA was particularly keen to try Japanese officials to seek revenge for the Japanese surprise attack on Pearl Harbour in Hawaii may well have merit. As no individual from the Allied nations was ever investigated, let alone prosecuted, it appeared as if only nationals of the countries that lost the war could have committed war crimes. This selectivity is nowadays regarded as a serious shortcoming that present-day tribunals have been keen to avoid.

Further deficiencies related to the defence counsel in both trials. Because the USA was influential in both tribunals, the proceedings on the whole had a rather adversarial feel. Native trials in both Germany and Japan were at the time and still to a large extent today quite inquisitorial. The proceedings therefore must have felt alien both to defendants and their counsel. As Tokyo Judge Röling observed, 'the majority of the judges were accustomed to an Anglo-Saxon trial and gradually many Anglo-Saxon features crept into the proceedings by majority decision of the court. Thus it became a kind of trial Japanese lawyers were not accustomed to' (Cassese and Röling, 1993: 36).

When this became apparent it was agreed that each defendant be assigned a US defence counsellor, better equipped to operate effectively at trial. On the other hand, it must also be said that there were distinct inquisitorial elements in both trials. Defendants were permitted to give unsworn statements at the end of the trial. That is a typically inquisitorial feature. Additionally, the rules of evidence were as relaxed as they often are in inquisitorial systems. Evidence merely had to be probative to be admitted and hearsay evidence was allowed, and very frequently used. There also was no jury.

Another significant shortcoming was the fact that there was no appeals procedure. Defendants simply did not have that right. Those convicted in Nuremberg could request only the Control Council of Germany (the temporary Allied forces' administration in Germany) to reduce or change their sentences. All requests were rejected, and 10 of the 11 defendants who received death sentences were hanged two weeks later (the eleventh, Hermann Göring, had committed suicide in prison while awaiting execution). Whatever its shortcomings, Nuremburg justice certainly was swift.

The Yugoslavia and Rwanda tribunals

After 50 years of relative silence two present-day *ad hoc* war-crimes tribunals emerged in the 1990s. Both the International Criminal Tribunal for the Former Yugoslavia (ICTY) and the International Criminal Tribunal for Rwanda (ICTR) came into existence. It was the first time that such bodies had existed under the umbrella of the United Nations.

The ICTY was established in 1993 by the UN's Security Council. Its specific assignment is to prosecute and sentence persons responsible for the violations of international humanitarian law in the Former Yugoslavia since 1991. The part of its statute that constitutes the Criminal Code consists of four clusters of crimes. These are grave breaches of the Geneva Convention 1949 (Article 2 of the Statute), violations of the laws and customs of war (Article 3), genocide (Article 4) and crimes against humanity (Article 5). Genocide is defined as:

> Any of the following acts committed with intent to destroy, in whole or in part, a national, ethnical, racial or religious group, as such:
> - killing members of the group;
> - causing serious bodily or mental harm to members of the group;
> - deliberately inflicting on the group conditions of life calculated to bring about its physical destruction in whole or in part;
> - imposing measures intended to prevent births within the group;
> - forcibly transferring children of the group to another group.

Another novelty within the Statute is the status of the offence of rape. When rape takes place as a part of a systematic and widespread campaign it might constitute a crime against humanity, or even genocide following a recent ruling at the Rwanda Tribunal, as was discussed in the previous chapter. The Statute also specifies that both individual and command responsibility can make one guilty of such offences. Finally, acts as well as failures to act in order to stop atrocities from occurring may constitute war crimes and may accordingly fall under both tribunals' jurisdiction. It is also worthy of note that crimes against humanity, often used as a catch-all term for war crimes and other crimes of a global calibre, are specifically defined in ICTY's Statute (Akvahan, 1993; International Criminal Tribunal for the Former Yugoslavia, 1993).

The sister court of the Yugoslav Tribunal, the Rwanda Tribunal (ICTR), came into operation in 1995. The Security Council Resolution that led to the establishment of the Tribunal was, ironically, voted against by the state of Rwanda itself. The state had three objections. First, it wanted the tribunal to be able to impose the death penalty. Second, it wanted to give the tribunal jurisdiction over crimes going back to 1990, instead of to 1994. Finally, Rwanda proposed that the tribunal be based in Rwanda and that local judges conduct the trials. None of Rwanda's proposals were implemented. The Tribunal cannot impose capital punishment, the jurisdiction was not put back to 1990, the tribunal is based in Tanzania and the judges are not Rwandan (Robinson, 1999). The Tribunal consists of two trial chambers in Arusha, Tanzania, and an appeals chamber at the ICTY in The Hague, shared by both tribunals. ICTR's first completed trial was that of Jean-Paul Akayesu, former major of a town called Taba. On 2 September 1998 he was found guilty of genocide and crimes against humanity. The verdict was historic in the sense that it was the first conviction by a UN tribunal for genocide.

Both tribunals' legislators were keen to ensure that they would improve on the Nuremberg and Tokyo tribunals. A few differences between those earlier tribunals and the ICTY, in particular, are therefore worth discussing. First, in the Nuremberg and Tokyo trials there were certain restrictions placed on the conduct of the defence. Any potential wrongdoing by the Allied forces was not to be discussed as it was ruled not relevant to the charges being brought. The ICTY, in contrast, is not intended to be, and clearly does not want to be seen to be, a victor's tribunal, and neither does the ICTR.

The judges at the ICTY and ICTR more accurately represent the world community than the benches in Nuremberg or Tokyo. In both present-day tribunals judges are appointed after a vote by the UN's General Assembly. Finally, the judges in Nuremberg relied, to a relatively large extent, on paperwork, because sizeable dossiers containing documentary evidence were available to them. This measure to enhance the trials' expedience helped to ensure that the Nuremberg trial took no more than 11 months to complete. The Tokyo trial lasted approximately two and a half years. Because, at the Yugoslav Tribunal, the principles of immediacy and orality are much more strictly adhered to, some trials there involving a single defendant have lasted as long as the Nuremberg trial as a whole.

A consequence of the prime importance of what happens in the courtroom is that many vulnerable witnesses have to testify in court when, in the more inquisitorial trial systems, they would often not need to. The Yugoslav Tribunal has the full modern range of technological options available to accommodate the needs of vulnerable witnesses, such as video links, masking devices for appearance as well as voice distortion, while, on occasion, a satellite link with a witness in the Former Yugoslavia has been used.

ICTY in action

By April 2014 the ICTY had indicted 161 individuals. Proceedings have been completed against 97. In total 67 people have been sentenced, and there have been 17 acquittals. The work of the Tribunal is expected to end in 2015 (see Steinberg, 2011 for a detailed and in-depth collection of chapters on ICTY's legacy). The first was Erdemović, who was sentenced to five years' imprisonment. He has since completed his sentence in Norway. Erdemović was a typical foot soldier, a member of a firing squad who was ordered to shoot prisoners in Srebrenica. He estimated he killed about 70 people. Erdemović has provided information on many other crimes and has testified against head of state Slobodan Milošević.

Tochilovski has explained that the style of trial proceedings is predominantly adversarial. He has argued that this decision was informed not so much by theoretical assumptions underlying modes of trial, but by practical concerns. The advisors most forthcoming in the preparatory stage were said to be from an adversarial background, most notably from the USA, so that an adversarial system of trial proceedings emerged as the natural choice (Tochilovski, 1998).

An obvious departure from the adversarial tradition is the absence of juries anywhere in the proceedings. A panel of three judges decides on guilt as well as on sentencing. A majority finding of 2–1 is sufficient for a guilty verdict, a state of affairs that has not escaped criticism (Pruitt, 1997). Another difference is that the prosecutor at the ICTY has extensive rights of appeal against acquittals. Defendants have, unlike in Nuremberg or Tokyo, absolute rights to appeal against any conviction (O'Brien, 1993).

It is worth investigating further the role of the judges at trial. After all, they are the actual decision-makers on guilt or innocence as well as on sentencing; in addition, the rules of procedure allow them considerable latitude to decide how to conduct a trial. Since judges work at the tribunal for a limited period of time after having been on the bench in their home countries for, probably, many years, it is not unreasonable to assume that judges might 'bring their domestic legal culture with them' when they sit at this international court. One might expect judges accustomed to an adversarial manner of trial proceedings to be more reactive, and judges from an inquisitorial tradition to conduct their trials in a more active and domineering fashion.

There is evidence for judges conducting their trials differently depending on their background (Pakes, 2000b). When comparing the behaviour of American presiding judge MacDonald with French presiding judge Jorda clear differences can be found. The French judge asked a greater number of factual questions and interrupted examinations more often. The bench in the case with the French presiding judge also called a number of witnesses itself. The bench over which the American judge presided did not.

As always when discussing inquisitorial-versus-adversarial modes of justice, the question of which is more appropriate emerges. It could be argued that in the case of war-crimes tribunals the answer to that question is relatively straightforward. Indeed, a good case can be made for a relatively inquisitorial mode of trial procedure. After all, the tribunal is more than a platform for conflict resolution. One of its aims is the discovery of the complete truth of what happened. The ICTY itself is quite clear on this:

> Ensuring that history listens is a most important function of the Tribunal. Through our proceedings we strive to establish as judicial fact the full details of the madness that transpired in the former Yugoslavia. In the years and decades to come, no one will be able to deny the depths to which their brother and sister human beings sank. And by recording the capacity for evil in all of us, it is hoped to recognise warning signs in the future and to act with sufficient speed and determination to prevent such bloodshed.
>
> (ICTY, 1998: paragraph 294)

It is hard to overestimate the importance of this aim. It would therefore be fitting if the way in which the tribunal does its business bears it in mind. We have seen that finding the truth is a characteristic associated with inquisitorial justice in which the judge actively pursues the presentation of evidence. An active judge, whose duty will encompass an obligation towards the finding of the truth, is more appropriate in this regard than judges who regard it as their role to witness the battle between prosecution and defence unfold. Tochilovski (1998) has phrased this as the choice between trials as either battle or as scrutiny, with a preference for the latter.

Slobodan Milošević on trial

The trial of former Head of State Slobodan Milošević exposes both the strengths and the weaknesses of the ICTY. The strengths are obvious: the arrest and transfer of Milošević to The Hague highlights the fact that no one is immune from prosecution for crimes against humanity. It shows that the Tribunal has muscle, something that was severely doubted during the early days of its operations. It is telling that prosecutions began mainly focusing on lower-rank individuals such as execution squad member Erdemović. Their prosecutions have subsequently yielded further information that allowed investigators to go after the 'big fish'. The Milošević trial began in 2002. Pressure put on the Serb government by the United Nations and the United States was probably instrumental in bringing that about, as Milošević seemingly remained virtually untouchable in his home country.

Milošević was set from the start to test the very foundations of the ICTY. He refused to plead and refused to be assisted by a defence lawyer. Instead he conducted his own defence and examined witnesses directly and probably with disingenuous objectives. Bass (2003: 82) describes one exchange as follows:

> Milošević asks, serving as his own counsel, 'Based on my information, your wife's name is [deleted]?' As the Prosecution objects furiously, pointing out that Lazarevic is in a witness relocation program and demanding that his wife's name be stricken from the record, Milosevic adds, 'His wife worked as a [deleted].' It is a blatant attempt at intimidation: you mess with me; I mess with your family.

Because he conducted his own defence, Milošević was given time to study the law. As he became increasingly unwell, the trial was also much delayed for that reason. Milošević died of natural causes in 2006. The trial that started in 2002 was nowhere near its conclusion. This raises pertinent issues of the speed of justice at the ICTY. Feinberg (2006) refers to it as a dawdling process of justice. In addition, the death of Milošević highlights another shortcoming: it simply halts all proceedings, which raises the question whether that is satisfactory for victims and for the aim of establishing an objective historical record of the conflict. This is a consequence of the resolute focus on individual responsibility: Milošević stood trial personally, not his regime or the country of which he was head of state. When he died, the wheels of justice ground to an abrupt halt (see Waters, 2013 for an in-depth treatment of the legacy of the Milošević trial).

The Rwanda Tribunal: legal landmarks

At the time of writing (in 2014) the Rwanda Tribunal has indicted 95 individuals. There have been 14 acquittals and six cases have been terminated. In 2014, 32 are serving their sentence while 12 have already completed their sentence. A number of cases have been passed on to national courts. The Tribunal is expected to complete its business at the end of 2014. Jean-Paul Akayesu was the first person to be convicted at the Rwanda Tribunal (Magnarella, 1997). A former school teacher and school inspector, he was extradited from Zambia in 1995 and was convicted of nine counts including genocide, for which he was sentenced to life imprisonment. Importantly, the Court established that rape could constitute genocide, a landmark ruling (Weinberg De Roca, 2005).

> The Trial Chamber held that rape, which it defined as 'a physical invasion of a sexual nature committed on a person under circumstances which are coercive', and sexual assault constitute acts of genocide insofar as they were committed with the intent to destroy, in whole or in part, a targeted group, as such. It found that sexual assault formed an integral part of the process of destroying the Tutsi ethnic group and that the rape was systematic and had been perpetrated against Tutsi women only, manifesting the specific intent required for those acts to constitute genocide.
>
> (*The Prosecutor v. Jean Paul Akayesu* (ICTR-96-4-T))

As the Tribunal has its own detention facilities but not its own prison, Akayesu is serving his sentence elsewhere, in Mali. The Rwanda Tribunal also saw convictions for incitement to genocide in relation to a television station and also with reference to the notorious *Kangura* newspaper. Its editor Hassan Ngeze was indicted by the Tribunal as well as some of its financiers. It famously called Tutsis cockroaches and preached hate and uttered threats against the Tutsi minority.

Finally, Jean Kambanda was head of state of Rwanda when the genocide commenced. His background was in banking. Charged with genocide, he pleaded guilty and was therefore the first head of state actually convicted by a modern-day international criminal tribunal. Despite his guilty plea, Kambanda has afterwards argued that he was a mere puppet, put in place by the military and that his guilt referred to feeling politically responsible, not necessarily criminally responsible. His sentence was upheld and Kambanda currently serves his sentence in Mali. The conviction of Kambanda shows that today, the Westphalian doctrine of state sovereignty is very much limited by international criminal law. Appeals to sovereignty or state immunity no longer serve as protection against the workings of these tribunals, so that even heads of state are no longer above international criminal law.

So how do both tribunals compare? Their statutes are highly similar and so are many procedures such as trial proceedings and the selection of judges. The courts share an appeals court. You would therefore expect both courts to operate rather similarly. Smeulers et al. (2013) found indeed that the acquittal rates were 13 per cent for ICTY and 14 per cent for ICTR. In 2013 the number of indictments was 118 (ICTY) and 74 (ICTR). In terms of sentencing the Rwanda Tribunal has imposed life sentences more regularly, in 21 of 61 convictions in 2013. In ICTY this figure was 4 out of 81. Prison sentences that were not life were also longer in Rwanda, 22.6 years average versus 15.9 in ICTY. The appeal rate is very similar, 80 per cent (ICTY) versus 82 per cent (ICTR).

Looking at the profile of those convicted we see interesting patterns. In terms of rank, only 9 (11.1 per cent) of ICTY's and 17 (27.8 per cent) of ICTR's convicted perpetrators could be said to be high ranked. This is in contrast to both tribunals after World War II where virtually all defendants were top brass. Interestingly, at ICTY, the vast majority of convicted perpetrators were military officials (83 per cent). At ICTR this was only 23 per cent, indicating the high involvement of civilians in the Rwanda genocide. The ICTY is different in the sense that it has tried individuals from more than one side of the conflict. This did not occur in either Nuremburg or Tokyo. Both modern-day tribunals have only convicted one female perpetrator. Biljana Plavšić was a political figure of Bosnian Serb origin who was a former professor of biology. She was initially charged with genocide but further to plea bargaining was found guilty of one count of crimes against humanity and sentenced to 11 years' imprisonment. She has served her sentence in Sweden. Pauline Nyiramasuhuko was a former minister in Rwanda, with a background in social work and a law degree. She was convicted of incitement to genocide and genocidal rape.

Finally, it was found that at ICTY 40.5 per cent of convicted perpetrators went to university. In Rwanda this was 50 per cent. Overall, across a range of tribunals, Smeulers et al. found that 95 per cent of perpetrators were married and 95 per cent had children. Very few had a criminal record prior to their involvement in human rights violations.

The International Criminal Court

Both the ICTY and ICTR have increased the profile of international justice tremendously. The next step, that probably is even more radical, is the establishment of a permanent International Criminal Court (ICC). In 1998 the decision was made to establish such a court at the Rome Conference. The reasons for its establishment have been given as follows.

The principal aim is to achieve justice for all. An international criminal tribunal has been described as the missing link in criminal justice. Its establishment will help to achieve justice for victims of genocide and crimes against humanity where in the past this was not achieved. Effective deterrence is another primary objective. It is hoped that those who would incite genocide, embark on a campaign of ethnic cleansing, murder or rape, or use children for barbarous medical experiments, should no longer find willing helpers. To what extent warmongers will indeed be deterred by the abstract threat of being tried before a tribunal in a foreign country remains to be seen.

Third, the International Criminal Court should enhance the prospects of a lasting peace. Although there is a question of the extent to which peace and justice may be achieved simultaneously, both the existing *ad hoc* tribunals and the ICC are clear in their intention to help to secure peace by bringing those responsible for war crimes to justice. Finally, this court should not suffer from the deficiencies of *ad hoc* tribunals, which by definition are established only after the fact. As investigations are best carried out when the events are still fresh, the ICC would have an obvious advantage.

The following quotation of the then UN Secretary General Kofi Annan illustrates the optimism and good will that underlies the establishment of a permanent war–crimes tribunal:

> In the prospect of an international criminal court lies the promise of universal justice. That is the simple and soaring hope of this vision. We are close to its realisation. We will do our part to see it through till the end. We ask you ... to do yours in our struggle to ensure that no ruler, no State, no junta and no army anywhere can abuse human rights with impunity. Only then will the innocents of distant wars and conflicts know that they, too, may sleep under the cover of justice; that they, too, have rights, and that those who violate those rights will be punished.
>
> (Kofi Annan, http://legal.un.org/icc/general/overview.htm)

The International Criminal Court Statute clearly defines what it deems a crime against humanity. It states that crime against humanity means any of the following acts when committed as part of a widespread or systematic attack directed against any civilian population, with knowledge of the attack:

(a) Murder;
(b) Extermination;
(c) Enslavement;
(d) Deportation or forcible transfer of population;
(e) Imprisonment or other severe deprivation of physical liberty in violation of fundamental rules of international law;
(f) Torture;
(g) Rape, sexual slavery, enforced prostitution, forced pregnancy, enforced sterilisation, or any other form of sexual violence of comparable gravity;
(h) Persecution against any identifiable group or collectivity on political, racial, national, ethnic, cultural, religious, gender or other grounds that are universally recognised as impermissible under international law, in connection with any act referred to in this paragraph or any crime within the jurisdiction of the court;

(i) Enforced disappearance of persons;
(j) The crime of apartheid;
(k) Other inhumane acts of a similar character intentionally causing great suffering, or serious injury to body or to mental or physical health.

Despite these seemingly good intentions, the practicalities of establishing a Statute have proved to be extremely difficult. A main bone of contention relates to the role and powers of the prosecutor. In many countries it was felt that the prosecutor should enjoy complete independence, in particular from the UN and its Security Council. Others, most notably the USA, felt that these powers should be constrained. The underlying reason is the idea that when a prosecutor has unlimited freedom in deciding where and when to investigate, this might hamper the maintenance of peace in those regions. It also involves the risk of frivolous or political prosecutions.

To counter such issues the suggestion was made that the UN Security Council have the final say with regard to giving the go-ahead for prosecutions. However, the fact that certain countries in the Security Council have the right to veto decisions might, in effect, mean that these countries are able to prevent prosecutions taking place. It has been argued that the USA's preference for this arrangement is a means to ensure that US nationals are unlikely ever to appear as defendants at the ICC.

The concession that has been made is that the Security Council's agreement is required when prosecutions are intended to be brought against individuals in non-UN member states. This occurred in May 2014 as it became clear that investigations in Syria were terminated further to a Russian veto in the Security Council. This shows the profound entanglement of justice, politics and international relations. The Security Council may also request prosecutions be halted for a one-year period. Nevertheless, the USA is one of the countries that has not ratified the Statute. Another non-signatory is Israel. It is debatable to what extent a tribunal that lacks the support of the USA can have an impact on the reinforcement of human rights on a global scale. After all, the tribunal will not have a police force, and will rely on states for funding, information and the apprehension of suspects. When the USA is unwilling to be involved, the court's ability to act could be severely curtailed.

The ICC was slow in getting off the ground for two reasons. The first is that it took four years for the UN resolution to gather the 60 ratifications required for it to formally become operational. The second is that the Court has had very little business in its early years. It has been controversial from the very start, with the USA, Israel, China and Russia so far refusing to ratify the UN resolution that established it.

Thus far the ICC case load is meagre. Four states have been referrals regarding ongoing situations in their country. These are Uganda, DR Congo, the Central African Republic and Mali. Two referrals have been made by the UN Security Council, regarding the situation in Darfur, Sudan and Libya. Two situations are examined through the initiative of the ICC's prosecutor. These are Kenya and Côte d'Ivoire. These investigations have led to 36 indictments. So far there have been three convictions (all now on appeal), five acquittals, and three indictees have died, most famously the former Libyan leader Muammar al-Gaddafi. Thomas Lubanga of DR Congo has the questionable honour of being the first accused to stand trial at the International Criminal Court. He led a rebel army called the Union of Congolese Patriots (UPC). The trial started in January 2009. Many of the charges concern the enlisting of child soldiers. He was convicted in 2012 and sentenced to 14 years in prison.

Meanwhile, the election of Barack Obama as US president might lead to a significant change of direction regarding the US attitude to the ICC. It was one of outright hostility for years although the position probably had softened somewhat near the end of George Bush's second term. When asked his position prior to his election Obama responded in a way that is highly encouraging:

> Now that it is operational, we are learning more and more about how the ICC functions. The Court has pursued charges only in cases of the most serious and systemic crimes and it is in America's interests that these most heinous of criminals, like the perpetrators of the genocide in Darfur, are held accountable. These actions are a credit to the cause of justice and deserve full American support and cooperation. Yet the Court is still young, many questions remain unanswered about the ultimate scope of its activities, and it is premature to commit the U.S. to any course of action at this time.
> (The American Society of International Law, 2008,
> www.amicc.org/docs/Obama%20on%20ICC.pdf)

Jessberger and Geneuss (2012) have argued that judging the performance of the ICC is difficult. One reason for that is the fact that in essence it serves three functions. The first is that of a criminal court. Apart from its practical value, which will always be limited due to resources and to the fact that selectivity is inevitably going to occur, there is real symbolic value in its existence. Tallgren (2002) says that the ICC serves as a loudspeaker echoing the values of the international community. But the ICC's second role is quite different: it is a watchdog court, or court of last resort: the ICC should only come into play when national courts cannot or will not undertake prosecutions. This is, Jessberger and Geneuss (2012) argue, somewhat at odds with the practice of states self-referring situations to the ICC. Is this using the Court as a last resort or does it in fact amount to outsourcing of prosecutions? Finally, the ICC can be construed as a security court. This is evident in cases where the UN Security Council refers cases to the ICC. That could mean that the ICC becomes part of the Security Council mission to restore peace in cases of ongoing conflict. That makes the Court part of a broader diplomatic network and may be governed by *realpolitik* rather than exclusively serving the interests of justice. This may politicise the ICC and make it become a tool to be used by the hegemonic nations with permanent seats on the UN Security Council. All this shows the highly delicate and multifaceted positioning that the ICC is subjected to.

All that said, the International Criminal Court will gain further credibility as well as increase its reputation should the United States indeed decide to come on board. That should put further pressure on other states that thus far fail to recognise the Court. Now that the business of the ICC is properly underway, practice at the Court may also over time convince the doubters. Thus, after a very hesitant start, perhaps the time for the ICC to blossom has now come, but we must remember that the security aspect of its functioning may always leave room for doubt as to the true motives behind ICC prosecutions.

The International Court of Justice

The final court I shall discuss is the International Court of Justice. This court has, for a long time, been the principal judicial organ of the United Nations. Its seat is at the Peace Palace in The Hague, the Netherlands. It began work in 1946, when it replaced the Permanent Court of International Justice that had been in operation at the same venue since 1922. Its main role is to settle, in accordance with international law, the legal disputes submitted to it by member states. (See www.icj-cij.org, which is the source for many of the details below.)

The court is composed of 15 judges, who are elected to nine-year terms of office by the United Nations General Assembly and Security Council, sitting independently of each other. It may not include more than one judge of any nationality. Elections are held every three years for one-third of the seats. The members of the court do not represent their governments but sit as independent magistrates.

The judges must possess the qualifications required in their respective countries for appointment to the highest judicial offices, or be jurists of recognised competence in international law. As is the case for the International Criminal Court the composition of the court has to reflect representatively the main cultures and the principal legal systems of the world. In 2009, the 15 judges were from Japan, Slovakia, China, Sierra Leone, Jordan, the USA, Germany, France, New Zealand, Mexico, Morocco, Russian Federation, Brazil, Somalia and the UK.

Only states may apply to, and their representatives appear before, the court. The cases that the court tends to be involved with include disputes between countries over land and maritime boundaries. As it is more of a civil-type court than one to do with criminal justice, this description will suffice here.

Conclusion

International criminal justice has intensified enormously since the end of World War II. The days in which dictators and organisers of genocide and other crimes against humanity could assume to be immune from prosecution have indeed gone. In order to understand how that came about, a number of observations are worth making. The first is to do with historic windows of opportunity. The end of World War II led to the establishment of two war crimes tribunals but historically more important were perhaps the establishment of the UN Declaration of Human Rights and the Geneva Conventions. The fall of the Berlin Wall was another watershed event signalling the end of the Cold War. Only since the 1990s was there sufficient political will to put tribunals in place, initially *ad hoc* but subsequently a permanent Court. Despite its slow start, its existence is of huge symbolic and of increasing practical importance.

What the International Criminal Court has failed to achieve, however is to erase the need for further *ad hoc* tribunals. *Ad hoc* international courts exist in many places such as a Special Court in Sierra Leone, Special Tribunals in Kosovo, as well as Extraordinary Chambers in Cambodia and the Tribunal for East Timor (Shraga, 2004). Within many areas devastated by war or dictatorial rule, there seems to be a strong desire to do justice against crimes against humanity, not in one international tribunal somewhere far away but in a local setting. It highlights the fact that international law is there to provide local justice. The International Court is unlikely to be the panacea. Instead, it is and probably should be a court of last resort.

A final development worth noting is that international law can be applied through national legislation. The UK has adopted the International Criminal Court Act 2001. It has incorporated into domestic law the offences contained in the Rome Statute that established the ICC. It also allows persons convicted by the ICC to serve prison sentences in the United Kingdom. That means that should a British citizen commit a crime that would fall under the ICC's jurisdiction, they can be effectively tried in domestic courts in the UK. Corporal Donald Payne was in fact the first individual convicted in 2006 under its provisions and convicted of inhumanely treating civilians in Iraq. The message is that the more nations adopt international law standards in their jurisdictions and utilise these effectively, the fewer cases are there for the ICC to pick up. That should ensure that it remains as intended, a court of last resort.

Further reading

Holá, B., Bijleveld, C., and Smeulers, A. (2012) Consistency of international sentencing: ICTY and ICTR case study. *European journal of criminology, 9*, 539–52.

Jessberger, F. and Geneuss, J. (2012) The many faces of the International Criminal Court. *Journal of international criminal justice, 10*, 1081–94.

Waters, T.W. (Ed) (2013) *The Milosevic trial: an autopsy.* Oxford: Oxford University Press.

Study questions

1   Why is evaluating the work of the International Criminal Court so difficult?
2   Outline and describe three achievements of the *ad hoc* tribunals ICTY and ICTR.
3   Outline and describe three shortcomings of ICTY and ICTR.

Chapter 12

Concluding comments

A number of current developments in criminal justice are as depressing as they are obvious. Prison rates worldwide are increasing steadily, despite accumulating evidence that imprisonment for the most part does more harm than good. We explained the punitive turn in Western democracies partly in terms of penal populism which involves an interplay between public discourse, governmental intent and the perceived wishes of the electorate. At the same time, punishment in less democratic states, nowhere more so than in China, is of a scale that dwarfs punishments in most other parts of the world. At the same time however, slow but steady progress is made towards a diminishing use of the death penalty although numerous examples to the contrary exist, with Egypt's recent mass trials that led to death penalty sentences an outrageous low point.

There is also good news: the Netherlands from 1950 to 1975 and Finland from 1950 to also have successfully achieved a dramatic reduction in prisoner numbers – important examples of decarceration. This shows that 'against the grain' policies can be successful in the long term although Pratt (2008b) does argue that Nordic penal exceptionalism is under threat, but in some locales more than others. Another interesting development is the rise of diversion and alternative dispute resolution in criminal justice. Although detailed research is required in order to come to terms with its exact nature and extent in various countries, there are hopeful signs of both a community orientation and an indigenisation of criminal justice procedures, away from punishment and towards a constructive dialogue between the various parties in conflict.

Finally, the rise of international justice must, despite reservations, be another example of developments that we can applaud. It ends the immunity that the architects of genocide and other crimes against humanity have enjoyed for much of human history. Through legal developments that bring sexual violence within the concept of genocide, and also the broadening of individual and command responsibility, international criminal justice seems to be more in tune with our knowledge of how such events occur. Despite the serious shortcomings of the International Criminal Court, simply not having such a court is no longer an option and there is hope that its influence will strengthen in the years ahead.

There are also hopeful signs in relation to the development and status of the field of comparative criminal justice. We can now say that some of our discipline's most prolific and influential scholars very explicitly engage in comparative research. The work of Aas is often quoted in this book and the work of eminent scholars such as Nelken (e.g. 2011), Bowling and Sheptycki (2012) and Crawford (2011) have raised the profile of the comparative project in criminology.

In addition the scope of the field is widening. There is now a rapidly growing area of comparative genocide. That that represents a major change for the better in criminology is something that few could argue with. In other areas, comparative research has seen remarkable developments as to the production of knowledge. In relation to the factors underlying prison rates, impressive work has taken place in the last decade (e.g, Lacey, 2011). Finally, globalisation, neoliberalisation and state crime are more in view than before. That helps ensure that comparative criminology remains at the cutting edge of social science, rather than as a niche endeavour. The fact that Nelken (2011) has devoted an edited collection to the very questions that globalisation asks of comparative criminology is telling.

Apart from punishment as a core concern, criminology is increasingly concerned with surveillance as a form of social control. Rather than controlling and correcting offenders after the fact the focus has shifted towards prevention as a key concern. Surveillance often occurs via CCTV and via the monitoring of Internet traffic and other forms of specialist technology. Surveillance does not only serve to spot or deter crime but also to monitor movement of people and goods. It is often said that surveillance and control is about stemming flows, controlling gateways and other forms of restricting movement. Borders are particularly meaningful in achieving this objective.

I have discussed globalisation at various points in this book. When we are looking for new directions in comparative criminal justice it is safe to assume that globalisation will affect virtually all future developments in comparative criminal justice. Although it is often emphasised that criminals travel more easily than ever before, it may well be the case that criminal justice notions still spread around the globe even more unrestrictedly. Jones and Newburn's (2007) work on policy transfer is important in understanding how these processes work. Similarly, the work of Andreas and Nadelmann (2006) demonstrates how global criminalisations occur and emphasises the role the global moral entrepreneurs play.

Globalisation means interconnectedness. The trend simply is that comparative criminal justice will be less about comparing distant and distinct entities and will be increasingly about the study of the flow of persons, goods and ideas that makes these once separate and self-contained arrangements more interconnected. Perhaps this is the most profound change that has taken place in the study of comparative criminal justice arrangements. It is no longer about pure difference but about, as Sheptycki puts it 'diffusely intermingled difference'.

There is of course a certain romanticism about old-fashioned comparative research. It was for the intrepid explorer, the traveller who leaves the comfort zone of home to immerse themselves in foreign climes and cultures. It is true that participant observation remains a key tool in comparative research, but for few if any researchers is the Internet not the starting point as well as a base for comparative research. Contemporary comparative research is essentially multimethod: researchers explore official publications via the web prior to speaking to officials in person. They read newspaper accounts and engage with citizen journalistic efforts before and after directly talking to people affected by criminal justice. They are informed and look for juxtapositions between information from the various sources. It is also the case in many places that reliable information is more easily acquired outside the country at issue than inside it. This is particularly the case where censorship is strong and other forms of state control are in place, as we saw is the case in China. That should not preclude visits so that the researcher can put their ear to the ground. However, it does emphasise that researching criminal justice in a place like China certainly in part needs to take place outside it. The despatialisation that globalisation has brought about also affects comparative study.

Just as new media have enhanced the study of comparative criminal justice, new media could also be used in order to enhance its impact. Just as sociology, and in its slipstream criminology, have discussed the possible emergence of public sociology and public criminology, perhaps there ought to be such a thing as public comparative criminology. It is perhaps now time to consider how to make major findings – on genocide, on state crime, on punitivity and the global crime drop – have more impact. It is perhaps the public face of comparative research that should be the focus of future debates.

Finally, comparative research allows us to be more precise in relation to how criminal justice systems develop. Globalisation as we have seen produces a drive towards convergence, but from below, tendencies towards difference remain strong. So what makes criminal justice systems more similar? The perception of common enemies, such as cyber-crime and terrorism, constitute a factor that binds criminal justice systems. They serve as a driving force for convergence: what are perceived as common threats will invite common responses, which will increase the similarities in criminal justice systems around the world. However, common threats are not the only way in which similarities between systems can be explained. A number of mechanisms for convergence have been described by Fairchild and Dammer (2001).

The first is foreign domination. This explains, as we have seen, changes to criminal justice in Japan, and also explains why many colonies or former colonies have criminal justice systems not dissimilar to those of the colonial powers. Just as the inquisitorial system of justice was exported across Europe during the Napoleonic era, so has the British Empire left a common-law legacy across the world. A second reason why systems might be similar is imitation. Many former colonies still look to the old colonial power for examples, and because the systems are often still quite similar, features from the one are often relatively easy to incorporate into the other.

A further reason for convergence is simultaneous development. This is the case with regard to measures against cyber-crime and terrorism: the threats are perceived in a similar way in various countries at the same time, and measures are developed that are similar (although by no means identical) as well. Many states, for instance, have adopted the FBI definition of terrorism.

A third reason relates to international regulation. Returning to the example of anti-terrorist legislation, international bodies such as the United Nations and the European Union specify the measures that members should take. Such specifications do not spell out exactly what needs to be done, but room for manoeuvre is often limited, and the resulting pieces of legislation are likely to be similar. The force of global prohibition regimes must also not be underestimated.

The opposing force, diversification or diversion, may arise from two mechanisms. The first is termed 'cultural persistence'. In the present context this can be defined as a tendency to resist the import of foreign programmes or structures and to persist with the arrangements that exist nationally. The stronger version of cultural persistence is indigenisation. While cultural persistence seeks to maintain a state of affairs, indigenisation seeks to change structures or processes so that they more closely resemble the 'original' or indigenous arrangements that existed in the past. This is certainly occurring in many former colonies. Under the indigenisation denominator fall certain arrangements such as the informal conflict-resolution processes that have been resurrected following the end of colonial rule.

A third set of processes may refer to pluralism. This can certainly be discerned in systems of justice so that trial and conflict resolution platforms become more patchwork-like. The detail of these patchworks will differ from one place to the next but pluralisation is a common factor in comparative criminal justice: Sharī'ah courts operate alongside secular criminal justice systems in an increasing number of countries; private security is in operation alongside the police; alternative dispute resolution functions as an addition to, and not a replacement for, regular arrangements. Pluralisation occurs at different levels: state governments may set legal boundaries within which local actors may find a great deal of room for manoeuvre. Local solutions, in particular in the realm of cannabis, may be picked up in other local areas in a way that simply bypasses the state. In this way, pluralisation may account for both an increased level of similarity as well as difference: similarity at the level of local implementations but difference in how the whole of the patchwork shapes up.

Fairchild and Dammer (2001) have also argued that change in criminal justice often comes about through a mixture of such converging and diverging forces. The example quoted is that of the Japanese police force. Initially, the very idea of a police force intended to deal with crime and public order was imported from the West. After its importation, which can be said to have been an instance of convergence via a process one could call imitation, it has developed into something that truly fits the Japanese context and has thus diversified away from the Western policing blueprint. Such an indigenised process of innovation highlights the value of culturally sensitive comparative criminal justice research.

Nevertheless, the globalisation of crime and of criminal justice is likely to increase the pressure on convergence. New measures against novel forms of crime are likely to be, to an extent, directed by international regulations, which will enhance their similarities. The fact that information about foreign criminal justice systems is easier to obtain than ever before also makes it more likely that policy-makers will look abroad for examples. The variety with regard to trial procedures, sentences and judicial decision-makers might well, in the future, become less bewildering than it is today.

On one hand, this constitutes a loss. However, criminal justice systems are not like the natural world, where we should celebrate diversity for its own sake. Increased requirements for communication and harmonisation provide rewards for convergence, and criminal justice systems will, after all, be judged on their effectiveness. And one can remain sure that as long as cultures, languages, public opinions and social discourses differ, so will criminal justice systems and the way they operate.

References

Aas, K.F. (2005) Getting ahead of the game: Border technologies and the changing space of governance. In: E. Zureik and M.B. Salter (Eds) *Global surveillance and policing: Borders, security, identity*. Cullompton, Devon: Willan, 194–214.

Aas, K.F. (2007) *Globalisation and crime*. London: Sage.

Abdo, M. (2011) Legal pluralism, Sharī'ah courts, and constitutional issues in Ethiopia. *Mizan law review, 5*, 72–104.

Abrahamsen, R. and Williams, M.C. (2006) Security sector reform: Bringing the private in. *Conflict, security and development, 6*, 1–23.

Akvahan, P. (1993) Punishing war crimes in the Former Yugoslavia: A critical juncture for the new world order. *Human rights quarterly, 15*, 262–89.

Alaska Justice Reform (1996) Village Alaska: Community characteristics and public safety. *Alaska justice reform, 12*, 1–5.

Alderson, J. (1979) *Policing freedom*. Plymouth: Macdonald and Evans.

Alvazzi del Frate, A. (1998) *Victims of crime in the developing countries*. UNICRI Publication no 57. Rome: UNICRI.

Alvazzi del Frate, A. (2010) Crime and criminal justice statistics challenges. In: S. Harrendorf, M. Heiskanen and S. Malby (Eds) *International statistics on crime and justice*. Helsinki: HEUNI and Vienna: United Nations Office on Drugs and Crime, 167–75.

Ambler, L. (2007) The people decide: The effect of the introduction of the quasi-jury system (Saiban-In Seido) on the death penalty in Japan. *NorthWestern University journal of international human rights, 6*, 1–23.

Amnesty International (2001) *Death penalty news, 3/4* (October 2001).

Amnesty International (2008a) *Philippines submission to the UN Universal Periodic Review. First session of the UPR working group, 7–18 April 2008*. Available on line: http://www. amnesty.org/en/library/asset/ASA35/006/2007/en/eec90aaf-a2e7-11dc-8d74-6f45f39984e5/asa350062007en.pdf (accessed 15/7/2014).

Amnesty International (2008b) *Ratifications of international treaties to abolish the death penalty*. Amnesty International, 31 December 2008.

Anderson, B. (1983) *Imagined communities*. London: Verso.

Anderson, M., Den Boer, M., Cullen, P., Gilmore, W.C., Raab, C.D. and Walker, N. (1995) *Policing the European Union: Theory, law and practice*. Oxford: Clarendon Press.

Andreas, P. (2011) Illicit globalization: myths, misconceptions, and historical lessons. *Political science quarterly, 126*(3), 403–25.

Andreas, P. and Nadelmann, E. (2006) *Policing the globe: Criminalization and crime control in international relations*. New York: Oxford University Press.

Aremu, A.O., Pakes, F. and Johnston, L. (2009) Locus of control and self-efficacy as means of tackling police corruption in Nigeria. *International journal of police science and management, 11,* 97–107.

Aromaa, K. and Heiskanen, M. (Eds) (2008) *Crime and criminal justice systems in Europe and North America 1995–2004.* Helsinki: HEUNI.

Ashworth, A. (1998) *The criminal process.* Oxford: Oxford University Press.

Auld, A. (2001) *Review of the criminal courts of England and Wales.* London: Lord Chancellor's Department.

Australian Bureau of Statistics (2006) *Law and justice statistics – Aboriginal and Torres Strait Islander people: a snapshot.* Canberra: Australian Bureau of Statistics.

Awit, J.G. (2007) Cardinal urges: Know more than inmates' dances. *Sun Star Cebu,* 7 November 2007.

Baker, B. (2013) Where formal and informal justice meet: Ethiopia's justice pluralism. *Journal of international and comparative law, 21,* 202–18.

Baker, B. and Scheye, E. (2007) Multi-layered justice and security delivery in post-conflict and fragile states. *Conflict, security and development, 7,* 503–28.

Baldwin, J. (1985) *Pre-trial justice: A study of case settlement in Magistrates' Courts.* Oxford: Blackwell.

Bannenberg, B. (2000) Victim–offender mediation in Germany. In: The European Forum for Victim–Offender Mediation and Restorative Justice (Ed) *Victim–offender mediation in Europe: Making restorative justice work.* Leuven: Leuven University Press, 251–79.

Barker, V. (2013) Nordic exceptionalism revisited: Explaining the paradox of a Janus-faced penal regime. *Theoretical criminology, 17,* 5–25.

Barr, H. (2001) Policing madness: People with mental illness and the NYPD. In: A. McArdle and T. Erzen (Eds) *Zero tolerance: Quality of life and the new police brutality in New York City.* New York: New York University Press, 50–84.

Barrett, A. and Harrison, C. (1999) *Crime and punishment in England: A source book.* London: UCL Press.

Bass, G.J. (2003) Milosevic in The Hague. *Foreign Affairs, 82,* 82–96.

Bauman, Z. (2013) *Modernity and the holocaust.* Chichester: Wiley.

Bayley, D.H. (1985) *A model of community policing: The Singapore story.* Washington, DC: US Department of Justice.

Bayley, D.H. (1991) *Forces of order: Police behaviour in Japan and the United States (2nd edition).* Berkeley: University of California Press.

Bayley, D.H. (1994) *Police for the future.* Oxford: Oxford University Press.

Bayley, D.H. (1996) Policing: The world stage. *Journal of criminal justice education, 7,* 241–51.

Bayley, D.H. (1999) Policing: The world stage. In: R. Mawby (Ed) *Policing across the world: Issues for the twenty-first century.* London: Routledge, 1–22.

BBC (2007) *Afghan judges' bodies discovered.* Available on line: http://news.bbc.co.uk/1/hi/world/south_asia/6925363.stm (accessed 15/7/2014).

Beck, U. and Sznaider, N. (2006) Unpacking cosmopolitanism for the social sciences: A research agenda. *British journal of sociology, 57,* 1–23.

Bedau, A.H. (1996) The United States. In: P. Hodgkinson and A. Rutherford (Eds) *Capital punishment: Global issues and prospects.* Winchester: Waterside Press, 45–76.

Bedau, A.H. and Ratelet, M.L. (1987) Miscarriages of justice in potentially capital cases. *Stanford law review, 40,* 21–79.

Beirne, P., and Nelken, D. (Eds) (1997) *Issues in comparative criminology.* Farnham: Ashgate/Dartmouth.

Bennett, R.R. (2011) Comparative criminological and criminal justice research and the data that drive them. *International journal of comparative and applied criminal justice, 33,* 171–92.

Benyon, J., Turnbull, L., Willis, A. and Woodward, R. (1993) *Police cooperation in Europe: An investigation.* Leicester: CSPO.

Benyon, J., Turnbull, L., Willis, A. and Woodward, R. (1994) Understanding police cooperation in Europe: Setting a framework for analysis. In: M. Anderson and M. Den Boer (Eds) *Policing across national boundaries.* London: Pinter, 46–65.

Birkbeck, C. (1993) Against ethnocentrism: A cross-cultural perspective on criminal justice theories and policies. *Journal of criminal justice education, 4,* 307–23.

Blackburn, A.G. and Matthews, M. (2011) Crime and punishment in Ethiopia: A country profile. *International journal of comparative and applied criminal justice, 35,* 167–81.

Block, L. (2012) European joint investigation teams: Political ambitions and police practices. In: S. Hufnagel, C. Harfield and S. Bronitt (Eds) *Cross-border law enforcement: Regional law enforcement cooperation: European, Australian and Asia-Pacific perspectives.* Abingdon: Routledge, 73–86.

Blom, M. and Smit, P. (2006) The prosecution service function within the Dutch criminal justice system. In: J-M. Jehle and M. Wade (Eds) *Coping with overloaded criminal justice systems: The rise of prosecutorial power across Europe.* Berlin/Heidelberg: Springer, 237–56.

Body-Gendrot, S. (2000) *The social control of cities? A comparative perspective.* London: Blackwell.

Bowling, B. and Sheptycki, J. (2012) *Global policing.* London: Sage.

Braithwaite, J. (1989) *Crime, shame and reintegration.* Cambridge: Cambridge University Press.

Brandts, C. and Field, S. (1995) Discretion and accountability in prosecution: A comparative perspective on keeping cases out of court. In: P. Fennell, C. Harding, N. Jörg and B. Swart (Eds) *Criminal justice in Europe: A comparative study.* Oxford: Clarendon Press, 127–48.

Bratton, W. (1997) Crime is down in New York City: Blame the police. In: N. Dennis (Ed) *Zero tolerance: Policing a free society.* London: Institute of Economic Affairs, 29–43.

Brison, K.J. (1999) Imagining a nation in Kwanga village courts, East Sepik Province, Papua New Guinea. *Anthropological quarterly, 72,* 74–85.

Brodeur, J.P. (1982) High policing and low policing: remarks about the policing of political activities. *Social problems, 30,* 507–20.

Brodeur, J.P. (2007) High and low policing in post-9/11 times. *Policing, 1*(1), 25–37.

Bruyn, S. (1966) *The Human perspective in sociology: The methodology of participant observation.* Englewood Cliffs, NJ: Prentice-Hall.

Bryman, A. (2012) *Social research methods (4th edition).* Oxford: Oxford University Press.

Button, M. (1999) Private security and its contribution to policing: Under-researched, under-utilized and underestimated. *International journal of police science and management, 2,* 103–16.

Button, M. (2002) *Private policing.* Cullompton, Devon: Willan.

Button, M. (2007) Assessing the regulation of the private security industry across Europe. *European Journal of criminology, 4,* 109–28.

Byrne, J. (2008) Russia to scrap jury trials for wide range of crimes. *Prison planet,* 13 December 2008.

Canivell, J.M. (no date) Spain. In: *The world factbook of criminal justice systems.* Available on line: http://www.bjs.gov/content/pub/ascii/WFBCJSPN.TXT (accessed 1572014).

Carcach, C. and McDonald, D. (1997) *National police custody survey.* Research and public policy series, no. 9. Canberra: Australian Institute of Criminology.

Cassese, A. and Röling, B.V.A. (1993) *The Tokyo Trial and beyond*. Cambridge: Polity Press.

Castberg, A.D. (1990) *Japanese criminal justice*. New York: Praeger.

Cavadino, P. and Dignan, J. (2011) Penal comparisons: Puzzling relations. In: A. Crawford (Ed) *International and comparative criminal justice and urban governance*. Cambridge: Cambridge University Press, 193–213.

Cheesman, N. (2011) How an authoritarian regime in Burma used special courts to defeat judicial independence. *Law and society review, 45*, 802–30.

Choe, D.H. (2013) Discretion at the pre-trial stage: A comparative study. *European journal of criminal policy and research, 20*, 1–19.

Chomsky, N. (1998) *Profit over people: Neoliberalism and global order*. New York: Seven Stories Press.

Christie, N. (1977) Conflicts as property. *British journal of criminology, 17*, 1–15.

Christie, N. (1994) *Crime control as an industry (2nd edition)*. London: Routledge.

Churchill, W. (1946) *Speech by Winston Churchill, Zürich Switzerland*. Available on line: http://www.coe.int/t/dgal/dit/ilcd/archives/selection/churchill/ZurichSpeech_en.asp (accessed 15/7/2014).

Clegg, I. and Whetton, J. (1995) In search of a Third World criminology. In: L. Noaks, M. Levi and M. Maguire (Eds) *Contemporary issues in criminology*. Cardiff: University of Wales Press, 26–51.

Clinard, M.B. and Abbott, D.J. (1973) *Crime in developing countries*. New York: Wiley.

Cohen, S. (1985) *Visions of social control*. Cambridge: Polity Press.

Cole, B.A. (1999) Post-colonial systems. In: R.I. Mawby (Ed) *Policing across the world: Issues for the twenty-first century*. London: UCL Press, 88–108.

Cole, F., Frankowski, S.J. and Gerz, M.G. (1987) Comparative criminal justice: An introduction. In: *Major criminal justice systems: A comparative study (2nd edition)*. Newbury Park: Sage, 15–26.

Comins-Richmond, W. (2004) Legal pluralism in the Northwest Caucasus: The role of Sharī'ah Courts. *Religion, state and society, 32*, 59–73.

Comte, A. (1865) *A General View of Positivism*, J.H. Bridges (Trans). Paris: Trubner and Co. (reissued by Cambridge University Press, 2009).

Corstens, G. (2008) *Het Nederlands strafprocesrecht (6th edition)*. Amsterdam: Kluwer.

Crawford, A. (Ed) (2011) *International and comparative criminal justice and urban governance*. Cambridge: Cambridge University Press.

Criminal Sanctions Agency (2003) *Prison service in Finland*. Helsinki: Ministry of Justice.

Crombag, H.F.M. (2003) Adversarial or inquisitorial: Do we have a choice? In: P.J. Van Koppen and S.D. Penrod (Eds) *Adversarial versus inquisitorial justice*. New York: Kluwer/Plenum, 21–5.

Crystal, J. (2001) Criminal justice in the Middle East. *Journal of criminal justice, 29*, 469–82.

Cumming, E., Cumming, I. and Edell, L. (1965) Policeman as philosopher, guide and friend. *Social problems, 12*, 276–86.

Damaska, M.R. (1986) *The faces of justice and state authority: A comparative approach to the legal process*. New Haven, Connecticut: Yale University Press.

Dardagan, H., Sloboda, J., Williams, K. and Bagnall, P. (2005) *Iraq body count: A dossier of civilian casualties 2003–2005*. Available on line: www.iraqbodycount.org (accessed 15/7/2014).

Davies, M., Croall, H. and Tyrer, J. (1998) *Criminal justice: An introduction to the criminal justice system of England and Wales*. London: Longman.

Day, L.E. and Vandiver, M. (2000) Criminology and genocide studies: Notes on what might have been and what still could be. *Crime, law and social change, 34,* 43–59.

De Figueiredo Dias, J. and Antunes, M.J. (1993) Portugal. In: C. Van Den Wijngaert, C. Gane, H.H. Kuhne and F. McAuley (Eds) *Criminal procedure systems in the European Community.* London: Butterworth, 317–38.

De Sousa Santos, B. (2010) *The European Arrest Warrant in law and in practice: A comparative study for the consolidation of the European law-enforcement area.* Brussels: European Commission.

Death Penalty Information Center (2008) *Facts about the death penalty.* Available on line: www.deathpenaltyinfo.org/Factsheet.pdf (accessed 15/7/2014).

Deflem, M. (2002) *Policing world society.* Oxford: Oxford University Press.

Deković, M., Slagt, M.I., Asscher, J.J., Boendermaker, L., Eichelsheim, V.I. and Prinzie, P. (2011) Effects of early prevention programs on adult criminal offending: A meta-analysis. *Clinical psychology review, 31,* 532, 544.

Della Porta, D. and Fillieule, O. (2004) Policing social protest. In: D. Snow, S. Soule and H. Kriesi (Eds) *The Blackwell companion to social movements.* Oxford: Blackwell. 217–41.

Den Boer, M.C.W. and Walker, N. (1993) European policing after 1992. *Journal of common market studies, 31,* 3–28.

Devi, S. (2012) Bahrain continues to target Shia doctors. *The lancet, 380,* 1296.

Dhanapala, J. (2002) Multilateral cooperation on small arms and light weapons: From crisis to collective response. *Brown journal of world affairs, 9,* 163–71.

Dillard, W.T., Johnson, S.R. and Lynch, T. (2003) A grande façade: How the Grand Jury was captured by government. *Policy analysis, no 476.* Washington: Cato Institute.

Dixon, K. (1977) Is cultural relativism self-refuting? *British journal of sociology, 28,* 75–88.

Dobryninas, A. (2005) Lithuania's anti-corruption policy: Between the 'West' and the 'East'? *European journal on criminal policy and research, 11,* 77–95.

Downes, D. (1988) *Contrasts in tolerance: Post-war penal policy in the Netherlands and England and Wales.* Oxford: Clarendon Press.

Duff, P. (1993) The prosecutor fine and social control: The introduction of the fiscal fine to Scotland. *British journal of criminology, 33,* 481–503.

Duff, P. (1999) The prosecution service: Independence and accountability. In: P. Duff and N. Hutton (Eds) *Criminal justice in Scotland.* Aldershot: Ashgate, 115–30.

Duff, P. (2000) The defendant's right to trial by jury: A neighbour's view. *Criminal law review,* 85–94.

Duff, P. (2001) The Scottish criminal jury: A very peculiar institution. In: N. Vidmar (Ed) *World jury systems.* Oxford: Oxford University Press, 249–82.

Duff, P. and Hutton, N. (1999) *Criminal justice in Scotland.* Aldershot: Ashgate.

Durkheim, E. (1895) *The rules of sociological method.* New York: The Free Press.

Dwyer, F. (2001) *Can the police make a difference: The New York City example.* Lecture delivered at the University of Portsmouth (May), unpublished.

Ebbe, O.N.I. (2000a) The unique and comparative features of criminal justice systems: Policing, judiciary and corrections. In: Ebbe (Ed) *Comparative and international criminal justice systems: Policing, judiciary and corrections (2nd edition).* Boston: Butterworth-Heinemann, 277–89.

Ebbe, O.N.I. (2000b) The judiciary and criminal procedure in Nigeria. In: Ebbe (Ed) *Comparative and international criminal justice systems: Policing, judiciary and corrections (2nd edition).* Boston: Butterworth-Heinemann, 183–203.

Ebbe, O.N.I. and De Olano, R.G.R. (2000) The criminal justice system in Argentina. In: Ebbe (Ed) *Comparative and international criminal justice systems: Policing, judiciary and corrections (2nd edition)*. Boston: Butterworth-Heinemann, 79–90.

Eberhardt, J.L., Davies, P.G., Purdie-Vaughns, V.J. and Johnson, S.L. (2006) Looking deathworthy: perceived stereotypicality of black defendants predicts capital-sentencing outcomes. *Psychological science, 17*, 383–6.

Ellis, T. and Hamai, K. (2006) Crime and criminal justice in modern Japan: From re-integrative shaming to popular punitivism. *International journal of the sociology of law, 34*, 157–78.

EMCDDA (2008) *Annual report: The state of the drugs problem in Europe*. Lisbon: EMCDDA.

EMCDDA (2012) *Annual report: The state of the drugs problem in Europe*. Lisbon: EMCDDA.

Erickson, S.K., Campbell, A. and Lamberti, J.S. (2006) Variations in mental health courts: Challenges, opportunities, and a call for caution. *Community mental health journal, 42*(4), 335–44.

Esping-Andersen, G. (1990) *The three worlds of welfare capitalism*. Cambridge: Polity Press.

Fairchild, E. and Dammer, R.D. (2001) *Comparative criminal justice systems (2nd edition)*. Belmost, California: Wadsworth.

Fairfax Jr, R.A. (2010) Grand Jury innovation: Toward a functional makeover of the ancient bulwark of liberty. *William & Mary bill of rights journal, 19*, 339.

Fallows, J. (2008) The connection has been reset. *The Atlantic*, March 2008. Available on line: http://www.theatlantic.com/doc/200803/chinese-firewall (accessed 15/7/2014).

Farmanfarmaian, R. (in press) Policing the Arab Spring: Discordant discourses of protest and intervention. In: D. Pritchard and F. Pakes (Eds) *Riot, unrest and protest on the global stage*. London: Routledge.

Fazel, S. and Danesh, J. (2002) Serious mental disorder in 23,000 prisoners: a systematic review of 62 surveys. *The lancet, 359 (12 February 2002)*, 545–50.

Fazel, S. and Yu, R. (2011) Psychotic disorders and repeat offending: systematic review and meta-analysis. *Schizophrenia bulletin, 37*, 800–10.

Feeley, M.M. and Simon, J. (1992) The new penology: Notes on the emerging strategy of corrections and its implications. *Criminology, 30*, 449–74.

Feinberg, G. (2006) The International Criminal Tribunal for the Former Yugoslavia: The establishment and evaluation of a unique concept in international justice administration. *War crimes, genocide and crimes against humanity, 2*, 87–113.

Ferrell, J., Hayward, K., Morrison, W. and Presdee, M. (Eds) (2004) *Cultural criminology unleashed*. London: GlassHouse Press.

Field, S. (1998) The legal framework of covert and proactive policing in France. In: S. Field and C. Pelser (Eds) *Invading the private: State accountability and new investigative methods in Europe*. Aldershot: Ashgate, 67–82.

Field, S., Alldridge, P. and Jörg, N. (1995) Prosecutors, examining judges and control of police investigations. In: P. Fennell, C. Harding, N. Jörg and B. Swart (Eds) *Criminal justice in Europe: A comparative study*. Oxford: Clarendon Press, 227–49.

Fijnaut, C. (Ed) (1993) *The internationalisation of police cooperation in Western Europe*. Deventer, the Netherlands: Kluwer.

Fijnaut, C. and Paoli, E. (2004) Comparative synthesis of Part I. In: C. Fijnaut and E. Paoli (Eds) *Organised crime in Europe: Concepts, patterns and control policies in the European Union and beyond*. Dordrecht: Springer, 228–35.

Findlay, P. and Duff, P. (Eds) (1988) *The jury under attack*. London: Butterworth.

Fionda, J. (1995) *Public prosecutors and discretion: A comparative study*. Oxford: Clarendon Press.

Fitzpatrick, P. (1982) The political economy of dispute settlement in Papua New Guinea. In: C. Sumner (Ed) *Crime, justice and underdevelopment*. London: Heinemann, 192–227.

Foglesong, T. (2008). Grand ambitions, modest scale. In: Open Society Foundations (Ed) *Justice initiatives*. London: Open Society Foundations, 4–11.

Foucault, M. (1979) *Discipline and punish: The birth of the prison*. New York: Vintage.

Fowler, G. (2008) *IOC Chief strives to deflect criticism of Chinese censorship*. Available on line: http://online.wsj.com/article/SB121769525318907505.html (accessed 15/7/2014).

Franke, H. (1990) Dutch tolerance: Facts and fables. *British journal of criminology, 30*, 81–93.

Fricker, R.L. (1990) A judiciary under fire. *ABA journal, 76*, 54–8.

Friedman, T.L. (2005) *The world is flat*. New York: MacMillan.

Friedrichs, O. (2013) Crimes of globalization as a criminological project. In: F. Pakes (Ed) *Globalisation and the challenge to criminology*. London: Routledge, 45–63.

Fukurai, H. (2007) The rebirth of Japan's petit quasi-jury and grand jury systems: A cross-national analysis of legal consciousness and the lay participatory experience in Japan and the U.S. *Cornell international law journal, 40*, 315–54.

Ganapathy, N. (2005) Critical realist reflections on crime and social control in Singapore. In: J. Sheptycki and A. Wardak (Eds) *Transnational and comparative criminology*. London: GlassHouse Press, 157–77.

Garland, D. (1990) *Punishment and modern society: A study in social theory*. Oxford: Clarendon Press.

Garland, D. (2001) *The culture of control: Crime and order in contemporary society*. Chicago: University of Chicago Press.

Garland, D. (2002) The cultural uses of capital punishment. *Punishment and Society, 4*, 459–87.

Geertz, C. (1983) Local knowledge: Fact and law in comparative perspective. In: C. Geertz (Ed) *Local knowledge: Further essays in interpretative anthropology*. New York: Basic Books, 229–45.

Geysel, F. (1990) Europe from the inside, *Policing, 6*, 338–54.

Ghodsi, E. (2004) Murder in the criminal law of Iran and Islam. *Journal of criminal law, 68*, 160–9.

Giddens, A. (2002) *Runaway world: How globalization is reshaping our lives*. New York: Routledge.

Gill, M. (2006) Not just joining the dots but crossing the borders and filling the voids: Constructing security networks after September 11th 2001. *Policing and society, 16*, 27–49.

Gilliéron, G. (2014). *Public prosecutors in the United States and Europe: A comparative analysis with special focus on Switzerland, France, and Germany*. Dordrecht: Springer.

Goldhagen, D. (1996) *Hitler's willing executioners*. London: Knopf Doubleday.

Goldsmith, A. and Sheptycki, J. (Eds) (2007) *Crafting transnational policing, police capacity-building and global policing reform*. Oxford: Hart.

Goldstein, H. (1977) *Policing a free society*. Cambridge, Massachusetts: Ballinger.

Gorringe, H. and Rosie, M. (2008). It's a long way to Auchterarder! 'Negotiated management' and mismanagement in the policing of G8 protests. *British journal of sociology, 59*, 187–205.

Green, P. and Ward, T. (2000). State crime, human rights and the limits of criminology. *Social justice, 27*, 101–15.

Greve, V. (1993) Denmark. In C. Van Den Wijngaert, C. Gane, H.H. Kuhne and F. McAuley (Eds) *Criminal procedure systems in the European Community*. London: Butterworth, 51–72.

Guia, M.J., Van der Woude, M. and Van der Leun, J. (Eds) (2012) *Social control and justice: Crimmigration in the age of fear*. The Hague: Eleven International Publishing.

Haberfeld, M.R. and Cerrah, I. (Eds) (2008) *Comparative policing: The struggle for democratization*. London: Sage.

Hagan, J. and Rymond-Richmond, W. (2008) Collective dynamics of genocidal victimization in Darfur. *American sociological review, 73*, 875–902.

Hagan, J. and Rymond-Richmond, W. (2009) Criminology confronts genocide: Whose side are you on? *Theoretical criminology, 13*, 503–11.

Hague, R., Harrop, M. and Breslin, S. (1998) *Comparative government and politics: An introduction (4th edition)*. Basingstoke: Macmillan.

Hänggi, H. and Bryden, A. (2005) *Security governance in post-conflict peacebuilding*. Geneva: Geneva Centre for the Democratic Control of Armed Forces (DCAF).

Hans, V. (2008) Jury systems around the world. *Annual review of law and social science, 4*, 275–97.

Hardie-Bick, J., Sheptycki, J. and Wardak, A. (2005). Introduction: Transnational and comparative criminology in a global perspective. In: J. Sheptycki and A. Wardak (Eds) *Transnational and comparative criminology*. London: GlassHouse Press.

Harris, C. (2010) Investigating homicide investigation in France. *Policing and society, 23*, 328–45.

Harrendorf, S., Heiskanen, M. and Malby, S. (Eds) (2010) *International statistics on crime and justice*. Helsinki: HEUNI.

Hartmann, A. and Kerner, H.J. (2004, April) Victim–offender mediation in Germany. In *Revista del Foro europeo para la Mediación entre el Autor y la Víctima y para la Justicia restauradora (Newsletter of the European Forum for Victim–Offender Mediation and Restorative Justice)*.

Heidensohn, F. (2006) Contrasts and concepts: Considering the development of comparative criminology. In: T. Newburn (Ed) *The politics of crime control*. Oxford: Oxford University Press, 173–96.

Heidensohn, F. (2007) International comparative research in criminology. In: R. King and E. Wincup (Eds) *Doing research on crime and justice (2nd edition)*. Oxford: Oxford University Press, 199–228.

Held, D. (Ed) (2000) *A globalizing world? Culture, economics and politics*. London: Routledge.

Hiebert, M.S. (2009) Theorizing destruction: Reflections on the state of comparative genocide theory. *Genocide studies and prevention, 3*, 309–39.

Hills, A. (2009) The possibility of transnational policing. *Policing & society, 19*(3), 300–17.

Hinton, M.S. and Newburn, T. (Eds) (2008) *Policing developing democracies*. London: Routledge.

Hirsch, A.J. (1992) *The Rise of the penitentiary*. New Haven, Connecticut: Yale University Press.

Hodgson, J. (2000) Comparing legal cultures: The comparatist as participant observer. In: D. Nelken (Ed) *Contrasting criminal justice*. Aldershot: Ashgate, 139–56.

Hodgson, J (2001) The police, the prosecutor and the *Juge d'instruction*: Judicial supervision in France, theory and practice. *British journal of criminology, 41*, 342–61.

Hodgson, J. (2002) Suspects, defendants and victims in the French criminal process: The context of recent reform. *International and comparative law quarterly, 51*, 781–816.

Hodgson, J. (2004) The detention and interrogation of suspects in police custody in France: A comparative account. *European journal of criminology, 1*, 163–99.

Hodgson, J.S. (2010) The French prosecutor in question. *Washington & Lee law review, 67*, 1361–411.

Holá, B., Bijleveld, C. and Smeulers, A. (2012) Consistency of international sentencing: ICTY and ICTR case study. *European journal of criminology, 9*, 539–52.

Home Office (2001) *Criminal statistics: England and Wales 2000*. London: HMSO.

Hood, R. (1996) *The death penalty: A world-wide perspective (2nd edition)*. Oxford: Clarendon Press.

Hopkins Burke, R. (Ed) (1998) *Zero tolerance policing*. Leicester: Perpetuity Press.

Hörnle, T. (2006) Democratic accountability and lay participation in criminal trials. In: A. Duff, L. Farmer, S. Marshall and V. Tadros (Eds) *The trial on trial: Volume two: Judgement and calling to account*. Oxford: Hart Publishers, 135–54.

Horton, C. (1995) *Policing policy in France*. London: Policy Studies Institute.

Howard, J. (1777) *The state of the prisons in England and Wales*. London: William Eyres.

Huber, B. (1996) Criminal procedure in Germany. In: J. Hatchard, B. Huber and R. Vogler (Eds) *Comparative criminal procedure*. London: British Institute of International and Comparative Law, 96–175.

Hucklesby, A. (2002) Bail in criminal cases. In: M. McConville and G. Wilson (Eds) *The handbook of the criminal justice process*. Oxford: Oxford University Press, 115–36.

Huggins, M.K. (2003) Moral universes of Brazilian torturers. *Albany law review, 67*, 527–35.

Huggins, M.K., Haritos-Fatouros, M. and Zimbardo, P. (2002) *Violence workers: Police torturers and murderers reconstruct Brazilian atrocities*. Berkeley: University of California Press.

IANSA (2007) *International action network on small arms*. Available on line: www.iansa. org (accessed 15/7/2014).

ICAC (2009) *Corruption reports*. Available on line: http://www.icac.org.hk/en/useful_ information/cr/index.html (accessed 15/7/2014).

Ignatieff, M. (1979) Police and people: The birth of Mr Peel's 'blue locusts'. *New society, 49*, 481–509.

International Criminal Tribunal for the Former Yugoslavia [ICTY] (1993) *Statute*. The Hague: ICTY.

International Criminal Tribunal for the Former Yugoslavia [ICTY] (1998) *Fifth Annual Report of the International Tribunal for the Prosecution of Persons Responsible for Serious Violations of International Humanitarian Law Committed in the Territory of the Former Yugoslavia since 1991*. The Hague: ICTY.

International Crisis Group [ICG] (2009) *Liberia: Uneven progress in security sector reform (Africa report N°148, executive summary and recommendations)*. Available on line: http://www. crisisgroup.org/~/media/Files/africa/west-africa/liberia/Liberia%20Uneven%20 Progress%20in%20Security%20Sector%20Reform.ashx (accessed 15/7/2014).

International Military Tribunal (1947) *Trial of the Major War Criminals before the International Military Tribunal, 'Blue Series', volume 1*. Nuremberg: IMT.

International Telecommunication Union (2007) *World telecommunication/ICT development report 2006*. London: ITU.

Jackson, J.D., Quinn, K. and O'Malley, T. (2001) The jury system in contemporary Ireland: In the shadow of a troubled past. In: N. Vidmar (Ed) *World jury systems*. Oxford: Oxford University Press, 281–318.

Jamieson, R. (1999) Genocide and the social reproduction of immorality. *Theoretical criminology, 3*, 131.

Jamieson, R. and McEvoy, K. (2005) State crime by proxy and juridical othering. *British journal of criminology, 45*, 504–27.

Jehle, J-M., Wade, M. and Elsner, B. (2008) Prosecution and diversion within criminal justice systems in Europe: Aims and design of a comparative study. *European journal on criminal policy and research, 14*, 93–9.

Jensma, F. (2008) Advocaat bij verhoor is een harde klap. *Volkskrant*, 8 December 2008.

Jessberger, F. and Geneuss, J. (2012) The many faces of the International Criminal Court. *Journal of international criminal justice*, *10*, 1081–94.

Jobard, F. (in press) Riots in France: Political, proto-political or anti-political turmoils? In: D. Pritchard and F. Pakes (Eds) *Riot, unrest and protest on the global stage*. London: Palgrave.

Johnson, H., Ollus, N. and Nevala, S. (2007) *Violence against women: An international perspective*. New York: Springer.

Johnston, J., Keyzer, P., Holland, G., Pearson, M., Rodrick, S. and Wallace, A. (2011) *Juries and social media: A report prepared for the Victorian Department of Justice*. Victoria: Victorian Department of Justice.

Johnston, L. (2000) *Policing Britain: Risk, security and governance*. Harlow, Essex: Longman.

Johnston, L. and Shearing, C. (2003) *Governing security*. London: Routledge.

Jones, T. and Newburn, T. (1998) *Private security and public policing*. Oxford: Clarendon Press.

Jones, T. and Newburn, T. (Eds) (2006) *Plural policing: A comparative example*. London: Routledge.

Jones, T. and Newburn. T. (2007) *Policy transfer and criminal justice: Exploring US influence over British crime control policy*. Maidenhead: Open University Press.

Jörg, N., Field, S. and Brandts, C. (1995) Are inquisitorial and adversarial systems converging? In: P. Fennell, C. Harding, N. Jörg and B. Swart (Eds) *Criminal justice in Europe: A comparative study*. Oxford: Clarendon Press, 41–56.

Jorgensen, D.L. (1993) *Participant observation: A methodology for human studies*. Thousand Oaks, California: Sage.

Joutsen, M., Lahti, R. and Pölönen, P. (2001) *Criminal justice systems in Europe and North America*. Helsinki: European Institute for Crime Prevention and Control.

Juska, A. and Johnstone, P. (2004) The symbiosis of politics and crime in Lithuania. *Journal of Baltic studies*, *35*, 346–59.

Kafka, F. (1925/1998) *The trial*, M. Schocken (Trans). New York: Schocken/Random House.

Kalven, H. and Zeisel, H. (1966) *The American jury*. Chicago: University of Chicago Press.

Kapur, R. (2012) Pink chaddis and SlutWalk couture: The postcolonial politics of feminism lite. *Feminist legal studies*, *20*, 1–20.

Karolak, S., Thomas Nefau, T., Bailly, E., Solgadi, A. and Levi, Y. (2010) Estimation of illicit drugs consumption by wastewater analysis in Paris area (France). *Forensic science international*, *200*, 153–60.

Karstedt, S. (2011) Liberty, equality and justice: Democratic culture and punishment. In: A. Crawford (Ed) *International and comparative criminal justice and urban governance*. Cambridge: Cambridge University Press, 356–85.

Karunaratne, N.H.A. (no date) Sri Lanka. In: *The world factbook of criminal justice systems*. Available on line: http://www.bjs.gov/content/pub/ascii/WFBCJSRI.TXT (accessed 15/7/2014).

Kauzlarich, D., Mullins, C.W. and Matthews, R.A. (2003) A complicity continuum of state crime. *Contemporary justice review*, *6*, 241–54.

Kelk, C. (2007) Enkele strafrechtelijke ontwikkelingen en de volkswil. *Justitiële verkenningen*, *33*, 44–56.

Kelling, G.L., Pate, T., Dieckman, D. and Brown, C.E. (1998) The Kansas City preventive patrol experiment: A summary report. In: D.H. Bayley (Ed) *What works in policing*. New York: Oxford University Press, 30–50.

Kelman, H.C. (1973) Violence without moral restraint: Reflections on the dehumanization of victims and victimizers. *Journal of social issues*, *29*, 25–61.

Kilibarda, K. (in press) From #Occupy to #IdleNoMore: Rethinking space, settler consciousness and erasures within the 99%. In: D. Pritchard and F. Pakes (Eds) *Riot, unrest and protest on the global stage*. London: Palgrave.

Kilchling, M. and Loschnig-Gspandl, M. (2000) Legal and practical perspectives on victim/offender mediation in Austria and Germany. *International review of victimology, 7*, 305–32.

King, M. and Brearley, N. (1996) *Public order policing: Contemporary perspectives on strategy and tactics*. Leicester: Perpetuity Press.

King, N.J. (2001) The American criminal jury. In: N. Vidmar (Ed) *World jury systems*. Oxford: Oxford University Press, 53–91.

Kirk, D. (2013). Opinion: The jury's out. *Journal of criminal law, 77*, 173–6.

Klein, N. (2007) *The shock doctrine*. London: Penguin.

Komiya, N. (1999) A cultural study of the low crime rate in Japan. *British journal of criminology, 39*, 369–90.

Kramer, R.C. and Michalowski, R. J. (2005) War, aggression and state crime: A criminological analysis of the invasion and occupation of Iraq. *British journal of criminology, 45*, 446–69.

Krug E.G., Dahlberg, L.L., James, A., Mercy, J.A., Zwi, A.B. and Lozano, R. (2002) *World report on violence and health*. Geneva: World Health Organisation.

Kruttschnitt, C. and Dirkzwager, A. (2011) Are there still contrasts in tolerance? Imprisonment in the Netherlands and England 20 years later. *Punishment and society, 13*, 283–306.

Kühne, H.H. (1993) Germany. In: C. Van Den Wijngaert, C. Gane, H.H. Kühne and F. McAuley (Eds) *Criminal procedure systems in the European Community*. London: Butterworth, 137–62.

Lacey, N. (2011) Why globalisation doesn't spell convergence: Models of institutional variation and the comparative political economy of punishment. In: A. Crawford (Ed) *International and comparative criminal justice and urban governance*. Cambridge: Cambridge University Press, 214–50.

Leander, A. and Van Munster, R. (2007) Private security contractors in the debate about Darfur: Reflecting and reinforcing neo-liberal governmentality. *International relations, 21*(2), 201–16.

Lee, J.H. (2009) Getting citizens involved: Civil participation in judicial decision making in Korea. *East Asia law review, 4*, 177–207.

Leib, E.J. (2008) A comparison of criminal jury decision rules in democratic countries. *Ohio State journal of criminal law, 5*, 629–44.

Leigh, L. and Zedner, L. (1992) *A report on the administration of criminal justice in the pretrial phase in France and Germany*. Royal Commission on Criminal Justice Research Study, no 1, London: HMSO.

Leishman, F. (1999) Policing in Japan: East Asian archetype? in R.I. Mawby (Ed) *Policing around the world*. London: UCL Press, 109–25.

Leishman, F. (2007) Koban: Neighbourhood policing in contemporary Japan, *Policing, 1*, 196–202.

Leveson, L.J.B.H.L. (2012) *An Inquiry into the Culture, Practices and Ethics of the Press : Executive Summary and Recommendations* [Leveson Report]. London: The Stationery Office.

Lewis, C. (2010) Recent changes in the English public prosecution service. *Pakistan journal of criminology, 4*, 71–82.

Lipsey, M.W. (1995) What can be learned from 400 studies on the effectiveness of treatment with juvenile delinquents? In: J. McGuire (Ed) *What works: Reducing reoffending*. Chichester: Wiley, 63–78.

Lloyd-Bostock, S. and Thomas, C. (2001) The continuing decline of the English jury. In: N. Vidmar (ed) *World jury systems*. Oxford: Oxford University Press, 53–91.

Lu, H. and Miethe, T.D. (2002) Legal representation and criminal processing in China, *British journal of criminology, 42,* 267–280.

Lynch, J.P. (2006) Problems and promise of victimization surveys for cross-national research. *Crime and justice: A review of research, 34,* 229–87.

Lyon, D. (2005) The border is everywhere: ID cards, surveillance and the other. In: E. Zureik and M.B. Salter (Eds) *Global surveillance and policing: Borders, security, identity.* Cullompton, Devon: Willan, 66–82.

Magnarella, P.J. (1997) Some milestones and achievements at the International Criminal Tribunal for Rwanda: The 1998 Kambanda and Akayesu cases. *Florida journal of international law, 11,* 517–38.

Maher, G. (1988) The verdict of the jury. In: M. Findley and P. Duff (Eds) *The jury under attack.* London: Butterworth, 40–55.

Maier-Katkin, D., Mears, D.P. and Bernard, T.J. (2009) Towards a criminology of crimes against humanity. *Theoretical criminology, 13,* 227–55.

Mannheim, H. (1965) *Comparative criminology* (2 Vols). London: Routledge.

Malby, S. (2010) Homicide. In: S. Harrendorf, M. Heiskanen and S. Malby (Eds) *International statistics on crime and justice.* Helsinki: HEUNI and Vienna: United Nations Office on Drugs and Crime, 7–19.

Marrani, D. (2009) *Palaces of justice or places of justice: The dilemma of post-modernity.* Working paper. Available on line: http://papers.ssrn.com/sol3/papers.cfm?abstract_id=1650535 (accessed 15/7/2014).

Martinson, R. (1974) What works? Questions and answers from prison reform. The *public interest, 35,* 22–54.

Mathiesen, T. (2012) Scandinavian exceptionalism in penal matters: Reality of wishful thinking? In: T. Ugelvik and J. Dullum (Eds) *Penal exceptionalism? Nordic prison policy and practice.* London: Routledge, 13–36.

Matthews, R. (2005) The myth of punitiveness. *Theoretical criminology, 9,* 175–201.

Mawby, R.I. (Ed) (1999) *Policing across the world: Issues for the twenty-first century.* London: UCL Press.

Mawby, R.I. (1999) Approaches to comparative analysis: The impossibility of becoming an expert on everywhere. In: Mawby (Ed) *Policing across the world: Issues for the twenty-first century.* London: UCL Press, 13–22.

Mawby, R.I. (2000) Core policing: The seductive myth. In: F. Leishman, B. Loveday and S. Savage (Eds) *Core issues in policing (2nd edition).* Harlow, Essex: Longman, 107–23.

McAra, L. (2008) Crime, criminology and criminal justice in Scotland. *European journal of criminology, 5,* 481–504.

McGuire, J. and Priestley, B. (1995) Reviewing 'what works': Past, present and future. In: J. McGuire (Ed) *What works: Reducing reoffending.* Chichester: Wiley, 3–34.

McKenzie, I.M. and Gallagher, G.P. (1989) *Behind the uniform: Policing in Britain and America.* Hemel Hempstead: Harvester Wheatsheaf.

McKenzie, N. (2005) *Beyond the fringe: Family group conferencing and its relationship with the criminal justice process.* PhD thesis, University of Portsmouth.

Mead, M. (1928) *Coming of age in Samoa: A psychological study of primitive youth for Western civilization.* New York: Morrow.

Mead, M. (1935) *Sex and temperament in three primitive societies.* New York: Morrow.

Mead, M. (1977) *Letters from the field.* New York: Harper.

Melossi, D., Sozzo, M. and Sparks, R. (2011) (Eds) *Travels of the criminal question: Cultural embeddedness and diffusion*. Oxford: Hart.

Merrills, J.G. and Robertson, J. (2001) *Human rights in Europe: A study of the European Convention of Human Rights (4th edition)*. Manchester: Manchester University Press.

Messner, S. and Rosenfeld, R. (2007) *Crime and the American Dream*. Belmont, California: Wadsworth.

Meyer, J. and O'Malley, P. (2005) Missing the punitive turn?: Canadian criminal justice, 'Balance,' and penal modernism. In: J.Pratt, D. Brown, M. Brown, S. Hallsworth and W. Morrison (Eds) *The new punitiveness: Trends, theories and perspectives*. Cullompton, Devon: Willan, 201–7.

Miers, D. (2001) *An international review of restorative justice*. Crime Reduction Research series, Paper 10, London: Home Office.

Missing Women Commission of Inquiry (Canada) (2012) *Comparative approaches to missing persons procedures: An overview of British, American and Australian policies*. Available on line: http://www.missingwomeninquiry.ca/wp-content/uploads/2010/10/Comparative-Approaches-to-MP-Procedures.pdf (accessed 15/7/2014).

Mitsilegas, V. (2012) The changing landscape of the criminalisation of migration in Europe: The protective function of European Union law. In: M.J. Guia, M. Van der Woude and J. Van der Leun (Eds) *Social control and justice: Crimmigration in the age of fear*. The Hague: Eleven International Publishing, 87–113.

Monjardet, D. (1995) The French model of policing. In: J.P. Brodeur (Ed) *Comparisons in policing: An international perspective*. Aldershot: Ashgate, 51–68.

Moody, S. and Tombs, J. (1982) *Prosecution in the public interest*. Edinburgh: Scottish Academic Press.

Morris, A. and Maxwell, G. (1998) Restorative justice in New Zealand: Family Group Conferences as a case study. *Western criminology review*. Available on line: http://wcr.sonoma.edu/v1n1/morris.html (accessed 15/7/2014).

Morrow, P. (1993) A sociolinguistic mismatch: Central Alaskan Yup'iks and the legal system. *Alaska justice forum, 10*, 1–7.

Mullins, C.W. (2009) He would kill me with his penis: Genocidal rape in Rwanda as state crime. *Critical criminology, 17*, 15–33.

Muncie, J. (2011) On globalisation and exceptionalism. In: D. Nelken (Ed) *Comparative criminal justice and globalization*. Farnham: Ashgate, 87–106.

Mylonopoulos, C. (1993) Greece. In: C. Van Den Wijngaert, C. Gane, H.H. Kuhne and F. McAuley (Eds) *Criminal procedure systems in the European community*. London: Butterworth, 163–84.

Naim, M. (2005) *Illicit: How smugglers, traffickers and copycats are hijacking the global economy*. New York: Doubleday.

Nakayama, K. (1987) Japan. In: F. Cole, S.J. Frankowski and M.G. Gerz (Eds) *Major criminal justice systems: A comparative study (2nd edition)*. London: Sage, 161–77.

Nederveen Pieterse, J. (2011) Global rebalancing: crisis and the East–South turn. *Development and change, 42*, 22–48.

Nelken, D. (1997) Understanding criminal justice comparatively. In: M. Maguire, R. Morgan and R. Reiner (Eds) *The Oxford handbook of criminology (2nd edition)*. Oxford: Clarendon Press, 559–73.

Nelken, D. (2009) Comparative criminal justice: Beyond ethnocentrism and relativism. *European journal of criminology, 6*, 291–311.

Nelken, D. (2010) *Comparative criminal justice: Making sense of difference*. London: Sage.

Nelken, D. (Ed) (2011) *Comparative criminal justice and globalization*. Farnham: Ashgate.

Nelken, D. (2011). Afterword: Studying criminal justice in globalising times. In: D. Nelken (Ed) *Comparative criminal justice and globalization*. Farnham: Ashgate, 183–210.

Neuberger, F. (2006) How can it happen that horrendous state crimes are perpetrated? An overview of criminological theories. *Journal of international criminal justice, 4*, 787–99.

Newburn, T. (1999) *Understanding and preventing police corruption: Lessons from the literature*. Police Research series, paper 110, London: HMSO.

Neyroud, P. and Beckley, A. (2001) *Policing, ethics and human rights*. Cullompton, Devon: Willan.

Nijboer, J.F. (1995) *Strafrechtelijk Bewijsrecht*. Nijmegen, the Netherlands: Ars Aequi Libri.

NRC Handelsblad (2007) Kabinet is tegen lekenrechtspraak. *NRC Handelsblad*, 18 July 2007.

O'Brien, J.C. (1993) The International Tribunal for Violations of International Humanitarian Law in the Former Yugoslavia. *American journal of international law, 87*, 639–59.

OCTA (2008) *EU Organised Crime Threat Assessment*. The Hague: Europol.

O'Keefe, T. (2011) *Flaunting our way to freedom? SlutWalks, gendered protest and feminist futures*. New Agendas in Social Movement Studies, November 2011, Maynooth: National University.

O'Malley, P. (2000) Criminologies of catastrophe? Understanding criminal justice on the edge of the new millennium. *Australian and New Zealand journal of criminology, 33*, 153–67.

Onekalit, C.A. (2013) Women in peacekeeping: The emergence of the all-female uniformed units in UNMIL and MONUSCO. *Conflict trends, 2*, 42–6.

Open Society Foundations (2011) Pretrial detention and torture: Why pretrial detainees face the greatest risk. London: Open Society Foundations. Available on line: http://ppja.org/regional-information/world/pretrial-detention-and-torture-06222011.pdf (accessed 15/7/2014).

Osmancik, O. (no date) Czech Republic. In: *The world factbook of criminal justice systems*. Available on line: http://www.bjs.gov/content/pub/ascii/WFBCJCZE.TXT (accessed 15/7/2014).

Owen, J. (2008) 14,000 knife victims a year. *Independent on Sunday*, 6 July 2008.

Pakes, F.J. (1999) The positioning of the prosecution service in England and Wales and the Netherlands: Lessons from one extreme to another. *Liverpool law review, 21*, 261–74.

Pakes, F.J. (2000a) League leaders in mid-table: On the major changes in Dutch prison policy. *Howard journal of criminal justice, 39*, 30–9.

Pakes, F.J. (2000b) Doing international justice: The International Criminal Tribunal for the Former Yugoslavia, the role of the judge. In: C.M. Breur, M.M. Kommer, J.F. Nijboer and J.M. Reijntjes (Eds) *New trends in criminal investigation and evidence*. Antwerp: Intersentia, 523–33.

Pakes, F.J. (2001) *Spiders in the web: Public prosecutors at work*. PhD dissertation, Leiden University, the Netherlands, unpublished.

Pakes, F. (2004) The politics of discontent: The emergence of a new criminal justice discourse in the Netherlands. *Howard journal of criminal justice, 43*, 284–98.

Pakes, F. (2007a) Dutch prisons: An international comparative perspective. In: M. Boone and M. Moerings (Eds) *Dutch prisons: Front runners in penal policy?* The Hague: Boom, 297–314.

Pakes, F. (2007b) *Pearls in policing*. The Hague: Police Academy of the Netherlands.

Pakes, F. (2007c) The changing nature of inquisitorial, adversarial and Islamic trials. In: D. Carson, B. Milne, F. Pakes, K. Shalev and A. Shawyer (Eds) *Applying psychology to criminal justice*. Chichester: Wiley, 251–64.

Pakes, F. (2007d) The Dutch prison boom: when the global and the 'glocal' collide. *Prison service journal, 176,* 15–20.

Pakes, F. (2010) The comparative method in globalised criminology. *Australian and New Zealand journal of criminology,* 43, 17–30.

Pakes, F. (2013) (Ed) *Globalisation and the challenge to criminology.* London: Routledge.

Pakes, F. (2013) Globalisation and criminology: An agenda of engagement. In: F. Pakes (Ed) *Globalisation and the challenge to criminology.* London: Routledge, 1–8.

Pakes, F. and Silverstone, D. (2012) Cannabis in the global market: A comparison between the UK and the Netherlands. *International journal of law, crime and justice,* 40, 20–30.

Pakes, F. and Winstone, J. (2005) Community justice: The smell of fresh bread. In: J. Winstone and F. Pakes (Eds) *Community justice: Issues for probation and criminal justice.* Cullompton, Devon: Willan, 1–15.

Pakstaitis, L. (2002) *Crimes of corruption in Lithuania.* Lecture delivered at the Institute for Criminal Justice Studies, University of Portsmouth (April), unpublished.

Paliwala, A. (1980) Law and order in the village: Papua New Guinea's village courts. In: C. Sumner (Ed) *Crime, justice and underdevelopment.* London: Heinemann, 192–227.

Park, R.Y. (2010) The globalizing jury trial: Lessons and insights from Korea. *American journal of comparative law,* 58, 525–82.

Passas, N. (1998) Globalisation and transnational crime: Effects of criminogenic asymmetries. *Transnational organised crime,* 4, 22–56.

Pellerin, H. (2005) Borders, migration and economic integration: Towards a new political economy of borders. In: E. Zureik and M.B. Salter (Eds) *Global surveillance and policing: Borders, security, identity.* Cullompton, Devon: Willan, 51–65.

Perkins, J. (2005) *Confessions of an economic hitman.* London: Random House.

Philips, C. (1981) *The Royal Commission on Criminal Justice Report.* London: HMSO.

Pickering, S. and McCulloch, J. (Eds) (2012) *Borders and crime: Pre-crime, mobility and serious harm in an age of globalization.* London: Palgrave Macmillan.

Pitch, T. (1995) *Limited Responsibilities.* London: Routledge.

Pradel, J. (1993) France. In: C. Van Den Wijngaert, C. Gane, H.H. Kuhne and F. McAuley (Eds) *Criminal procedure systems in the European Community.* London: Butterworth, 105–36.

Pratt, J. (2008a) Scandinavian exceptionalism in an era of penal excess – part I: The nature and roots of Scandinavian exceptionalism. *British journal of criminology,* 48, 119–37.

Pratt, J. (2008b) Scandinavian exceptionalism in an era of penal excess – part II: Does Scandinavian exceptionalism have a future? *British journal of criminology,* 48, 275–92.

Pratt, J. and Clark, M. (2005) Penal populism in New Zealand. *Punishment and society,* 7, 303–21.

Pratt, J. and Erikson, A. (2012) In defence of Scandanavian exceptionalism. In: T. Ugelvik and J. Dullum (Eds) *Penal exceptionalism?: Nordic prison policy and practice.* Abingdon: Routledge, 235–59.

Pratt, J., Brown, D., Brown, M., Hallsworth, S. and Morrison, W. (Eds) (2013) *The new punitiveness.* London: Routledge.

Pritchard, D. and Pakes, F. (Eds) (in press) *Riot, unrest and protest on the global stage.* London: Routledge.

Pruitt, R.C. (1997) Guilt by majority in the International Criminal Tribunal for the Former Yugoslavia: Does this meet the standard of proof 'beyond reasonable doubt'? *Leiden journal for international law,* 10, 557–78.

Punch, M. (1985) *Conduct unbecoming.* London: Tavistock.

Punch, M. (1997) The Dutch criminal justice system: A crisis of identity. *Security journal, 9*, 177–814.

Punch, M. (2009) *Police corruption: deviance, accountability and reform in policing.* Cullompton, Devon: Willan.

Punch, M. and Naylor, T. (1973) The police: A social service. *New society, 17*, 358–61.

Reichel, P.L. (1999) *Comparative criminal justice systems: A topical approach (2nd edition).* Upper Saddle River, New Jersey: Prentice Hall.

Reiner, R. (2000a) *The politics of the police (3rd edition).* Hemel Hempstead: Harvester Wheatsheaf.

Reiner, R. (2000b) Romantic realism: Policing and the media. In: F. Leishman, B. Loveday and S. Savage (Eds) *Core issues in policing (2nd edition).* Harlow, Essex: Longman, 523–66.

Reporters without Borders (2008) *IOC accepts organized online censorship.* Reporters without Borders press release, 30 July 2008.

Rezeai, H. (2002) The Iranian criminal justice under the Islamization project. *European journal of crime, criminal law and criminal justice, 10*, 54–69.

Richmond, D.C. (2000) The changing boundaries between federal and local law enforcement. In: P. MacDonald and J. Munsterman (Eds) *Boundary changes in criminal justice organizations.* Washington, DC: US Department of Justice, 81–111.

Roberts, J.V. and Hough, M. (2009). *Public opinion and the jury: An international literature review.* Ministry of Justice research series, 1/09. London: Ministry of Justice.

Robinson, C.D. and Scaglion, R. (1987) The origin and evolution of the police function in society: Notes toward a theory. *Law and society review, 21*, 109–53.

Robinson, G. (1999) *Crimes against humanity: The struggle for global justice.* London: Penguin.

Roberts, J.V., Stalans, L.J., Indermaur, D. and Hough, M. (2002) *Penal populism and public opinion: Lessons from five countries.* Oxford: Oxford University Press.

Rosenthal, R. (1991) *Meta-analytic procedures for social research.* Newbury Park, California: Sage.

Ross, J.I. (2000) *Varieties of state crime and its control.* Monsey, New York: Criminal Justice Press.

Ross, J.I. (Ed) (2013) *The globalization of supermax prisons.* New Brunswick, New Jersey: Rutgers University Press.

Rothe, D.L., Ross, J.I., Mullins, C.W., Friedrichs, D., Michalowski, R., Barak, G., Kuazlarich, D. and Kramer, R.C. (2009) That was then, this is now, what about tomorrow? Future directions in state crime studies. *Critical criminology, 17*, 3–13.

Rothman, D.J. (1990) *The Discovery of the asylum: Social order and disorder in the New Republic (2nd edition).* Boston: Little Brown.

Rubinstein, W. (2004) *Genocide: A history.* London: Pearson.

Ruihua, C. (2003) The detention system in China. In: E.P. Mendes and A. Lalonde-Roussy (Eds) *Bridging the global divide on human rights: A Canada–China dialogue.* Aldershot: Ashgate, 39–52.

Ruiz Vadillo, E. (1993) Spain. In: C. Van Den Wijngaert, C. Gane, H.H. Kühne and F. McAuley (Eds) *Criminal procedure systems in the European Community.* London: Butterworth, 383–400.

Salas, L. (no date) Venezuela. In: *The World Factbook of Criminal Justice Systems.* Available on line: http://www.bjs.gov/content/pub/ascii/WFBCJVEN.TXT (accessed 15/7/2014).

Sanders, A. (2002) Prosecution systems. In: M. McConville and G. Wilson (Eds) *The handbook of the criminal justice process.* Oxford: Oxford University Press, 149–65.

Savelsberg, J.J. (2011) Globalization and states of punishment. In: D. Nelken (Ed) Comparative criminal justice and globalization. Farnham: Ashgate, 69–86.

Savitt, D.N. and Gottlieb, B. (1983) Pennsylvania Grand Jury practice. Harrisburg, Pennsylvania: Banks-Baldwin.

Scerri, E.R. (2006) The periodic table: Its story and its significance. Oxford: Oxford University Press.

Schmalleger, F. (2006) Criminal justice: A brief introduction. Prentice Hall: Pearson.

Schönteich, M. (2008) The scale and consequences of pretrial detention around the world. In: Open Society Foundations (Ed) Justice initiatives. London: Open Society Foundations, 11–43.

Seltzer, T. (2005) Mental health courts: A misguided attempt to address the criminal justice system's unfair treatment of people with mental illnesses. Psychology, public policy, and law, 11(4), 570–86.

Shafer, N.E. and Curtis, R. (1997) Alaska Supreme Court: Fairness and access problems and recommendations. Alaska justice forum, 14, 1–8.

Shalev, S. (2009) Supermax: controlling risk through solitary confinement. Cullompton, Devon: Willan.

Shammas, V.L. (2014) The pains of freedom: Assessing the ambiguity of Scandinavian penal exceptionalism on Norway's Prison Island. Punishment and society, 16, 104–23.

Shaw, M. (2012) From comparative to international genocide studies: The international production of genocide in 20th-century Europe. European journal of international relations, 18, 645–68.

Shearing, C. and Wood, J. (2003) Nodal governance, democracy and the new 'denizens'. Journal of law and society, 30, 400–19.

Sheehan, A.V. (1975) Criminal procedure in Scotland and France. Edinburgh: HMSO.

Shelley, L.I. (1999) Post-socialist policing: Limitations on institutional change. In: R.I. Mawby (Ed) Policing around the world: Issues for the twenty-first century. London: UCL Press, 75–87.

Sheptycki, J.W.E. (Ed) (2000) Issues in transnational policing. London: Routledge.

Sheptycki, J.W.E. (2005) Relativism, transnationalisation and comparative criminology. In: J.W.E. Sheptycki and A. Wardak (Eds) Transnational and comparative criminology. London: GlassHouse Press, 69–88.

Sheptycki, J. (2011) Transnational and comparative criminology reconsidered. In: D. Nelken (Ed) Comparative criminal justice and globalization. Farnham: Ashgate, 145–62.

Shraga, D. (2004) The second generation of UN-based tribunals: A diversity of mixed jurisdictions. In: C.P.R. Romano, A. Nollkaemper and J.K. Kleffner (Eds) Internationalized criminal courts: Sierra Leone, East Timor, Kosovo and Cambodia. Oxford: Oxford University Press, 15–38.

Simon, R.J. (1977) The jury: Its role in American society. Lexington, Massachusetts: Lexington Books.

Singleton, N., Meltzer, H. and Gatward, R. (1998) Psychiatric morbidity among prisoners in England and Wales. London: Office for National Statistics.

Skolnick, J. and Bayley, D. (1988) The new blue line. New York: Free Press.

Sloat, A. (2004) Integrating women: The gendered dimension of EU enlargement. Paper presented at Second Pan-European Conference; Standing Group on EU Politics Bologna, 24–6 June 2004.

Small Arms Survey (2008) Small arms survey: Risk and resilience. Cambridge: Cambridge University Press.

Smeulers, A. (2002) *What transforms ordinary people into gross human rights violators?* Paper prepared for ECPR in Torino, 22–7 March 2002.

Smeulers, A., Holá, B. and van den Berg, T. (2013) Sixty-five years of international criminal justice: The facts and figures. *International criminal law review, 13*, 7–41.

Smith, C.J. (2011) Comparative methods: Going beyond incorporating international research methods with traditional methods. *International journal of comparative and applied criminal justice, 33*, 211–28.

Solzhenitsyn, A. (1973) *The Gulag Archipelago*. Boulder, Colorado: Westview Press.

Souryal, S.S. (1987) The religionization of a society: The continuing application of Sharī'ah law in Saudi Arabia. *Journal for the scientific study of religion, 26*, 429–49.

Souryal, S.S., Potts, D.W. and Alobied, A.I. (1994) The penalty of hand amputation for theft in Islamic justice. *Journal of criminal justice, 22*, 249–65.

Spencer, J.R. (2013) Extradition, the European Arrest Warrant and human rights. *The Cambridge law journal, 72*, 250–3.

Spielmann, A. and Spielmann, D. (1993) Luxembourg. In: C. Van Den Wijngaert, C. Gane, H.H. Kühne and F. McAuley (Eds) *Criminal procedure systems in the European Community*. London: Butterworth, 261–78.

Steadman, H.J., Davidson, S. and Brown, C. (2001) Mental health courts: Their promise and unanswered questions. *Psychiatric services, 52*, 457–8.

Steinberg, R.H. (Ed) (2011) *Assessing the legacy of the ICTY*. Leiden: Martinus Nijhoff Publishers.

St. Eve, A.J. and Zuckerman, M.A. (2012) Ensuring an impartial jury in the age of social media. *Duke law & technology review, 11*, 1–29.

Stiglitz, J. (2002) *Globalization and its discontents*. London: Penguin.

Storch, R.D. (1976) The policeman as domestic missionary: Urban discipline and popular culture in Northern England 1850–1880. *Journal of social history, 9*, 481–509.

Stumpf, J. (2006) The crimmigration crisis: Immigrants, crime, and sovereign power. *American University law review, 56*, 367–419.

Stumpf, J. (2013) Two profiles of crimmigration law. In: F. Pakes (Ed) *Globalisation and the challenge to criminology*. London: Routledge, 91–109.

Swart, A.H.J. (1993) The Netherlands. In: C. Van Den Wijngaert, C. Gane, H.H. Kühne and F. McAuley (Eds) *Criminal procedure systems in the European Community*. London: Butterworth, 279–316.

Tak, P.J.P. (1986) *The legal scope of non-prosecution in Europe*. HEUNI publication series, no. 8, Helsinki: HEUNI.

Tak, P.J.P. (1999) *The Dutch criminal justice system: Organization and operation*. TheHague: Wetenschappelijk Onderzoek- en Documentatiecentrum (WODC).

Takayanagi, K. (1963) A century of innovation: The development of Japanese law 1868–1961. In: R. von Mehren (Ed) *Law in Japan: Legal order in a changing society*. Cambridge, Massachusetts: Harvard University Press, 14–40.

Tapley, J. (2005) Improving confidence in criminal justice: Achieving community justice for victims and witnesses. In: J. Winstone and F. Pakes (2005) *Community justice: Issues for probation and criminal justice*. Cullompton, Devon: Willan, 237–56.

Taylor, R. (2006) *The great firewall of China*. BBC. Available on line: news.bbc.co.uk/1/hi/programmes/click_online/4587622.stm (accessed 15/7/2014).

Terrill, R.J. (2012) *World criminal justice systems: A comparative survey*. Oxford: Newnes.

TE-SAT (2008) *EU terrorism situation and trend report*. The Hague: Europol.

Thaman, S.C. (2001) Europe's new jury systems: The cases of Spain and Russia. In N. Vidmar (Ed) *World jury systems*. Oxford: Oxford University Press, 319–51.

Thaman, S.C. (2007) The nullification of the Russian jury: Lessons for jury-inspired reform in Eurasia and beyond. *Cornell international law journal, 40*, 355–428.

Tochilovski, V. (1998) Trial in international criminal jurisdictions: Battle or scrutiny? *European journal of crime, criminal law and criminal justice, 6*, 55–60.

Tombs, S. (2012) State–corporate symbiosis in the production of crime and harm, *State crime, 1*, 170–95.

Törnudd, P. (1993) *Fifteen years of decreasing prisoner rates in Finland* (Research Communication 8/93). Helsinki: National Research Institute of Legal Policy.

Uglow, S. (2002) *Criminal Justice (2nd edition)*. London: Sweet and Maxwell.

Umbreit, M.S. and Armour, M.P. (2011) Restorative justice and dialogue: Impact, opportunities, and challenges in the global community. *Washington University journal of law and policy, 36*, 65–89.

Umbreit, M. and Coates, R. (1992) *Victim offender mediation: An analysis of programs in four States in the US*. Minneapolis: University of Minnesota, Center for Restorative Justice and Peacemaking.

Umbreit, M. and Greenwood, J. (1998) *National survey of victim offender mediation programs in the US*. Minneapolis: University of Minnesota, Center for Restorative Justice and Peacemaking.

United Nations (2006) *In-depth study on all forms of violence against women*. Report of the Secretary-General, New York, United Nations (A/61/122/Add.1.).

UNODC (2008) *World drug report*. Available on line: www.unodc.org/unodc/en/data-and-analysis/WDR-2008.html (accessed 15/7/2014).

Upham, F.K. (1987) *Law and social change in postwar Japan*. Cambridge, Massachusetts: Harvard University Press.

Urquhart, P.D. (1998) *The police integrity commission in New South Wales*. Paper presented to the 13th World Conference of the International Association for Civilian Oversight of Law Enforcement, Seattle, Washington (October 1998).

Valenti, J. (2011) SlutWalks and the future of feminism. *Washington post*, 3 June 2011. Available on line: http://www.washingtonpost.com/opinions/slutwalks-and-the-future-of-feminism/ 2011/06/01/AGjB9LIH_story.html (accessed 15/7/2014).

Van den Wijngaert, C. (1993) Belgium. In: C. Van Den Wijngaert, C. Gane, H.H. Kühne and F. McAuley (Eds) *Criminal procedure systems in the European Community*. London: Butterworth, 1–50.

Van der Leun, J. and Van der Woude, M. (2011) Ethnic profiling in the Netherlands? A reflection on expanding preventive powers, ethnic profiling and a changing social and political context. *Policing and society, 21*, 444–55.

Van der Leun, J. and Van der Woude, M. (2012) A reflection of crimmigration in the Netherlands. In: M.J. Guia, M. Van der Woude and J. Van der Leun (Eds) *Social control and justice: Crimmigration in the age of fear*. The Hague: Eleven International Publishing, 41–60.

Van Dijk, J.J.M. (2010) Highlights of International Crime Victims Survey. In: M. Natarjan (Ed) *International crime and justice*. Cambridge: Cambridge University Press, 462–70.

Van Dijk, J.J.M. and Tseloni, A. (2012) Global overview: International trends in victimization and recorded crime. In: J.J.M. Van Dijk, A. Tseloni and G. Farrell (Eds) *The international crime drop*. London: Palgrave MacMillan, 11–36.

Van Dijk, J.J.M., Mayhew, P. and Killias, M. (1990) *Experiences of crime across the world: Key findings from the 1989 International Crime Survey*. Deventer: Kluwer.

Van Dijk, J.J.M., Tseloni, A. and Farrell, G. (Eds) (2012) *The international crime drop*. London: Palgrave MacMillan.

Van Dijk, J.J.M., van Kesteren, J.N. and Smit, P. (2008) *Criminal victimisation in international perspective: Key findings from the 2004–2005 ICVS and EU ICS*. The Hague: Boom Legal Publishers.

Van Duyne, P.C. (2007) OCTA 2006: The unfulfilled promise. *Trends in organized crime, 10*, 120–8.

Van Kesteren, J., Mayhew, P. and Nieuwbeerta, P. (2001) *Criminal victimisation in seventeen industrialised countries: Key findings from the 2000 International Crime Survey*. The Hague: Scientific Research and Development Centre.

Van Koppen, P.J. and Penrod, S.D. (Eds) (2003) *Adversarial versus inquisitorial justice*. New York: Kluwer/Plenum.

van Nuijs, A.L., Castiglioni, S., Tarcomnicu, I., Postigo, C., de Alda, M.L., Neels, H. and Covaci, A. (2011) Illicit drug consumption estimations derived from wastewater analysis: A critical review. *Science of the total environment, 409*, 3564–77.

Van Swaaningen, R. (2011) Critical cosmopolitanism and global criminology. In: D. Nelken (Ed) *Comparative criminal justice and globalization*. Aldershot: Ashgate, 125–44.

Van Traa, M. (1997) The findings of the parliamentary inquiry viewed from an international perspective. In: M.G.W. Den Boer (Ed) *Undercover policing and accountability from an international perspective*. Maastricht, the Netherlands: European Institute of Public Administration, 15–25.

Vidmar, N. (2001a) A historical and comparative perspective on the common law jury. In: N. Vidmar (Ed) *World jury systems*. Oxford: Oxford University Press, 1–52.

Vidmar, N. (2001b) The jury elsewhere in the world. In: N. Vidmar (Ed) *World jury systems*. Oxford: Oxford University Press, 421–47.

Vogel, F. (2003) The public and private in Saudi Arabia: Restrictions on the powers of committee for ordering the good and forbidding the evil. *Social research, 70*, 749–68.

Vogler, R. (1996) Criminal procedure in France. In: J. Hatchard, B. Huber and R. Vogler (Eds) *Comparative criminal procedure*. London: British Institute of International and Comparative Law, 14–95.

Vogler, R. (2005) *A world view on criminal justice*. Aldershot: Ashgate.

Von Hofer, H. (2003) Prison populations as political constructs: The case of Finland, Holland and Sweden. *Journal of Scandinavian studies in criminology and crime prevention, 4*, 21–38.

Waddington, P.A.J. (1999) *Policing citizens*. London: UCL Press.

Waddington, P.A.J. (2000) Public order policing: Citizenship and moral ambiguity. In: F. Leishman, B. Loveday and S. Savage (Eds) *Core issues in policing (2nd edition)*. Harlow, Essex: Longman, 156–75.

Wacquant, L. (1995) The pugilistic point of view: How boxers think and feel about their trade. *Theory and society, 24*, 489–535.

Wacquant, L. (2005) The great penal leap backward: Incarceration in America from Nixon to Clinton. In: J. Pratt, D. Brown, M. Brown, S. Hallsworth and W. Morrison (Eds) *The new punitiveness: Trends, theories and perspectives*. Cullompton, Devon: Willan, 3–26.

Wacquant, L. (2008) *Urban outcasts: A comparative sociology of advanced marginality*. Cambridge: Polity Press.

Wadham, J. (1998) Zero tolerance policing: Striking the balance, rights and liberties. In: R. Hopkins Burke (Ed) *Zero tolerance policing*. Leicester: Perpetuity Press, 49–56.

Wagenaar, W.A., Van Koppen, P.J. and Crombag, H.F.M. (1993) *Anchored narratives: The psychology of criminal evidence*. Hemel Hempstead: Harvester Wheatsheaf.

Walby, S. and Allen, J. (2004) *Domestic violence, sexual assault and stalking: Findings from the British Crime Survey*. Home Office Research Study no 276. London: Home Office.

Walker, C. and Whyte, D. (2005) Contracting out war? Private military companies, law and regulation in the United Kingdom. *International and comparative law quarterly, 54,* 651–90.

Walker, N. (1991) *Why punish?* Oxford: Oxford University Press.

Walmsley, R. (2006) *World female imprisonment list: Women and girls in penal institutions, including pre-trial detainees/remand prisoners*. London: King's College.

Walmsley, R. (2008a) *World prison population list (7th edition)*. London: King's College.

Walmsley, R. (2008b) Trends in prison population 1995–2004. In: K. Aromaa and M. Heiskanen (Eds) *Crime and criminal justice systems in Europe and North America 1995–2004*. Helsinki: HEUNI, 149–68.

Walmsley, R. (2013) *World prison population list (10th edition)*. Available on line: http://www.prisonstudies.org/sites/prisonstudies.org/files/resources/downloads/wppl_10.pdf (accessed 15/7/2014).

Wardak, A. (2005) Crime and social control in Saudi Arabia. In: J.W.E. Sheptycki and A. Wardak (Eds) *Transnational and comparative criminology*. London: GlassHouse Press, 91–116.

Washburn, K.K. (2008) Restoring the grand jury. *Fordham law review, 76,* 2333–88

Waters, T.W. (Ed) (2013) *The Milosevic trial: An autopsy*. Oxford: Oxford University Press.

Weber, L. and Pickering, S. (2011) *Globalization and borders: Death at the global frontier*. Basingstoke: Palgrave-MacMillan.

Weber, L. and Pickering, S. (2013) Exporting risk, deporting non-citizens. In F. Pakes (Ed) *Globalisation and the challenge to criminology*. London: Routledge, 110–28.

Weinberg De Roca, I.M. (2005) Ten years and counting: the development of international law at the ICTR. *New England journal of international and comparative law, 12,* 69–80.

Whyte, D. (2007) The crimes of neo-liberal rule in occupied Iraq. *British journal of criminology, 47,* 177–95.

Whyte, W.F. (1943) *Street corner society*. Chicago: University of Chicago Press.

Wilson, J.Q. and Kelling, G.L. (1982) Broken windows: The police and neighborhood safety. *Atlantic Monthly, 249,* 29–38.

Williams, P. (2003) Transnational organized crime and the state. In: R. Bruce Hall and T.J. Biersteker (Eds) *The emergence of private authority in global governance*. New York: Cambridge University Press, 161–5.

Wing Lo, T. (2000) An overview of the criminal justice system in Hong Kong. In: O.N.I. Ebbe (Ed) *Comparative and international criminal justice systems*. Boston: Butterworth-Heinemann, 113–27.

Wolfreys, J. (2000) Controlling state crime in France. In: J.I. Ross (Ed) Varieties of state crime and its control. Monsey, New York: Criminal Justice Press, 119–48.

Wood, E.J. (2010) Sexual violence during war: Variation and accountability. In: A. Smeulers (Ed) *Collective crimes and international criminal justice: An interdisciplinary approach*. Antwerp: Intersentia.

Woolford, A. (2006) Making genocide unthinkable: Three guidelines for a critical criminology of genocide. *Critical criminology, 14,* 87–106.

Wootten, H. (1991) *Regional report of inquiry in New South Wales, Victoria and Tasmania*. Royal Commission into Aboriginal Deaths in Custody. Canberra: Australian Government Publishing Service.

Wright, A. (2002a) *Policing: An introduction to concepts and practice*. Cullompton, Devon: Willan.

Wright, A. (2002b) *Human rights and police ethics*. Portsmouth: University of Portsmouth, Institute for Criminal Justice Studies.

Young, J. (1971) *The drugtakers*. London: Paladin.

Young, J. (1999) *The exclusive society*. London: Sage.

Young, J. (2004) Voodoo criminology and the numbers game. In: J. Ferrell, K. Hayward, W. Morrison and M. Presdee (Eds) *Cultural criminology unleashed*. London: GlassHouse Press, 13–28.

Zedner, L. (1995) Comparative research in criminal justice. In: L. Noaks, M. Levi and M. Maguire (Eds) *Contemporary issues in criminology*. Cardiff: University of Wales Press, 8–25.

Zimbardo, P.G. (1969) The human choice: Individuation, reason, and order versus deindividuation, impulse, and chaos. *Nebraska symposium on motivation, 17,* 237–307.

Zimring, F. (2003) *The contradictions of American capital punishment*. Oxford: Oxford University Press.

Index

Page numbers in *italic* refer to tables.